THE DISTANCE TEACHING UNIVERSITIES

The Distance Teaching Universities

Edited by
GREVILLE RUMBLE AND KEITH HARRY

CROOM HELM
London & Canberra

ST. MARTIN'S PRESS
New York

© 1982 Greville Rumble and Keith Harry
Croom Helm Ltd, 2-10 St John's Road, London SW11

British Library Cataloguing in Publication Data

The Distance teaching universities.
　　1. Correspondence schools and courses
　　I. Rumble, Greville　　II. Harry, Keith
　　378'.17　　　LC5915

ISBN 0-7099-2230-2

First published in the United States of America in 1982
All rights reserved. For information write:
St. Martin's Press, Inc., 175 Fifth Avenue, New York, N.Y. 10010

Library of Congress Cataloging in Publication Data
Main entry under title:

The Distance teaching universities.

　　Includes index.
　　1. University extension – Addresses, essays, lectures.
2. Independent study – Addresses, essays, lectures.
I. Rumble, Greville. II. Harry, Keith.
LC6219.D57　　1982　　　378'.1554　　　82-42559
ISBN 0-312-21323-9

Printed and bound in Great Britain by
Biddles Ltd, Guildford and King's Lynn

CONTENTS

A NOTE ON THE CONTRIBUTORS

Alec Fleming is Staff Tutor in Educational Studies at the UK Open University, where he has worked since 1972. In 1978-80 he was seconded from the OU as a member of the British Project Team at the Allama Iqbal Open University, Pakistan.

Keith Harry joined the UK Open University in 1975. He is currently Documentation Officer of the International Documentation Centre for Distance Learning at the UKOU.

Arthur James joined the UKOU in 1972. He is Staff Tutor in Educational Studies with a particular research interest in distance education in Spanish speaking countries, and has visited the Universidad Nacional de Educación a Distancia in Spain.

Desmond Keegan is Head of the School of General Studies at the Open College of Further Education in Adelaide, South Australia, which post he has held since 1975. He is a joint executive editor of the international journal *Distance Education*, which he founded in 1979. During 1981 he was Visiting Professor of Distance Education at the Fernuniversität in the Federal Republic of Germany.

Robert McCormick joined the UK Open University ten years ago, and is now Senior Lecturer in the Faculty of Educational Studies. He has a particular interest in distance education in developing countries, was seconded for a year to the Allama Iqbal Open University in Pakistan, and has visited the Central Broadcasting and Television University in Beijing, People's Republic of China.

Greville Rumble joined the UKOU in 1970 and is now Senior Assistant Secretary in Academic Administration Division. Between 1976 and 1979 he undertook three technical assistance missions related to the Universidad Estatal a Distancia project in Costa Rica, and four consultancy missions to the Universidad Nacional Abierta in Venezuela. In 1980-81 he was Visiting Consultant in the Planning Vicerectorate at UNED, and during this period he also undertook a study of the economics of UNA as part of a research programme funded by the Organisation of American States.

David Seligman joined the British Broadcasting Corporation's Open University Productions unit in 1970, and is now Executive Producer (Social Sciences). He has advised on media and media integration in a number of projects and has visited Everyman's University in Israel.

Doug Shale joined Athabasca University in 1976 and is now Head of the Office of Institutional Studies there.

6

EDITORS' PREFACE AND ACKNOWLEDGEMENTS

It is our hope that this book will prove useful to practitioners and decision-makers interested in exploiting the potential of distance education at the university level. We are well aware that, in restricting our attention to those few universities mainly founded in the 1970s to teach only at a distance, we have ignored a much older and more widespread tradition of distance teaching in universities. We hope that the Introduction and Chapter 1, while they fall far short of a treatise on the development of universities and university-level distance teaching, go some way towards redressing this balance. Nevertheless, we felt that the institutions which we have called the "distance teaching universities" and which have attracted so much attention in the last few years warranted consideration in their own right. The heart of the book is thus the nine case studies of particular distance teaching universities around the world.

Throughout the book we have attempted to ensure factual accuracy and reasonable interpretation of the evidence, and wherever possible we have tried to check this. In the final analysis, however, we accept full responsibility for any errors which may have been committed.

It would be impossible to name everyone who has contributed in one way or another to this book. However, we particularly wish to mention the following: Dr. Stephen Griew, President of Athabasca University; Professor Zun Hua Wang of the Central Broadcasting and Television University, Beijing, People's Republic of China; Dr. Chester Zelaya, Rector of the Universidad Estatal a Distancia in Costa Rica, and Dr. Ronald García, the Executive Vice-rector; Dr. Otto Peters of the Fernuniversität, Federal Republic of Germany, and Professor Börje Holmberg of the same university; Dr. Avshalom Shohat, Director of Course Development at Everyman's University, Israel; Dr. A. Mohiuddin, Vice-Chancellor of the Allama Iqbal Open University, and Professor A. Qayyum, and Mrs. A. Quaraishi; at the Universidad Nacional de Educación a Distancia, Dr. Eduardo López, Dr. José Luis Lorente, Sr. Agustín Mengod, Dr. Pío Navarro, Sr. Emilio Nogales, Sr. José Antonio Roldán, Sr. Carlos Roura, Sr. Francisco Velasco, and Sr. Joaquín Valverde; at the UK Open University, Mr. John Dodd, Professor Michael Neil, Mr. Brian Ramsden, Professor Ralph Smith, and Mr. Godfrey Woodward; Ing. Antonio Francés, Director of Strategic Planning and Institutional Evaluation at the Universidad Nacional Abierta, Venezuela; Dr. George Borden of the Department of Communication at the University of Delaware; and the Editorial Universidad Estatal a Distancia, San Jose, Costa Rica, for permission to make use of material from Greville Rumble's forthcoming book, *La Universidad Estatal a Distancia: una evaluación.*

Finally we are particularly grateful to Mrs. Anne Rumble for her help in editing the final manuscript, and to Mrs. Gwen Green of Stantonbury Parish Print for preparing the camera ready copy.

Greville Rumble
Woburn Sands

Keith Harry
Grafton Regis

7

ABBREVIATIONS

Most of the abbreviations used within this book are specific to the chapters in which they arise, and are introduced as necessary by the chapter authors. However, the following ones are used throughout the book.

AIOU   Allama Iqbal Open University (Pakistan)

AU   Athabasca University (Alberta, Canada)

CCTU   Central China Television University (People's Republic of China), more properly known as the Central Broadcasting and Television University.

DTU(s)   Distance Teaching University(ies)

EU   Everyman's University (Israel)

FeU   Fernuniversität (Federal Republic of Germany)

OU   Open University (sometimes used as a generic term but in chapter 9 used to refer to the British Open University - but see also UKOU)

UNA   Universidad Nacional Abierta (Venezuela)

UNDP   United Nations Development Programme

UNED   Universidad Estatal a Distancia (Costa Rica)

UNED   Universidad Nacional de Educación a Distancia (Spain)

UNESCO   United Nations Educational, Scientific and Cultural Organisation

UNICEF   United Nations Childrens' Fund

UKOU   United Kingdom Open University

Academic degrees are also referred to in their abbreviated form: e.g. BA - Bachelor of Arts; B Admin - Bachelor of Administration; B Ed - Bachelor of Education; BGS - Bachelor of General Studies; B Phil - Bachelor of Philosophy; MA - Master of Arts; M Ed - Master of Education; M Phil - Master of Philosophy; PhD - Doctor of Philosophy.

8

INTRODUCTION

Greville Rumble and Desmond Keegan

In 1971 the United Kingdom's Open University (UKOU) began teaching students. Cyril Houle, Professor of Education at the University of Chicago, commented "For some not-easily-defined reason, the Open University instantly became a worldwide topic of concern ... among both educators and the general public" (Houle, 1974: 35), while another American observer noted: "So great has been the flow of visitors to this institution that it is becoming a mark of distinction among American educators to be able to say that one has not visited the Open University" (Valley, 1972: 106).

Within a few years of the foundation of the UKOU a number of other 'open' or 'distance' universities had been established in both developed and developing countries.

These universities, in the main established in the 1970s (see chapter 1, Table 1.1), are called the *distance teaching universities* in this book.

They reflect, as Chapter 11 shows, a concern with the need to widen access to university level education. This concern dates back, in the United States of America, to the passing of the Morrill Act in 1862, the foundation of the Land Grant universities, and the beginnings of the idea of a university extension movement related to the notion that "the campus is the state". In England, the Extension Movement emerged in the 1870s, and by 1884 its leaders were pressing, unsuccessfully, for "a part-time, non resident teaching university operating a system of academic credits" (Marriott, 1981: 15).

Linked to the extension movement was the idea that a university should actively *teach* students who could not attend regular classes on campus. Members of the British Extension Movement argued that the free studies system, by which students register for a degree, study independently, and sit university examinations, was inadequate. Such a system had been adopted by the University of London under its revised charter of 1858, when (except in medicine) the attendance requirement was lifted and London degrees were open to any male candidates who could pass the tests. It was argued that this turned the University of London into a huge machinery of examinations which did little to foster a university education.

9

Students registered for University of London examinations could, however, obtain tuition from various commercial colleges, some of which offered correspondence courses.

This is not the place to chronicle the long and sometimes chequered history of the correspondence institutions. It is enough to note that they date back 130 years to the middle of the nineteenth century, and that it was inevitable that at some point universities would begin to build on their experience to utilise correspondence teaching methods to provide tuition for students of their own. Thus, in the United States of America, for example, the first university-sponsored correspondence programme was founded and organised by the University of Chicago in 1891.

Again, this is not the place to chart the development of correspondence and distance education programmes within universities in general, although Chapter 1 provides some indications of the extent and richness of this provision.

The existence of such programmes, coupled with the fact that independent correspondence schools and colleges had been shown to be viable propositions, made the development of distance teaching universities - that is, universities wholly or almost exclusively dedicated to distance teaching - a matter of time.

The first distance teaching university, properly so called, was the University of South Africa. Originally established as a conventional university, it had as a result of constitutional changes to its constituent colleges, to seek a new role. In 1946 it began teaching by correspondence, and it was reconstituted in 1951 to provide degree courses for external students only.

The foundation of distance teaching universities in the 1970s stemmed in part from an increased concern (itself dating from the late 1950s and 1960s) for greater equality of opportunity of access to higher education. This led not only to an expansion of conventional universities to provide places for more school leavers, but to the feeling that higher education should be made available to those adults who had at an earlier stage in their careers missed the opportunity to attend a university. Coupled with this was an increasing belief (particularly in the 1970s) in the need for adults to have access to educational opportunities throughout their lives, in order to renew or update their knowledge.

By its very nature, distance education was well suited to meeting the needs of such adults, yet, at least in the United Kingdom, there was a reluctance on the part of the conventional universities to meet this need (Perry, 1976: 5).

It therefore became clear that if action was going to be taken in the United Kingdom, the government had to initiate it by itself proposing the establishment of a distance teaching institution. The early history of the UKOU makes it clear that it was the personal influence and commitment of a few politicians which ensured the foundation of that university (Hall *et al*, 1975: 231).

The novelty of the UKOU, its success, and the worldwide interest it attracted, made it certain that some countries would follow the example of the United Kingdom and found distance teaching universities of their own. However, not every country has done so, not least because in some of them (e.g. Australia) there is a well-developed and successful tradition of distance education embedded in the existing universities.

Before we consider briefly the provision of distance education by universities in general (Chapter 1) and the development and characteristics of the distance teaching universities in particular (Chapters 2 to 12), it is as well to delineate clearly the field of education with which we are dealing, and to indicate which educational traditions come within the terminology we are using and which do not.

Distance education is a generic term that includes the range of teaching/learning strategies variously referred to as *correspondence education* or *correspondence study* in both developed and developing countries; as *home study* or *independent study* in the United States of America; *external studies* in Australia; *télé-enseignement* in France; *Fernstudium* or *Fernunterricht* in Germany; *educación a distancia* or *enseñanza a distancia* in Spanish speaking countries and *teleducação* in Portuguese.

Exactly what these terms mean has been the subject of some debate. *Distance education* has been proposed as the general term for this whole area of education. *Distance teaching* would then refer to the institutional role of providing education at-a-distance (and hence appears in the title of this book), and *distance learning* to the students' role in the process.

Related terms such as *open learning, non-traditional studies, outreach* and *off-campus* programmes, and *telemathic* teaching also appear in the literature. The meaning of these various terms has been discussed

11

by Moore (1977), Holmberg (1980) and Keegan (1980). These methods are usually contrasted with *conventional* or *traditional* forms of education.

We ourselves find the term *open learning* unsatisfactory in an administrative sense, nor do we favour the use of the term *open university* to describe this type of institution, although it is used in the name of existing DTUs in Pakistan, Sri Lanka, Thailand, the United Kingdom and Venezuela. 'Open education' and 'open university' are imprecise terms in constant need of clarification.

In their book *Open Learning*, Mackenzie, Postgate and Scupham describe well the difficulties and advantages of the term 'open':

> Open learning is an imprecise phrase to which a range of meanings can be, and is, attached. It eludes definition. But as an inscription to be carried in procession on a banner, gathering adherents and enthusiasms, it has great potential. For its very imprecision enables it to accommodate many different ideas and aims. (1975: 15).

In the case of the UKOU the original inspiration of the term *open university* stemmed from four factors: the openness of the university in respect of (1) people, since it would not debar applicants on account of their lack of educational qualifications; (2) place, in the sense that learning would be home based and not restricted to classrooms or a campus; (3) the use of new methods of teaching and (4) ideas. However, not all of these features are to be found in other 'open' universities.

The concept of *openness* is linked to the idea of access to educational opportunities. It goes beyond the extent to which the rules and regulations governing registration of students are restrictive of entry to a particular institution, to include the degree to which it is actually practicable for an individual to avail himself or herself of the learning facilities provided (Neil, 1981: 37). Distance and other geographical constraints and the ability to have access to the teaching medium in use are factors, here, so that "openness of access is positively and highly correlated with the extent to which an institution is dedicated to distance-learning" (Neil, 1981: 37).

Distance education itself involved a separation between the teacher and the learner. Thus Sims (1977: 4) says:

The unique and distinguishing feature in the correspondence education process is that the learner is at a distance from the teacher for much, most or even all of the time during the teaching-learning process.

However, this separation of teacher and learner does not preclude supplementary face-to-face sessions (Holmberg, 1980: 107).

A related concept is that of *independent study*. The fact that the student is separated from the teacher places great emphasis on the former's ability to study on his own initiative. Wedemeyer (1971: 550) defined independent study as follows:

Independent study consists of various forms of teaching-learning arrangements in which teachers and learners carry out their essential tasks and responsibilities apart from one another, communicating in a variety of ways for the purpose of freeing internal learners from inappropriate class pacings or patterns, of providing external learners with opportunities to continue learning in their own environments, and of developing in all learners the capacity to carry on self-directed learning.

Wedemeyer's definition still involves an element of communication between teacher and learner at some point in the process. As such it is related to concepts of distance education which stress the independent self-pacing nature of the student's learning. It is not enough to say that independent study is learning on one's own without establishing the context within which a student exercises his or her independence. Total independence takes one into areas covered by, for example, teach-yourself books and educational broadcasting in which the element of two-way communications essential in distance teaching is absent.

Keegan (1980: 33) suggests that the main elements in any definition of distance education are:

*   The separation of teacher and learner which distinguishes it from face-to-face lecturing.
*   The influence of an educational organisation which distinguishes it from private study.
*   The use of technical media, usually print, to unite teacher and learner and carry the educational content of the course
*   The provision of two-way communication so that the student

may benefit from or even initiate dialogue, which distinguishes if from other uses of educational technology.

* The teaching of students as individuals and rarely in groups, with the possibility of occasional meetings for both didactic and socialisation purposes.

* The participation in a more industrialised form of education (based on the view that distance teaching is characterised by division of labour; mechanisation; automation; application of organisational principles; scientific control; objectivity of teaching behaviour; mass production; concentration and centralisation).

Elsewhere Kaye and Rumble (1981: 18-19) provide a semi-operational and descriptive definition of *distance learning systems* in which they identify the key features of these systems in respect of their students, teaching materials and methods, and organisational and cost structures.

References

1. Hall, P., Lund, H., Parker, R. and Webb, A. (1975) 'Change, Choice and Conflict in Social Policy'. London: Heinemann.
2. Holmberg, B. (1980) 'Aspects of Distance Education'. Comparative Education, 16, 2, 107-119.
3. Houle, C.O. (1974) 'The External Degree'. San Francisco: Jossey-Bass.
4. Kaye, A. and Rumble, G. (1981) 'Distance Teaching for Higher and Adult Education'. London: Croom Helm.
5. Keegan, D. (1980) 'On defining distance education'. Distance Education, 1, 1, 19-45.
6. Mackenzie, N., Postgate, R. and Scupham, J. (1975) 'Open Learning: Systems and Problems in Post Secondary Education'. Paris: Unesco.
7. Marriott, S. (1981) 'A Backstairs to a Degree. Demands for an open university in late Victorian England'. Leeds: University of Leeds Department of Adult Education and Extramural Studies.
8. Moore, M. (1977) 'A Model of Independent Study'. Epistolodidaktika. 1977/1, 6-40.
9. Neil, M. (1981) 'Education of Adults at a Distance'. London: Kogan Page.
10. Perry, W. (1976) 'Open University. A personal account by the first Vice-Chancellor'. Milton Keynes: Open University Press.
11. Sims, R.S. (1977) 'An inquiry into correspondence education processes: policies, principles and practices in correspondence education systems worldwide'. Paris: Unesco. Unpublished.
12. Valley, J. (1972) 'External Degree Programs'. In Gould, S.B. and Cross, K.P. (editors) 'Explorations in Non-Traditional Study'. San Francisco: Jossey-Bass.
13. Wedemeyer, C.A. (1971) 'Independent Study'. In 'The Encyclopedia of Education'. Vol. 4 ed. L.C. Deighton. New York: MacMillan.

Chapter 1

DISTANCE TEACHING AT UNIVERSITY LEVEL

Desmond Keegan and Greville Rumble

A SURVEY OF DISTANCE TEACHING AT UNIVERSITY LEVEL

In spite of the attention paid the DTUs in the 1970s, distance education is not a recent phenomenon. Programmes using distance teaching methods have existed at further education level (technical and vocationally-orientated courses) for 130 years and at higher education level (university and university-orientated college courses) for 100 years.

United Kingdom: The University of London

In many ways the story begins with the foundation of the University of London in 1836. At first the University's functions were limited to the conduct of examinations and the conferring of degrees. Responsibility for teaching was vested in approved colleges or institutions and students who wished to sit an examination had to follow a course of instruction in one of these. In 1858, however, this restriction was removed and anyone could be admitted for degree studies provided they had passed the Matriculation Examination and paid the entrance fee.

This change paved the way for the growth of private correspondence colleges which prepared students for University of London examinations, and enabled them to study independently for the degree, without any formal tuition.

In 1898 the University of London was reconstituted as a teaching university. Institutions were able to apply to become schools of the University and teach 'internal students'. This restructure, however, left the University with a continuing responsibility for the examination of 'external students' who presented themselves for a degree. In 1970 about one third of the external students were either preparing themselves for the examinations by independent study or were tutored by private correspondence colleges such as University Correspondence College and Wolsey Hall.

In 1970, with the foundation of the British OU, the University of London began to review its policies. It decided that external students attending full-time courses in tertiary level non-university institutions should be provided for under the aegis of the Council for National Academic Awards, whilst overseas students should be the responsibility of their own government. The University of London also decided that from September 1977 its external degrees would be open only to private study students resident in the United Kingdom. The last overseas students will be examined in 1985.

The University of London now provides home-based students with the opportunity to study privately towards certain specialised degrees which are not provided by the OU. Its system also allows students to study with greater flexibility, and even intermittently if circumstances make this necessary, over the initial eight year registration period. (In contrast, the UKOU student is required to follow a course of instruction geared to a fixed academic year and hence has less overall flexibility.)

Of the 10,348 United Kingdom based students studying in July 1980 for a first degree or diploma, at least 46 percent were taking correspondence courses and a further 31 percent were studying by 'other methods' which includes independent study in their own home.

New Zealand and South Africa

The influence of the University of London in the acceptance of external studies as a legitimate and academically valid means of obtaining a degree can be seen in New Zealand and South Africa. The University of New Zealand was initiated in the 1880s as an examining body which later sponsored extramural study. In 1963 it transferred to the newly chartered Massey University the responsibility for extramural tuition of the majority of external students in the country.

Another institution which was based on the University of London was the University of the Cape of Good Hope, which was founded in 1873 and which awarded degrees on the basis of study undertaken at one of eight colleges in South Africa. Renamed the University of South Africa in 1916, its constituent colleges gradually became universities in their own right. As a result of these changes the University of South Africa (UNISA) had to seek a new role. In 1946, therefore, it began to teach by correspondence and in 1951 it was reconstituted to provide degree courses for external students.

UNISA is one of the forerunners of the DTUs. It achieved full autonomy in 1964 and is today a flourishing *correspondence-based university* with 56,000 students in 1981, and employing 1,000 full-time lecturers and 1,600 administrative personnel. It strives to present itself as an ordinary university in all respects except for the fact that its students study at home. It appoints full-time staff and, like conventional universities, offers all its degrees at Bachelors, Masters and Doctoral levels in six faculties: Sciences, Law, Arts, Education, Economic and Management Sciences, and Theology.

Adminstratively UNISA is a centralised organisation with few study centres. It relies mainly on printed materials with audiocassettes, videotapes, slides and telephone tuition regarded as secondary teaching materials; rejects the large course team approach in favour of full-time UNISA faculty writing all materials on a largely individual basis; emphasises the learning package rather than student support services; and insists on a major research commitment from staff. It calls its distance teaching method 'teletuition'.

Australia

Distance education at university level is provided by five Australian universities:
*   University of Queensland at Brisbane since 1911
*   University of New England at Armidale since 1955
*   Macquarie University in Sydney since 1967
*   Murdoch University in Perth since 1975
*   Deakin University at Geelong since 1977

All of these are conventional universities with New England, Murdoch and Deakin having a major commitment to external studies.

The Act establishing the University of Queensland in Brisbane in 1909 made provision for the teaching of university level courses by correspondence. The egalitarian and utilitarian philosophy which characterised the University of Queensland Act was due to its foundation in a new state, huge in area, thinly populated, economically reliant on primary industry and politically dominated by rural voters who wanted a university that would serve the interests of government and industry throughout the state and not just in the capital city.

The directions taken by the University of Queensland correspondence programme seventy years ago have influenced Australian external studies ever since: the synchronisation of study programmes for external and internal students; the use of the same examinations leading to the award of identical degrees for both; and the same assistance to external and internal students from the full-time academic staff. In 1949 the University of Queensland set up a separate department of external studies with its own professor and lecturers - a mini-open university within a conventional university - a structure it maintains to this day.

In 1955 the University of New England at Armidale was set up with a major commitment to external studies. Its dictum that all university staff should have two responsibilities - one for a class of conventional on-campus students and the other for an off-campus group, has come to be known as the *New England model* or the *Australian integrated mode* and constitutes a specifically distinct type of distance teaching provision. Under two influential directors, Howard C. Sheath (1955-1973) and Kevin C. Smith (1973 -), it has had a marked effect on Australian external studies at university and college level, influenced the UKOU (Perry, 1972: 13), and has been copied in Zambia, Fiji, Jamaica and Papua New Guinea.

At Murdoch University (founded in 1975) external enrolments in 1980 constituted 46 percent of total enrolments. Each course is designed and prepared by a single academic staff member in consultation with an academic from the External Studies Unit. Emphasis is placed on one-to-one tuition by correspondence, telephone and computer, rather than on study centre provision or compulsory attendance. At Deakin University (founded in 1976) the 2,600 external enrolments in 1980 comprised 55 percent of total enrolments. Course materials, which are prepared by teams of academic staff and other specialists, are designed in the first instance for off-campus use but may then be used on-campus. There is a network of study centres and student support services modelled on the UKOU's system.

In 1980, the 14,109 external enrolments in Australian universities constituted 8.7 percent of enrolments in all 19 Australian universities (only 5 of which taught at a distance).

The influence of the OU led the Whitlam Labour Government in 1973 to set up a commission on the founding of an open university in Australia. The commission rejected the idea of a DTU for Australia and voted in favour of the existing provision. It feared that "if it were to limit its recommendations to the creation of a single major institution like the British Open University, it might actually reduce the likelihood of existing institutions adopting innovatory policies" (Karmel,

1975, para. 8.2) and "in the Committee's judgment it is doubtful whether the market for off-campus courses in Australia would be large enough and homogeneous enough to produce such economies (of scale)" (8.25).

United States of America

The foundation of a correspondence programme at Illinois State University in 1874 can be taken as the start of distance education at university level in the USA. The idea that universities should take education to the general adult public was reflected in the early growth of the extension movement.

Formal courses have served the needs of external students since 1891 when William Rainey Harper organised the first university-sponsored correspondence programme in America as a formal part of the University of Chicago, and in 1906 correspondence teaching was introduced into the University of Wisconsin, a university that was to have a long and fruitful association with university programmes at a distance.

In the United States distance education courses at university level have usually been provided by independent study divisions within the extension colleges of conventional universities. In 1981 sixty-four such departments were affiliated to the Independent Study Division of the National University Extension Association of the United States of America. An example is the independent study department of Extension College of the University of Minnesota, which College also embraces the University Without Walls (a contract programme containing some contract and some distance study) and other non-traditional structures.

A number of other innovative institutions have emerged in the past decade. Empire State College, for example, was established in 1971 within the State University of New York system. Students who register with the College have to plan their own programme. They can take formal courses at other institutions, study independently or under guidance from a tutor, work with other students on a particular project, or take organised self-instructional programmes such as correspondence, programmed learning or televised courses (Houle, 1974: 97-8).

Elsewhere in the USA, limited use of UKOU teaching materials occurred from 1972/3 at Rutgers University, the University of Houston, and the University of Maryland; and efforts have been made to

19

transplant the UKOU idea, either wholly or in part, to the United States.

Recent developments in America, however have favoured the formation of materials production institutions meeting the needs of several universities. One example of these is the University of Mid-America (UMA). UMA is a regional institution serving seven mid-Western states. Students from nine state universities can enrol on its courses, which consist largely of printed materials, although some are based on television series. The state universities themselves provide tutorial support where possible, examine the students, and award credit.

The Union of Soviet Socialist Republics (USSR)

University level distance teaching in the USSR has a history going back to 1926. It was given a considerable boost following the end of the Second World War and, in the light of the experience then gained, was regulated by the 1958 Educational Reform Act (Subramanian, 1971: 178-80). Peters (1965: 105), surveying distance teaching at the university level in the early 1960s, identified eleven *distance teaching universities* in the USSR:

*   Northwestern Polytechnic Distance Teaching University, Leningrad.
*   Union Polytechnic Distance Teaching University, Moscow.
*   Ukranian Polytechnic Distance Teaching University, Kharkov.
*   Union Polytechnic Distance Teaching University, Kirov.
*   The seven Union Distance Teaching Universities for special disciplines (usually branches of engineering) all with their central institution in Moscow.

These Soviet distance teaching universities were based on a didactic strategy which has two bases: individual study from printed materials, and regular face-to-face meetings (seminars or consultations) which may be replaced by correspondence when distances are too great. In addition, Severtsev (1975: 40-42) reports widespread use of broadcasting and audio-visual systems to reach dispersed populations.

Today higher education planning in the USSR is based on the need to establish "for each specialisation . . . optimum proportions between the different types of education (full-time, evening or distance) with due regard to the special characteristics of education methods in each discipline and the branches of the economy for which specialists must be provided" (Ternov, 1978: 18). Distance education is seen to have two functions in the USSR. It provides educational opportunities for adults in employment and underlines the democratic character of education. Distance study at university level is seen to provide a satisfactory linking between study and productive work; to solve the problem of continuing professional education in engineering and to give people in employment the opportunity to learn a second career (Gorochow, 1979: 16).

In 1979, 2.2 million people were enrolled in university courses at a distance or in the evenings. This constitutes 40 percent of all university enrolments in the USSR. There were fourteen DTUs and over 100 evening and distance departments of conventional universities which offered courses in 267 disciplines. Millions of graduates have qualified in undergraduate and postgraduate programmes without ceasing to contribute to the GNP during the course of their studies.

German Democratic Republic (DDR)

Fernstudium in the German Democratic Republic, *Studia Zaochne* in Poland and similar forms of university distance education in Czechoslovakia and other socialist republics of central and eastern Europe received their present administrative and didactic structure in the 1950s. A specifically distinct model of distance education known as the *consultation model* has been developed especially in the German Democratic Republic. Of all the major forms of university distance education it is the one that places the most emphasis on compulsory face-to-face meetings and suggests that if distance study programmes are to be a success they must be structured as nearly as possible to conventional education.

Thirty of the 54 universities and university-level institutions in the DDR offer degrees at a distance.

The basic university degree programme (*Diplom*) lasts five and a half years as opposed to four years full-time on-campus. The distance study programme begins with a residential study school at which students are introduced to distance learning skills and receive the printed learning materials. Then the programme is continued by private study interspersed with compulsory fortnightly seminars or consultations. The 1:1 rhythm between lectures and private study in conventional university programmes is replaced by a 1:5 rhythm between consultations and private study in distance education. There is no correspondence element. The consultations are used for guidance, clarification, motivation, assessment of knowledge and abilities and the development of individual study skills.

In the final years of study the consultations are replaced by four or five intensive sessions lasting several days each and in the final year an extensive thesis is undertaken. The law *Anordnung über die Freistellung von der Arbeit* (GB1. 1Nr. 31) of the 1st July, 1973 grants 48 days paid study leave per year to students enrolled in scientific disciplines and 36 days for the social sciences. A further three months paid study leave in the final year of study is awarded by the law for the thesis (*Diplomarbeit*). As the distance study programme is planned between the student, the university and the student's firm, the thesis frequently takes the form of a research project of value to the enterprise and a position of higher responsibility is earmarked for the student on completion of the distance study programme. The fees of 120 Marks per year (1982) are paid by the firm if it officially sponsors the student.

The administrative structure of distance education at university level in the DDR comprises a Central Office for Distance Education set up in 1969 in Dresden, the university in which the student is enrolled, and a network of fourteen universities which provide consultation centres for the subject being studied - one of which should be relatively close to the student's place of residence.

The Central Office receives all applications for admission, prepares curricula, gives methodological guidance for authors and ensures production of the study materials, which are the same for all universities in the DDR. It also supervises the organisation and running of the consultation centres in the universities. Learning materials are developed by small groups of university professors meeting under the guidance of the central office. Today there are 1,675 centrally produced courses of which 1,000,000 copies are distributed annually (Dietze, 1978: 23).

Enrolments in 1981 are on the decline, due mainly to the growing lack of financial incentive for employees with the five and a half year *Diplom* as against their colleagues without it. An upsurge of enrolments is anticipated when a growing population bulge reaches the workforce about 1988. Nevertheless the 15,000 distance students enrolled in 1980

constituted 11.5 percent of all university enrolments in the DDR.
Unlike the USSR, the DDR has no DTUs nor has it any plans to change the comprehensive university level distance teaching system it has developed. This system produced in the period 1950-1975, 90,000 university graduates or 28 percent of total graduates in the period - while the students maintained their role in the workforce. A new emphasis is today being placed on the value of distance education for post-graduate awards (Möhle, 1978:10).

Canada, France, India, Latin America and elsewhere

It is not the place of this book to review in detail the development and current provision of distance teaching in universities on a world-wide basis. Such a review has not been undertaken since the work of Otto Peters in the early and mid-1960s.

By way of conclusion attention is drawn to:

* *Canada*, where distance education at university level was initiated at Queen's University, in Kingston, Ontario, in 1889. Today twenty Canadian universities have correspondence or distance education departments.

* *France*, where 18 of the 75 French universities have Centres de télé-enseignement universitaire (CTUs), with an enrolment in 1980 of 15,000.

* *India*, where Correspondence Directorates exist in 23 universities and in some other institutions of higher education.

* *Latin America*. Escotet (1980: 51-68) lists various Latin American universities with distance systems - for example, the distance studies projects at the University of Antioquia and the Javeriana University in Colombia.

Extensive treatment of distance education in a number of countries is to be found in Peters' book *Texte zum Hochschulfernstudium* (1971) which contains chapters on the USA by Wedemeyer, Bern and Childs; South Africa (Raedel), Australia (Sheath); Japan (Nishimoto); Sweden (Holmberg); England (Hawkridge); DDR (Möhle); Poland (Bandura); Czechoslovakia (Singule and Kamiac); USSR (Zavjolov) and People's Republic of China (Chou Li).

Conclusion

When the German scholar Otto Peters undertook a fundamental

comparative study of all distance teaching institutions in the Eastern and Western world in the early 1960s, his analysis of universities then teaching at a distance led him to the conclusion that "Distance teaching universities exist only in the Soviet Union and South Africa" (1965: 105). He cited the eleven universities listed above in the section on the Soviet Union and UNISA in the Republic of South Africa.

In the 1970s a new kind of institution, foreshadowed by UNISA, emerged: the autonomous multi-media distance teaching universities (DTUs) with which this book deals. These institutions are listed in Table 1.1.

By eliminating the lecture hall, seminar room and university library and placing the student at home, the DTUs have presented the most radical challenge yet to the traditional concept of a university. They also show specific differences from the Russian and South African foundations that preceded them. These differences are:

* The acceptance of a new "open" philosophy so that from many points of view they *are* open universities. This openness is reflected in some by an open admissions policy.

* The adoption of a broader curriculum by some of the recent foundations.

* The use of the new electronic and communications technology of the 1970s and 1980s.

Other DTUs are in the planning stage. The University of the Air in Japan is due to open in 1984; the Nigerian Open University, the bill for which was rejected in October 1981 by the legislature, but is likely to be resubmitted; and a Palestinian Open University, for which a feasibility study was carried out by Unesco during 1979-80. There is a proposal for an American Open University, building on the experience of the University of Mid-America at Lincoln, Nebraska. There are also proposals for open universities in a number of other countries (e.g. Portugal, Denmark, Finland). These proposals suggest that the 1980s will see the development of further DTUs although it is unlikely that there will ever be a great number of them.

The DTUs have been seen as the most striking development in higher education structures in recent decades, while the success and acclaim with which some of them have been met suggests that they will con- stitute a permanent component of the higher education sector of a number of national educational systems in the 1980s and 1990s.

24

Table 1.1 : Distance Teaching Universities (with their dates of incorporation)

University	Date of incorporation	
Open University, Milton Keynes, United Kingdom	1969	OU (UK)
Universidad Nacional de Educación a Distancia, Madrid, Spain	1972	UNED Spain
Free University of Iran, Tehran, Iran	1973	FUI
FernUniversität, Hagen, Federal Republic of Germany	1974	FeU
Everyman's University, Tel-Aviv, Israel	1974	EU
Allama Iqbal Open University, Islamabad, Pakistan	1974	AIOU
Athabasca University, Edmonton, Alberta, Canada	1975 †	AU
Universidad Nacional Abierta, Caracas, Venezuela	1977	UNA
Universidad Estatal a Distancia, San Jose, Costa Rica	1977	UNED Costa Rica
Sukhothai Thammathirat Open University, Bangkok, Thailand	1978	STOU
Central Broadcasting and Television University, Beijing, China and 28 Local Television Universities	1978	CCTU
Sri Lanka Open University, Nawala, Sri Lanka	1981	SLOU
Open University, Heerlen, Netherlands	1981	OU (Netherlands)

† as recorstituted

A TYPOLOGY OF DISTANCE TEACHING
AT UNIVERSITY LEVEL

As will be clear from the previous section, there is a wide range of universities which teach at a distance besides the DTUs which are the subject of this book.

A first attempt to group them is implied in Peters' 1971 classification of the institutions he presents into western and eastern models of distance education at university level (Table 1.2). Peters' division reflects the fundamental differences in administration and didactic structures between a study programme based on printed materials plus correspondence or media communication in the western models, and the eastern models based on printed materials plus face-to-face consultations.

Table 1.2 : Otto Peters' Western and Eastern models of distance teaching at university level.

	Examples of Western models		Examples of Eastern models
U.S.A.	University of Wisconsin University of Nebraska	D.D.R.	Karl-Marx Universitat, Leipzig
South Africa	UNISA	Poland	
Australia	University of New England	Czecho-slovakia	Karls University, Prague
Japan	Chuo, Hosei, Keio universities, etc.	U.S.S.R.	Northwestern Poly-technic Distance Teaching University, Leningrad
Sweden	Hermods		
United Kingdom	Open University	People's Republic of China	

El-Bushra (1973: 13-15) identified six categories of institutions providing for external students at university level:
* Institutions dealing exclusively with external students (e.g., the UKOU).
* Institutions which offer facilities for external examinations but provide no actual teaching (e.g. the External Degrees Service of the University of London).

* Institutions where the correspondence unit operates under a single department (e.g. the School of Education at the University of the South Pacific).

* Institutions which accept both internal and external students in the same teaching department and in which the correspondence unit is an administrative and supervisory body (e.g. the University of New England in Australia).

* Institutions where the correspondence department takes responsibility not only for administering the courses, but also for teaching them (e.g. the University of Queensland in Australia).

* Institutions which offer correspondence courses in co-operation with other bodies (e.g. Massey University in New Zealand).

Neil (1981) has recently developed a typology in which he distinguishes between autonomous distance learning systems operating as institutions in their own right and those which operate as the distance learning "wing" of a conventional educational institution (Neil, 1981: 126). He bases his conception of institutional autonomy on four key areas of control: finance, examination and accreditation, curriculum and materials, and delivery and student support systems (ibid.: 140). He then goes on to identify five types of distance learning systems:

* 'Centre-periphery' models in which a central headquarters has total control over the activities of its local centres (e.g. UKOU).

* Associated centre models (in which the headquarters does not have control over its centres in one or more areas) (e.g. UNED, Spain).

* Dispersed centre models (e.g. Coastline Community College, California) in which the institution is "embedded" throughout the community.

* 'Switchboard' organisational models (e.g. the Norsk fjernundervisning) which have enabling, co-ordinating, initiating and approving roles in the development of distance education programmes but do not themselves teach.

* Service institution models (e.g. the Deutsches Institut für Fernstudien an der Universität Tübingen) which work in co-operation with other institutions on distance learning projects, but which neither teach nor have students.

In 1982 Keegan developed a simplified typology of distance teaching institutions for use in one of the course units developed for the Graduate

Diploma in Distance Education of the South Australian College of Advanced Education in Adelaide. He omitted institutions that do not both enrol and teach students (e.g. University of London External Degree Service, University of Mid-America, Deutsches Institut für Fernstudien at Tübingen) and proposed as the basis of the typology whether the institution was established solely for distance education or was a mixed or hybrid institution having both distance and conventional students (see Figure 1.1).

Figure 1.1 : Keegan's typology of distance teaching at university level.

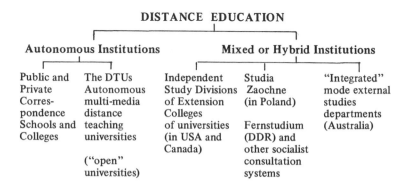

On the basis of our review of distance teaching in universities we have developed the following typology for universities which teach at a distance. As in Neil and Keegan's typologies the basic distinction is between autonomous distance teaching systems and those mixed or hybrid systems which teach both distance and conventional students. We have identified seven basic organisational structures, as follows:

Autonomous, centrally controlled DTUs. Organisations of this type teach wholly at a distance and are clearly identified with a single institution. As universities, they determine their own curriculum and design their own materials (or buy in materials on their own initiative); they have a clear responsibility for their own examinations and accreditation; determine their own delivery and student support systems; and have a reasonable degree of financial autonomy. Examples of this type include the UKOU, EU, AU and UNED Costa Rica.

Autonomous, decentralised DTUs. Organisations of this type teach wholly at a distance and are clearly identified with a single institution. They share the characteristics of the preceding group, but have a lower degree of control over their delivery and student support systems, which are handled by associated centres. UNED Spain and the CCTU in the People's Republic of China are institutions of this type.

Essentially autonomous distance teaching universities operating within a federated university structure encompassing both conventional campuses and a distance teaching unit. The Télé-université in Quebec falls within this category. The Télé-université is an autonomous unit operating under the University of Quebec Board of Governors, which Board also oversees the management of the University's largely autonomous campuses at Montreal, Trois Rivières, Rimouski and Chicoutimi, as well as a number of more specialised institutions.

Autonomous centralised distance teaching systems with a high degree of control using facilities based in and run by conventional universities. Organisations of this type cannot be equated with a single institution, but are better regarded as distance teaching 'systems'. An example of this kind of system is found in the DDR where the Central Office for Distance Education, a Government Ministry at Dresden, exerts a fair degree of control and is responsible for admitting students, preparing curricula, overseeing materials design and production, and supervising the organisation and running of the 'consultation' centres. The latter essentially operate as distance education departments within the conventional universities.

Mixed mode, uni-departmental model. In this model a special distance teaching department is established within a conventional university to both administer the system and teach the courses. The External Studies Department at the University of Queensland is of this kind.

Mixed mode, multi-departmental model. This model is also referred to as the *Australian integrated mode* or the *New England model* because it originated in Australia at the University of New England. In this model academic staff are responsible for teaching both internal and external students, and the External Studies Department is an administrative and not an academic unit.

Mixed mode, multi-institutional model. An example of this approach is found at Massey University in New Zealand, which is a mixed mode institution teaching its own campus-based and external students.

However, Massey University has an additional responsibility as the sole provider of university level correspondence courses in the country, and as such registers on appropriate courses the external students of other universities for tuition purposes only. Such students sit Massey's examinations but the accreditation is done in the name of their 'home' university.

However, while we find this typology helpful, in practice it can be very difficult to draw dividing lines between the models listed above.

Conclusions

The DTUs are a relatively new development. While they present a radical challenge to the traditional concept of a university, they have, as we have shown, developed out of a wider context, and it is important to recognise that there is another tradition of mixed distance and conventional teaching universities which is both older and more widespread than the autonomous DTUs that are the subject of this book.

The next chapters (2 to 10) provide case studies of nine of the institutions listed in Table 1.1; case studies of the Free University of Iran by Beardsley (1975) and Goodenough (1978) have been published elsewhere. In the final chapters (11 and 12) we attempt to identify certain common characteristics of the DTUs and assess their success to date.

Many of the DTUs have already achieved a name for excellence and we believe that they can be regarded as permanent structures within the higher education systems which they serve. At a time when further DTUs are in the process of being established, and when a number of governments are considering founding a DTU, it seems opportune to survey the institutions now operating and report on their progress. It is in this context that we hope that this book will prove useful.

References

1. Beardsley, J. (1975) 'The Free University of Iran'. In Mackenzie, N., Postgate, R., and Scupham, J., (editors) (1975) 'Open Learning'. Paris: Unesco.
2. Dietze, G. (1978) 'Zur Leitung und Planung der Hochschulfernstudiums in der DDR'. In Möhle, H. (ed.) 'Hoch-und Fachschulfernstudium in der DDR und in Entwicklungsländern Afrika'. Leipzig: Karl-Marx Universität.
3. El-Bushra, J. (1973) 'Correspondence Teaching at University'. Cambridge: International Extension College.

4. Escotet, M.A. (1980) 'Tendencias de la Educación Superior a Distancia'. San Jose: Editorial UNED.
5. Goodenough, S. (1978) 'A case study in distance learning systems: The Free University of Iran'. Milton Keynes: Open University Centre for International Co-operation and Service. Mimeograph.
6. Gorochow, (1979) 'Hauptwege zur Fervollkommnung des Fernstudiums in der UdSSR'. In Dietze, G. (ed.) 'Referate und Beiträge: 4 Internationales Wissenschaftunches Seminar zum Hochschulfernstudium'. Dresden: Ministerium für Hoch- und Fachschulwesen.
7. Houle, C.O. (1974) 'The External Degree'. San Francisco: Jossey-Bass Publishers.
8. Karmel Report (1975) 'Open Tertiary Education in Australia. Final Report of the Committee on Open University to the Universities Commission'. Canberra: Australian Government Publishing Service.
9. Möhle, H. (1978) 'Das in das einheitliche Sozialistische Bildungswesen der DDR integrierte Hochschulfernstudium, seine Grundkonzeption und sein Ergebnisse'. In Möhle, H. (ed.) 'Hoch- und Fachschulfernstudium in der DDR und in Entwicklungsländern Afrika'. Leipzig: Karl-Marx Universität.
10. Neil, M. (1981) 'Education of Adults at a Distance'. London: Kogan Page.
11. Perry, W. (1972) 'The Early Development of the Open University. Report of the Vice-Chancellor, January 1969- December 1970'. Milton Keynes: The Open University.
12. Peters, O. (1965) 'Der Fernunterricht. Materialien zur Diskussion einer neuen Unterrichtsform'. Weinheim: Beltz.
13. Peters, O. (1971) 'Texte Zum Hochschulfernstudium'. Weinheim: Beltz.
14. Severtsev, V. (1975) 'Case Study of the Development of Higher Education in the USSR'. Paris: Unesco. ED/76/WS/1.
15. Subramanian, S. (1971) 'Education by correspondence in Sweden, Russia and Poland'. In Glatter, R. and Wedell, E.G. (1971) 'Study by correspondence. An enquiry into correspondence study for examinations for degrees and other advanced qualifications'. London: Longmans.
16. Ternov, I.M. (1978) 'Education Orientated Towards Professional Employment'. In International Association of Universities (1978) 'The Right to Education and Access to Higher Education'. Paris: IAU.

31

Chapter 2

ATHABASCA UNIVERSITY, CANADA

Doug Shale

Athabasca University, the newest of the four Alberta universities, is presently situated in Edmonton, the provincial capital. The University is currently in the process of relocating to the town of Athabasca, a small rural community some 145 kilometres to the north of Edmonton.

PROVINCIAL PROFILE

Geography

Alberta has a total area of 661,000 square kilometres and comprises one-fifteenth of the total area of Canada. The varied terrain encompasses the foothills of the Rockies in the south-west; the boreal forest of the north, broken by the farmlands of the Peace River region; the ice-scoured plain of the Canadian Shield in the north-east; and the prairie parklands and grasslands of the centre and south.

Population

The population is ethnically diverse. Predominantly urban, 51 percent of the total population of 2.1 millions (1980) live in Edmonton (0.51 million) and Calgary (0.56 million). Roughly 50 percent of the population is 24 years of age or younger; 27 percent is in the age range 25-44; and 11 percent 65 or older. Of the 1.46 million considered to be of working age, 1.2 million are economically active.

Economy

The oil and gas industry dominate the economy, accounting for 53 percent of the total net value of production, followed by construction (22 percent), manufacturing (13 percent), and agriculture (10 percent).

Communications

There were 148,000 kilometres of roads in 1979 with 1.6 million registered vehicles (0.95 million cars). Two major railways link Alberta with the rest of Canada, and there are 3 main provincial railways. In addition, the province has extensive internal airservices.

The considerable size of Alberta and the relative geographic isolation of many of its inhabitants make communications a vital concern. There is an extensive radio and television broadcasting network which in 1979 consisted of 38 AM and 11 FM radio broadcasting stations; 28 AM and 31 FM rebroadcast stations; 11 television stations; and 101 television rebroadcast stations. Major centres also receive broadcasts from U.S. stations via cable. There is a television set in virtually every household and some 80 percent of the households have colour TV. The average house has more than one radio. Most of the TV and radio broadcasting is privately owned. However, the Alberta government has established a corporation called ACCESS which is responsible for providing educational radio and television programming. A communications satellite is used to provide some programming to the remote northern regions of the province. There are 9 daily newspapers which reach over 80 percent of all households in Alberta, and there are well over one hundred weekly newspapers. The province has an extensive telephone system with some 1.5 million phones in service in 1979. A radio-telephone link provides for communication with isolated areas not reached by terrestrial telephone lines.

EDUCATIONAL PROFILE

The ten provinces and two territories in Canada are joined together by a federal system of government under which the federal and provincial governments have established areas of jurisdiction. The legislative responsibilities of these two levels of governments are established by the British North America Act and under one of the sections of this Act education is identified as a provincial responsibility. Education in Alberta is compulsory for children 6 to 16 years of age. There are preschool programmes for some of the children 4 to 6 years of age but these are not universally available. School programmes consist of

3 general levels: Elementary education, which provides for the first six years of schooling; Secondary education, which provides for the next six years of schooling; and Post-Secondary education, which includes university-level study, training in the arts, and technical, vocational and industrial training.

The Post-Secondary section of the educational system comprises four universities, the Banff Centre, ten public colleges, three private colleges, two technical institutes, four adult vocational centres, and a petroleum industry training centre. Although all of these institutions receive financial support from the government, students are expected to make a significant contribution to the costs of their education through payment of fees. Because of the provision within the BNA Act assigning responsibility for education to the provinces, the financing of education is also a provincial responsibility. However, the federal government has historically contributed substantially to support the costs of university education. The current arrangement involves a transfer of tax points to the Province and a cash payment pegged to changes in the gross national product with the provinces administering these monies in accordance with provincial priorities.

ATHABASCA UNIVERSITY (AU)

Origins

As was the case throughout the rest of Canada, full-time enrolments at universities in Alberta burgeoned through the sixties. By the late sixties enrolment pressures at the University of Alberta were particularly acute with this institution reaching what was regarded as the upper limit to its growth. Athabasca University was established in 1970 largely in response to these enrolment pressures and was to have been a conventional campus-based university offering innovative undergraduate programmes in arts, science and education. The Order in Council establishing the University enjoined it "to explore and to institute, if deemed desirable, new procedures in curriculum organization and instruction", and the early academic planning proceeded in this spirit. The university was to have been located in St. Albert, a city (then a town) adjoining Edmonton. In the latter part of 1970 there occurred a juxtaposition of events that lead to the abandonment of what Hughes

(1980) has called "the first Athabasca University". The major event was the ascendance to power of the Progressive Conservative Party, ending thirty-six years of Social Credit government. The new Cabinet immediately undertook extensive reviews of major projects initiated under the previous regime, Athabasca being one of these. Unfortunately for the University, by this time it was apparent that the projected rates of growth in full-time enrolments would not be realised. In May, 1972, the government issued a policy statement which suspended all physical facilities planning. However, in this same statement the government expressed approval of the academic plan that had been developed, and authorised the Governing Authority "to continue academic planning by undertaking a pilot project which would test in a practical setting various dimensions of the Athabasca University model. The pilot study would, in effect, be a research and development project in advanced education". The pilot project as it was envisaged at that time ". . . would involve a group of approximately 250 students with the necessary academic and professional staff operating in temporary quarters". The University grasped at this opportunity and proceeded to plan in accordance with the direction indicated. However, as Hughes (1980: 19) points out ". . . Athabasca University's efforts to set the pilot project in motion became just another disillusioning false start". The practicalities of hiring staff, attracting students, and acquiring physical facilities under the limited 4 to 5 year commitment the government was prepared to give, virtually guaranteed the project would be stillborn. In addition, the higher educational establishment was still not prepared to support another campus-based institution. The zeitgeist of the day was lifelong learning and ". . . a break with the institutional tradition of a central place for learning" (Worth, 1972). Consequently, in December, 1972 the government issued another Order in Council which established Athabasca University again and appointed an interim governing body. This Order in Council: "empowers and authorizes the Athabasca University Interim Governing Authority to undertake a pilot project for the production, testing and application of learning systems to provide study programmes in the arts and sciences leading to an undergraduate degree, and for the application of technology and new procedures to improve educational opportunities for adults generally". However, Athabasca University was still regarded as a pilot project which was to end in 1975.

Although AU was "re-established" with a mandate distinctly

35

different from what was originally intended, some of the educational innovations planned for in those early days lead directly to a number of major policies adopted by the University such as an open admission policy, which enables students to enter the University at any time and to withdraw from it at any time; and a policy of self-pacing and self-directed study through a learning system. The practicalities of designing its own learning systems and the observed success of the British Open University in its early days led AU into distance education directed at adults who, for various reasons, might not otherwise have access to university study. As part of the pilot project, the University produced a core of three courses and began registering students in October, 1973. By the time the pilot project period ended in November, 1975, the University had convinced the government that the concept of distance education could be made to work in Alberta, and that a need for such an educational service existed. Consequently, at that time the government - through yet another Order in Council - granted permanent status to Athabasca University as an undergradute, degree granting institution. However, no legislative commitment had yet been made to the University. Finally, in April, 1978, the University was formally established under the authority of the Universities Act, and at the same time a permanent Governing Council was appointed to replace the Interim Governing Authority which had been in place since 1970. The issue of a facility for the University was left hanging, although the Minister had stated during the budget debates of April, 1978: "There has been no judgement as to a permanent location . . . this will have to occur now that Athabasca University has been given a permanent mandate." This matter was not to be resolved until March, 1980.

Students

Although the Athabasca University student population is very diverse in its characteristics, it has been relatively consistent in this diversity. Data gathered on all students for the years 1977-78 to 1980-81 indicate that the relative distribution of male and female students has remained quite stable over these years with females representing between 59 and 62 percent of the student body. Most of the students have been in the 25-44 age range with the percentage increasing somewhat from 60 percent in 1977-78 to 67 percent in 1980-81. The percentage of students in the 18-24 age range has decreased slightly from a high of

25 to a low of 22, and the percentage of students aged 45 and older has remained stable at 11 - 12. As might be expected, the age and sex distributions of AU students are very similar to those of students who study part time at the conventional universities in Alberta.

Homemakers have consistently been the largest "occupational" group, although the proportionate size of this group has diminished from a high of 16 percent in 1977-78 to 8 in 1980-81. Nurses constitute the next largest group, followed by teachers, students and the retired, and clerical occupations. Each of these groups is of a similar size - 5 to 7 percent of the student body. In all, students listed some 100 different job titles with about 90 percent reporting they were either employed or maintaining a household.

The general level of previous educational background of AU students has increased steadily; the number of students with less than complete high school education has declined from 31 percent in 1977-78 to 16 in 1980-81, and the number of students with complete high school has increased steadily from 69 to 84 percent in the same period. While the number of students with some university experience has remained fairly constant at 22 - 25 percent, the number of previous degree holders has increased from 5 to 16 percent.

Although the University attracts students from all parts of Alberta, more students are situated in the northern part of the province than in the south. An analysis of the 1980-81 body of students indicated that approximately 70 percent of these students are located in one or other of the Albertan cities, whereas approximately 67 percent of the total Alberta population is located in these centres. Some 47 percent of this group of students come from the cities of Edmonton and Calgary compared to 51 percent of the Alberta population. The University also draws students from most of the other provinces and the two territories, although the numbers are modest. In 1980-81, about 28 percent of the total AU student population consisted of out of province students. Most of the out of province students are from British Columbia and are due largely to special arrangements the University has with North Island College.

Students have consistently reported that the most important reason for their undertaking university study is to prepare for a future career and the next most important reason is for personal development. They also state that the main reason they are studying with Athabasca University is because of the flexibility of starting and completing courses virtually at any time throughout the year and the freedom to set their own study schedule. Students consider the next most important feature to be the advantages of studying at home, thereby remaining in their own communities.

Academic Programmes

Athabasca University currently offers three undergraduate level degree programmes: a Bachelor of Arts; a Bachelor of General Studies (B.G.S.); and a Bachelor of Administration. These degree programmes each require that a student accumulate 90 credits, which is equivalent to three years of full-time study. The University offers individualised degree study programmes within the applied and liberal studies areas in which a framework is provided for students to choose and organise courses according to what they need and want. University determined programmes are also offered in which the choice and organisation of courses is regulated by the University. Programmes are also offered which are designed to facilitate students' completing degree programmes at other institutions. AU has collaborated with the Faculties of Nursing of both of the Universities of Calgary and Alberta to produce post-basic Nursing Transfer Programmes designed to minimise the amount of time students would have to spend on the campuses to obtain a bachelors degree in nursing. Similarly, a transfer programme in Social Work has been developed in co-operation with the University of Calgary. A general transfer programme is available which could provide students with sufficient credits to satisfy the requirements of the first two years of study in general arts and science degree programmes at the other Albertan universities. A non-programme admission category is available for students who wish to register on AU courses that interest them without having to meet any programme requirements. The University used to offer a certificate course in Public Administration in collaboration with the Blue Quills Native Education Council, but this programme was discontinued in 1980. Most AU students are admitted to the University as non-programme students, and roughly one-third of the students active in 1980-81 were in this category. The Bachelor of Administration programme which is the fastest growing of the programmes, has the next largest number of active students - 22 percent in 1980-81, an increase of 7 percent on 1979-80. About one-fifth of active students have typically registered in the general transfer programme. Less than 15 percent of active students have registered in the BA and BGS programmes. The University conferred its first degrees in 1976-77, and has awarded a total of 29 to date. Table 2.1 displays the number and kind of degrees awarded by year.

Table 2.1 : Number of Graduates by Degree Conferred

Degree Granted	1976-77	1977-78	1978-79	1979-80	1980-81
B.G.S.	2	--	5	5	9
D.A.	--	--	--	3	2
B. Admin.	--	--	--	--	3
Totals.	2	--	5	8	14

(Source: AU Fact Book, 1980-81)

The attractiveness of the BGS programme is largely due to a provision within its regulations allowing the acceptance of large numbers of university level credits earned at other recognised post-secondary institutions. In fact, it is possible for a student to amass enough credit through the credit transfer and consolidation provision within the BGS programme to earn his degree without having to complete any AU courses. The first degrees conferred by AU were for BGS programmes of this kind.

Courses

Athabasca University differentiates three levels of courses: there are preparatory courses which are designed to prepare students for university level study in certain disciplines - currently mathematics and French; junior courses, which are introductory level courses; and senior courses, which assume some appropriate level of prior learning and which may require specific pre-requisites. AU courses are normally either six-credits or three-credits in weight, which corresponds to the three and six semester-hours of credit designations used at other universities. The University also currently offers three general interest psychology courses for which no credit is awarded. Courses are offered in four academic areas of study: Administrative Studies, Sciences,

Social Studies and Humanities. There are also a relatively small number of courses that are generically designated as Applied Studies courses because of their specific relationships to professional programmes.

The difficulties and costs involved in producing university courses to be delivered at a distance are now well-known (for example, see Perry, 1976). However, in the years of the pilot project AU undertook to design its courses "from the ground up". To a large degree, this was a consequence of attempting to accommodate the educational philosophy persisting from the planning surrounding the "first Athabasca University". In fact, the first three courses the University developed were designed to match very closely, early intentions to establish interdisciplinary "fields of study" in: Environmental Problems; Human Community; and Humanities (Athabasca University - Academic Concept, 1971). A fourth course was planned which would have matched the fourth "field of study" identified in the Academic Concept document, Communications: however, this latter course was never produced. In producing its first courses, the University continued with an early interest in "learning systems", two consequences of which were attempts to use a variety of media in presenting course content, and the adoption of the course team concept pioneered by the British Open University. Because these courses took a considerable length of time to produce and were very costly, the University subsequently sought ways to produce courses more quickly and cheaply. As a result, efforts to use a variety of media diminished and courses came to be based more and more on printed material. There was also a significant shift in emphasis from a course development process wherein substantial amounts of instructional material had to be written, to a model wherein commercially available texts and manuals were used as the instructional core. As the complexity of the course development process diminished, course team operations became simpler and the course team grew smaller (Stringer, 1980: 14). The University also increased its efforts to acquire courses produced by other institutions. Despite meeting with a host of problems in adopting and adapting courses produced elsewhere (Daniel and Forsythe, 1979), the University has been able to supplement its course offerings substantially by acquiring courses from the Open University in the UK, Coastline Community College in the USA, Laurentian University and the Télé-Université in Canada, and others. Athabasca University and the Open Learning Institute in BC have worked jointly on the development of several courses and the experience has been that such collaboration ameliorates many of the problems usually associated with using courses produced elsewhere. This arrangement has been of considerable benefit to both institutions.

AU has experimented with delivering traditional lecture style courses in selected locations throughout the province, as a means of responding quickly to specific local demands. The University also offers a number of reading courses at the senior level which are similar in design to reading courses offered at traditional universities, except that instructor-student contact is by telephone. At various times and in various selected locations, AU offers seminar-supported courses, which are courses based primarily on home-study instructional materials, but for which an instructor is provided. These courses have study schedules that are determined by the schedule of seminar meetings. A few courses have also been offered at some locations by teleconferencing. These latter courses may simply be home-study packaged courses supported through regular teleconferencing sessions led by an instructor or tutor. However, they may also be hybrid courses in which much of the learning results from the oral interaction among the instructor and students with printed materials providing the information on which the teleconferencing sessions are based.

However, the home-study course remains the mainstay of the AU instructional system. These courses are designed to be self-instructional, and they are essentially self-contained. All required textbooks, study guides, audio-cassette tapes, workbooks, references, and other materials are included in a course materials package that is mailed to the student. Courses which have a laboratory component are offered in certain locations only, depending on student demand and whether the University can arrange for the laboratory facilities. Some courses have television and/or radio components associated with them. The radio programmes have been broadcast over private stations and a station run by ACCESS, the provincial educational media corporation. In the Fall of 1980, the University also began narrowcasting a series of radio programmes through a Subsidiary Communications Multiplex Operation (SCMO) facility made available by ACCESS. Television programmes have been delivered through a variety of distribution systems, largely via cable. Unfortunately, even with a network of distribution systems some students are not able to receive course television programmes. Difficulties with scheduling programmes and unreliability in some aspects of the distribution system cause additional problems.

Consequently, the University makes television programmes available on video-tapes that may be viewed at some of the Regional Learning Centres located throughout the province. It has been involved with ACCESS in delivering some television programmes by satellite on an experimental basis. However, AU has produced relatively few television and radio programmes of its own despite its early considerable interest in multi-media instruction. In fact, the University produced only one course which used television and that was for the first course developed. The costs and difficulties associated with producing quality television were the major factors that led the University away from developing its own programmes. When ACCESS was established, it was expected to provide television production support to educational institutions including AU, and this arrangement has led to the joint production of some TV programmes. Most of the television and radio programmes offered by AU have been acquired by purchasing courses from other institutions. In 1980-81, the University offered a total of 74 hours of television programmes over 6 courses, and 85 hours of radio programmes over 4 courses.

Course Development

Home-study courses have typically been produced by course teams consisting of a subject matter expert, an instructional developer, a visual designer and an editor, with one of these individuals assuming additional duties as course team manager. The subject matter expert is responsible for selecting the content covered by a course, and he usually reviews and chooses the textbooks and other prepared materials to be used in the course. If appropriate instructional materials are not commercially available, the subject matter expert may write much of the instruction himself. In the early days after the pilot project phase, and as the University struggled to produce more courses more quickly, many subject-matter experts were retained on a part-time or consulting basis. Since that time the trend has been toward hiring full-time academic staff to fill this role, although AU continues to use a significant number of external consultants. The instructional developer works with the subject matter expert to ensure that the content is organised so that it may be learned more easily. He or she also helps the subject matter expert prepare practice questions and exercises, as well as examinations. The visual designer is responsible for the format, lay-out, and physical production of the materials. The editor's role is to ensure that all materials are well written. As Stringer (1980) has pointed out, not all course teams have been constituted in this manner, and the University has experimented with different kinds of course teams in an effort to find effective and efficient ways to produce courses.

Student Support Services

The most important element in the University's academic support to students is the tutor. When students enrol in a home-study course, they are automatically assigned a tutor who becomes the students' immediate contact with the University. Tutors answer students' questions about course content and administrative matters, and generally introduce a personal element into the solitude that is distance study. Tutors may also be involved in marking and commenting on student assignments, and in organising seminars, discussion groups, or workshop sessions. All students have toll-free telephone access to tutors from anywhere in Canada.

Tutors are part-time members of staff recruited from throughout the province and employed under a contract that must be renewed annually. They typically have Masters degrees or relevant experience in a discipline closely related to the course being tutored. Tutors are currently paid on the basis of their experience, the number of students assigned, and the type of course being tutored. Since the University first instituted the tutorial system in 1976, the number of tutors has increased from 22 to 91 (as of March, 1981). The hiring and administration of tutors is the responsibility of a unity called Regional and Tutorial Services. This unit looks after matters pertaining to tutor contracts, terms and conditions of employment, payment of fees and expenses, and so on. Regional and Tutorial Services also provides orientation and staff development programmes for tutors. However, a tutor's primary contact with the University is through a course co-ordinator, to whom the tutor is responsible for all academic matters related to courses and students. The course co-ordinator, who is an academic with qualifications equivalent to those in faculties at other universities, is available to provide tutors and students with additional information about course content as required.

Learning centres, which are administered through Regional and

Tutorial Services, have been established in various communities throughout the province. These centres, which are often situated in local schools or libraries, provide students with access to a range of supplementary learning materials. All centres stock supplementary reading materials and some have computer terminals, television, and other audio-visual resources. Students may also come to learning centres to study or to write examinations. In addition to these learning centres the University has established regional offices in Calgary and Ft. McMurray. These regional offices were originally established to provide students in these communities with a limited range of information and student services. Consideration has been given to locating more student service functions in regional offices, and various trials are now being conducted. The University is also considering establishing regional offices in other locations. AU has negotiated arrangements with some other post-secondary institutions whereby students of these institutions enrol in AU courses and are examined by the University, with tutorial and other support services being provided by the institutions. The most notable of these has been the arrangement AU has with North Island College in British Columbia.

In addition to providing students with course packages, tutors, and scheduled learning sessions, AU offers other services to students to help them achieve maximum benefit from their studies. Student Development Services, which is an organisational unit within the University, gives students advice on career and educational planning and help in selecting and organising programmes of study. This unit also provides students with information on a wide variety of topics such as how AU operates, how to arrange for the transfer of AU credits to a programme elsewhere, and what type of programme would best accommodate a particular combination of career, educational, and personal goals. Student Development Services currently produces three publications to facilitate communication between the University and its students: the AU magazine which contains information of general interest about the University and its activities; the Student Handbook which provides students with advice on study skills and more detailed information than is given in the Calendar on such matters as registering on courses and dealing with problems; and a Student Directory designed to provide students with an opportunity to get in touch with other students.

Library Services are available to students who require various library reference materials such as books, journals, newspapers and maps.

Students may borrow materials from the AU library by dropping in, by writing to the library, or by telephoning. The University library also cooperates with the libraries of the other Albertan universities to extend access to library services for AU students. Through a system of interlibrary loans, students may obtain materials from major libraries throughout Alberta.

Student Administration

AU has an open admissions policy. There are no academic requirements for entry to the University, and the only constraints are that students must be eighteen years of age or older and live in Canada. In most cases, students may enrol in AU courses at any time of the year. Students may proceed through courses at their own pace and complete courses when they are ready. The University generally requires that they complete a 3-credit course within six months and a 6-credit course within twelve months. The student may, because of extenuating circumstances, be allowed to suspend study for up to six months. Students may also obtain an extension to the time allowed for completion of a course at a cost of 10 dollars a month until completion. However, extensions are granted only if the student has remained active in the course.

Tuition fees currently are 82.50 dollars for a 3-credit course and 165 dollars for a 6-credit course. Payment of tuition fees entitles a student to all course materials, including textbooks, and to tutorial support and other services for as long as a student's registration is active. Tuition fees are waived for those 65 years of age and older. The typical AU student will enrol in only one course per year, although some attempt more than one, the proportion for 1980-81 being 1.4 enrolments per student.

Because students are able to register on and complete courses at any time, AU does not have an academic year or academic terms. Consequently, it has adopted the fiscal year as the time period for which it reports data about its operations. In actuality, much of the University's activities follow the two term cycle used at other Albertan universities. Most course production schedules are established so that new courses are first offered in September-October or January-February, and advertising is generally synchronized to these time periods. It follows that the majority of course enrolments occur at these times. However, there are significant numbers of enrolments throughout the other months. The flexibility allowed by the University in regard to start dates and rate of course completion requires a sophisticated computer-based system of administration. AU currently uses an on-line management system.

Student Assessment and Examinations

The University's early concern with educational innovation led it to adopt the "Mastery Model" instructional programme during the pilot project phase. In retrospect, this model can be regarded as a natural consequence of the spirit of educational egalitarianism prevailing at that time, because of the commitment within the model to the assumption that most people can attain academic mastery of a subject if they are provided with adequate instruction and sufficient time. Some of the operational consequences resulting from the implementation of this model were: extensive course design based on behavioural objectives; substantial diagnostic evaluation of learning throughout courses; the provision of additional instructional opportunities and time for those students who require them; and the establishment of 80 percent as the pass mark, with the assessment system being criterion-referenced rather than norm-referenced. Substantial practical problems arose from the implementation of the model, and many of its distinguishing features were considerably altered. However, vestiges of the Mastery Model may be seen in AU's current instructional and assessment practices. Many courses are still developed according to defined goals or learning objectives that are drawn from the course content and descriptive of it. Student grades are based on the degree to which students achieve these goals and learning objectives, and are expressed in percentages. Students are not explicitly graded on a curve, and the entire range of the percentage scale is used. The University has established 60 percent as the passing grade in its courses, a grade which the University considers to reflect a better than marginal performance and an adequate preparation for subsequent courses in the same subject. There are a few courses that are still based on the 80 percent pass mark but these are administered differently from the other courses.

Some courses are still structured into discrete blocks of material with assessment performed, grades assigned, and credit awarded for each block. Within certain limits the University will accept for credit towards its degrees, credits earned in the partial completion of its courses. However, this assessment practice, which required a considerable amount of formal examination (up to six exams in some courses), has largely been replaced by continuous assessment. Formal exams are still required in most courses, but the average number of examinations per course has been reduced substantially. Formal examinations are all supervised. When a student is ready to write an exam, he or she notifies the University. If there is a learning centre near the student, the examination may be written there. However, if such an arrangement is not possible, the student may nominate as a supervisor, a resident of the community who occupies a position of public responsibility. The marking of examinations occurs at the University's central offices, unlike the marking of assignments which is distributed to tutors.

Governance and Organisation

When the University was given permanent status, it adopted a unicameral governance system in which the Governing Council assumed the powers and duties of a conventional Board of Governors with respect to financial and administrative matters, and of a General Faculties Council/Senate with respect to academic affairs. The maximum number of members on the Governing Council has been set at twenty-three. The Chairman is appointed by the Government, and twelve public members are appointed by the Minister. Five academic staff members and one support staff member are elected by the respective groups of staff, and there is one student representative. The President and two of the Vice-presidents are members ex-officio. A recent review of the committee arrangement supporting this structure has resulted in a distribution of responsibilities that is more akin to bicameral governance. In particular, responsibility for academic affairs has been delegated to an Academic Council consisting of a broad representation of staff.

The chief academic and administrative officer is the President of the University. The University has three Vice-presidents, each of whom heads one of the University's three operational divisions: Learning Services, which is responsible for academic functions; University Services, which provides administrative services in support of the University's academic operations; and Finance and Facilities, which is responsible for financial affairs and facilities planning.

From an operational point of view, the University's two primary academic functions, course development and programme services delivery, cut across organisational lines. As AU has grown, it has tried various organisational structures to accommodate these academic functions. The interested reader is referred to the Athabasca University Annual Reports (1975-76 to 1980-81) for a history of these. Currently, the programme areas, which are Liberal Studies and Administrative Studies, administer the production of courses and exercise budgetary control of this process. This was formerly the responsibility of a separate unit called Course Development. In addition, the programme areas provide much of the subject matter expertise required to produce course content. Courses are delivered and administered by course co-ordinators who are academic staff within the programme areas.

Other units involved in the production of courses are: Instructional Development, which provides expertise in making courses instructionally effective; Editorial Services, which ensures that subject matter is presented in clear, readable English; and Media Services, which provides expertise in the effective visual presentation of course content and is responsible for the physical production of course materials. Units primarily concerned with providing support services to students are: Regional and Tutorial Services, which is responsible for administering the system of tutors and for co-ordinating the use of various delivery mechanisms such as television, radio, teleconferencing, and satellite; Student Development Services, which provides students with inform-ation and advice on career and educational planning; and the Registry, which is responsible for student administration and student records. The Library, Computing Services, and Course Materials also provide students with support services. There are other units within the Uni-versity that essentially provide administrative support to instructional activities or are concerned with institutional management.

Costs

Table 2.2 displays a variety of data about Athabasca University per-taining to enrolments, courses, staffing, and costs. Comparative data are provided for six years. As the data indicate, the University has grown rapidly. Although there has been a decrease in some rates of increase, it is expected that the University will continue to grow at a relatively rapid rate at least until 1985-86.

Table 2.2 : Data on AU Operations, 1975-76 to 1980-81.

	1975-76	1976-77	1977-78	1978-79	1979-80	1980-81
Total Courses Available 1.	3	16	31*	59*	66*	95*
Total Credits Available	18	90	138	240	273	390
No. of courses by mode of delivery -						
Packaged:	2	12	17	29	42	50
Instructor-delivered:	1	3	14	26	14	11
Seminar-supported:	–	1	–	4	1	17
Teleconferencing:	–	–	–	–	–	1
Reading Courses:	–	–	–	–	9	16
New Enrolments by Programme of Study -						
Liberal Studies:	726	1255	1525	2790	3145	4112
Admin. Studies:	–	15	291	942	1434	1501
Non-credit:	–	–	8	152	83	77
TOTAL ENROLMENTS:	726	1270	1824	3884	4662	5690
TOTAL WEIGHTED ENROLMENTS: 2	726	1250	1702	3116	3587	4252
Operating Expenditures in Current Dollars (000)	1118	1986	2511	3772	4485	5965
Staff Complement - Full-time						
Professional:	32	42	49	56	66	84
Full-time Support:	20	26	46	63	65	71
Tutors:	–	–	22	43	70	91

Notes:

* *Includes non-credit courses*

1. *If a course was offered in two different delivery modes, it is counted as two course offerings.*

2. *Weighted enrolments = (enrolments in 3-credit courses÷2) + (enrolments in 6-credit courses)*

Source: Athabasca University Fact Book, 1980-81.

These data may be used to derive a measure of the relative efficiency of the University based on the annual enrolment figures and the operating expenditure figures (appropriately adjusted). However, this is a very coarse indicator of the University's performance, and is an incomplete, perhaps ambiguous descriptor.

Table 2.3 presents the results of a detailed analysis of unit costs at AU conducted by Snowden (1980) that distributes costs over course development, programme/services delivery, and institutional "management" functions. Costs are expressed in 1980 dollars. "Institutional" costs are expressed as a percentage of total expenditures.

Table 2.3 : Unit costs at Athabasca University, 1977-78 to 1980-81

Year	Course Development Cost per Credit of Course Development Load	Programme/Services Delivery Cost per Weighted Enrolment	Institutional Costs
1977-78 Actual	$19 510	$580	42%
1978-79 Actual	$12 500	$565	37%
1979-80 Actual	$11 285	$525	38%
1980-81 Budget	$14 635	$535	40%

Note: Course development load was defined in the cost study to include course maintenance, course revision and course replacement activities. Because the cost and activity data required to determine the unit costs directly attributable to such activities was not available, an assumption was made that the cost of maintaining or revising a course over its variable lifetime is not greater than the cost of developing a new course. By making a further assumption that the average course lifetime is 5 years, course development load was determined to be "course credits under development" plus one-fifth of "course credits in delivery".

(Source: Snowden, 1980: 26)

Concluding Remarks

By most standards, Athabasca University has had a tempestuous and crisis-laden past. That it has survived, let alone done as well as it has, is something approaching a minor miracle. However, there are many challenges that the University will have to meet in the coming years and there are many issues to be resolved. Some of the issues currently being considered or likely to be considered are:

1. Pacing - this is an issue that has arisen quite regularly within the University. At various times and with various people supporting the arguments, pacing has been touted as: a solution to the ubiquitous "attrition" problem; a shoring-up of the academic stature of the University; or an administrative necessity required to save the institution from collapsing under the burden of maintaining a very complicated student administration system. Some proponents of pacing argue for the necessity of introducing group learning situations, such as residential sessions, so that an element of socialisation is introduced into the learning process. Much of the dilemma experienced by AU on this issue seems to be a result of a conflict of values. The University was originally established to be open to adults in Alberta wherever they might reside, and at whatever time they might wish. Although there are definitions of pacing that do not necessarily diminish this openness, most definitions do introduce some form of constraint, and consequently a number of difficult trade-offs will have to be made before the matter can be laid to rest.

2. Technology - the utilisation of technology is a standard conundrum in distance education, and every institution in the business has had to come to terms with which technologies to use, how to use them effectively, and how to contend with the substantial costs usually associated with them. Costs are a particular concern for AU because the University has very limited resources with which to reach a small, widely dispersed population. Despite these very substantial constraints, AU is expected to show strongly in the application of technologies to higher education - if only because of the original concept proposed for the University. These expectations undoubtedly are heightened because the institution exists in an environment in which the general benefits of technology in other fields of endeavour are widely apparent.

3. Regionalisation - it has always been a goal of the University to provide students with educational opportunities within their home communities. However, it has not been clear what range of services could be usefully offered and how this might best be managed given AU's limited resources. Experience elsewhere, particularly at the British Open University, has made AU wary of establishing costly regional offices that are scaled-down versions of the central office. However, the University is planning to open a limited number of centres at which it would be possible for students to register, pay fees, obtain materials, and receive advice and information. These centres would also incorporate current functions of learning centres. Depending on the success of these operations, AU may expand this network in the future.

4. Course development - every institution involved in distance education very quickly realizes that course development is a costly and time-consuming endeavour, and every institution seeks to reduce the money and time that must be invested. As mentioned in earlier sections, AU has sought to do this by adopting courses acquired from other institutions, by collaborating with other institutions to produce courses that may be shared, by modifying the role of the course team in the production process and the models of production used, and by vesting responsibility for both course development and course delivery in the programme areas, rather than continuing to have a separate functional unit responsible for developing courses. However, the collaborative development of courses is likely to become the single most important means of increasing the efficiency of this process.

5. Governance - the University adopted the unicameral governance structure in the belief that concentrating the responsibility and authority for both academic and administrative affairs in one body would allow the institution to respond in a more timely and concerted manner to service demands placed on it (Daniel and Smith, 1979: 69). Although this has undoubtedly been realised to some extent, the Governing Council has experienced a corporate schizophrenia because of its divided responsibilities and membership. With the large number of staff on the Council, its role as public trustee is open to question by the government - and similarly its role as an advocate of academic affairs is open to question by the University's staff because of the presence of the public members. Although AU's unicameral system is entrenched in legislation and regulations, the University has recently revised its committee structure to introduce elements of conventional bicameral governance. Pressures had existed within the University for some time to separate academic and administrative affairs, and the conflicts of interest inherent in the unicameral system were apparent every year when terms and conditions of employment were being negotiated. However, the nascent schism opened widely under the pressure of circumstances that have presented the University with a challenge equal to those it has had to meet in the past. In March, 1980, the

Minister of Advanced Education and Manpower announced that as part of the Government's avowed policy of decentralisation, "the town of Athabasca has been chosen as the permanent site for Athabasca University".

6. *Relocation* - the Government's decision to move the University from Edmonton to Athabasca, a town of some 1800 people, 145 kilometres to the north, was greeted with shock and disbelief by the University's Council and staff alike. The Council ultimately accepted the decision, leading the president of the day to resign and the staff to become embittered. Although it is now clear that the University and its staff must live with the reality of the move - which is scheduled for 1984 - considerable time and energy are being consumed one way or another in accommodating to this reality. The University faces great uncertainties in the next few years and one can only speculate about how well it will survive its latest "challenge".

References

1. Athabasca University (1971) 'Academic Concept'. Edmonton: Athabasca University.
2. Athabasca University (1981) 'Fact Book, 1980-81'. Edmonton: Athabasca University, Office of Institutional Studies.
3. Daniel, J.S. & Forsythe, K. (1979) 'Experience with using courses from other institutions'. Paper presented to the Open University Conference on the Education of Adults at a Distance, Birmingham, U.K., 18-23 November 1979.
4. Daniel, J.S. & Smith, W.A.S. (1979) 'Opening Open Universities: The Canadian Experience'. Canadian Journal of Higher Education, 9, 2, 63-74.
5. Hughes, L.J. (1980) 'The First Athabasca University'. Edmonton: Athabasca University.
6. Perry, W. (1976) 'The Open University'. Milton Keynes: Open University Press.
7. Snowden, B.L. (1980) 'Report on Impacts, Consequences, and Costs of Relocation'. Edmonton: Athabasca University, Commission for Relocation Planning.
8. Stringer, M. (1980) 'Lifting the course team curse'. Teaching at a Distance, 18, 13-16.
9. Worth, W. (1972) 'A Choice of Futures'. Edmonton: Queen's Printer, Commission on Educational Planning.

Chapter 3

THE CENTRAL BROADCASTING AND TELEVISION UNIVERSITY, PEOPLE'S REPUBLIC OF CHINA

Robert McCormick

COUNTRY PROFILE

Geography

9.6 million square kilometres. There are enormous physical and climatic variations with the high plateaux and desert basins of the West and North experiencing cold winters, low annual rainfall, and in the northern deserts, hot summers, which contrast both with the hot humid summers and cold dry winters of the hills and plains of 'North China' and Lower Yangtze, and the tropical climate of southern China.

Population

1,000 millions (1980 estimates), but possibly higher; a census was taken in 1981.

The population is culturally and racially homogeneous (94 percent Han Chinese) but with significant numbers of different minority groups (55). Modern Standard Chinese (Mandarin) is the official language based upon the northern dialect and it is used in all schools and other educational institutions as the language of instruction. There are, however, many local languages which are quite distinct from the national language. There is a single written language standard throughout China. Since liberation in 1949 the characters have been simplified and romanisation (Pin yin) has been introduced.

The birth rate in 1979 was 1.8 percent. 36 percent of the population is under 15 years old, more than 50 percent is below 25, and 86 percent below 50. 87 percent of the population live in rural areas on some 50,000 communes. The non-agricultural labour force is 95 millions with an estimated 20 millions unemployed. Most of the population live in the east, particularly the North China Plain, i.e. around the plains through which the Yangtze and Huangho - the two great rivers of China - pass.

Economy

The main activity is in agriculture but in volume terms China is a leading world industrial power with manufactured goods (and crude oil) making up more than half of its export earnings. Following the Cultural Revolution the four modernisations (covering agriculture, industry, defence, and science and technology) were promoted to an extent that the 1976-85 ten year plan proved too ambitious, resulting in a balance of payments deficit. 1979-1981 was a period of 'readjusting, restructuring, consolidating and improving' prior to a more realistic ten year plan. China hopes to become a modern developed economic power by the year 2000. The major economic problems are: an underdevelopment of transport and communications and a shortage of qualified technicians and researchers.

Communications

Roads:	890,000 km mostly well graded but unmetalled. 83 percent of the communes can be reached by road.
Vehicles:	95 million bicycles, 60,000 cars, 30,000 buses and 409,000 lorries.
Rail:	48,000 km.
Air:	160 internal routes - 500 weekly flights.
Telephones:	3.7 millions.
Television:	One national channel, from Central China Television (CCTV) in colour, 32 stations all producing programmes in local dialects. Estimates of the number of receivers vary; there are probably around two million sets, with an annual production rate of 2.4 millions in 1980. China hopes to have a satellite by the mid-eighties.
Radio	99 radio stations and 118 million receivers with an annual production of 28.7 millions in 1980.
Cinemas:	1386: there is currently some concern about competition from television broadcasting of feature films.
Newspapers:	Annual circulation was 13.080 million copies (1978). The main national daily *Renmin Ribao (People's Daily)* has a circulation of 7 millions.
Post offices:	67,000.

55

EDUCATIONAL PROFILE

Structure

There are three basic levels: primary, 6 years; secondary, 6 years, divided into junior and senior cycles of three years each; and higher, usually of 4 years duration. Schooling is not compulsory by Law. There are a variety of part-time schools and colleges which run in parallel to the formal full-time schooling. A system of key schools for the best students, abolished during the Cultural Revolution, has been reintroduced at all levels.

Participation

There are 146 million pupils in 1 million primary schools representing 94 percent of the age group. 88 percent of primary graduates go on to junior secondary schools. There are 65 million secondary students in 20,000 schools. The proportion of females is: primary 45 percent; secondary 41 percent; higher 24 percent.

Standards

Since the Cultural Revolution there has been great concern about raising standards which had fallen during that period. Now there is keen competition particularly for entrance to the key schools. Examinations control transition between the three levels.

Higher Education

Policy is under the control of the Ministry of Education which also directly controls some key northern institutions. All other institutions are under control of provincial or municipal education departments and certain other ministries (e.g. Light Industry). All presidents of universities are directly appointed by the government. The direct control by the Ministry of Education or local government etcetera includes finance.

With the reintroduction of examinations for entry to university there has been intense competition. Some 4.6 millions sat the national examination for some half-million places. Entry is given on the basis of marks, with regional quotas being given to each institution. There is some degree of student choice of courses and institution. To enter one of the key universities a minimum pass mark is set. There is a maximum age of 28 but students typically enter at 25. This will decrease as newly graduated secondary school students become the main entry group. (Prior to 1977 students had to work for a number of years before entering university.)

There is a long tradition of spare and part-time education with some 160,000 students in higher education, many of them working in factories.

THE CENTRAL BROADCASTING AND TELEVISION UNIVERSITY (CCTU)

Origins

The Central Broadcasting and Television University (usually called Central China Television University - CCTU) in its present form started preparing courses in 1978 and was launched in February 1979. A preliminary start had already been made in 1977 with courses in English, electric circuits and mathematics offered through 'open broadcasting', by the Ministry of Education and the Education Department of the Chinese Central Television (CCTV). But the origins of CCTU go back further than this. The Beijing Television College (now connected with CCTU as the Beijing Broadcasting and Television University), opened in 1960 with five departments: mathematics, physics, chemistry, Chinese and English. Its teaching was through television, correspondence material and face to face teaching (Abe, 1961). From the period 1960-66 some 8,000 students graduated with another 50,000 students studying a single subject. The Cultural Revolution disrupted television and Beijing TV College was closed. Indeed all educational television suffered and, for example, Shanghai's 'open broadcasting' did not resume until 1975.

Not only can China boast one of the world's earliest television universities, it has a long tradition of correspondence education dating from the beginning of the century. Although such education has been developed at university level, through special departments attached to universities, the establishment of the CCTU is the first attempt to set up a national, multi-media, distance learning institution. The process that led to its establishment started in 1978 when a steering committee met, made up of representatives from various ministries, Education, Broadcasting, Administration, Electronics, Finance, Commerce, Posts and Telecommunications, as well as other bodies: the National Planning Commission, Trade Unions, the Central Committee of China Youth League, etcetera. The committee, which reported to the State Council (the supreme governing body in China), was chaired by the Minister of Education, with the Director of the Central Broadcasting Bureau as the vice-chairman. This committee produced a report in June 1978 which led to the establishment of the University.

Its aims are to promote the modernisation of China, to raise the level of scientific education, and to repair the damage done to education by the 'gang of four'. Given the growth in the concept and practice of distance learning over the last decade or so, the committee saw a unique opportunity to use this approach to learning as a way of responding both to the limitations of places and to those whose higher education was denied during the Cultural Revolution. The awakening interest in international efforts in the field of distance learning was shown by various visits to the British Open University by delegations from China and by an article in the *People's Daily* ('A University without students' [*Yisuo 'meiyou xuesheng' de Daxue*] , 3 March 1979) on the British Open University by one of the members of a delegation (Chen lin - a professor of English who is a teacher in CCTU).

China provides distance learning with a unique challenge: to cope with the economic, demographic and geographic conditions of the country. The single autonomous institution, as characterised by the British OU, cannot be adopted uncritically in China. The CCTU is a central body responsible for course design and material preparation but there are 28 Local Television Universities (LTU), one under each of the Municipal or Provincial Education Bureaux, who are responsible for the registration and organisation of students.

Students

A consideration of the enrolment figures (Table 3.1) indicates why the CCTU has to consider a decentralised model of a distance learning system. They also show a remarkable achievement in the first few years of the University's operation.

Table 3.1 : CCTU enrolments.

Year of intake	1979	1980	1981	1982
Number of enrolments	273,060*	144,026	NIL	280,000+

    * *continuing enrolments*
    + *estimated*

Of the 417,086 students registered in 1981, 92,714 graduated with a single subject certificate (mostly in English) leaving 324,372 students continuing in 1981. There was no 1981 intake because of insufficient transmission time to repeat the first year courses. Of the continuing students 167,962 are full-time (i.e. released from work on full-pay), and 156,410 half and spare-time students. Half-time students spend the equivalent of three working days per week studying, and spare-time students have to make up their work-time because of morning television viewing. (It appears that students who are not formally registered can 'follow' the courses and sit the exams.)

No precise data on students exists at national level but most of them come from the following occupational groups: secondary school teachers, civil servants, technicians and factory workers. (The following figures for the 1979 intake have however been given to visitors: 42 percent workers, 38 percent secondary school teachers, and 20 percent government and army cadres.) For Beijing TVU (one of the LTU's) the occupations of students are given in Table 3.2.

Table 3.2 : Beijing TVU student occupations for 1979 intake.

Occupation	Number of Students	%
Workers	11,543	39.7
Government functionaries	3,472	12.0
Technicians	9,240	31.8
Teachers	3,411	11.8
People's Liberation Army	1,396	4.8
Total	29,062	100.1

There were also reported to be 572 young school leavers registered with Beijing TVU in 1981.

The average age of students nationally was 29 years for the 1979 intake, and 23 years for the 1980 intake. (In Beijing TVU the average age in 1979 was 28.2 years.) There are no national figures for the sexes. In addition to the number of students in Beijing (see Table 3.2), it is also reported that the province of Shanxi with a population of 30 millions in 1979 had 11,000 students registered in some 500 classes.

All students must be senior secondary school graduates, although this does not imply that they hold a particular qualification. To be admitted, students must pass an entrance examination which, although it is national, is different from that sat by students wishing to enter a conventional university, in that it aims to ensure that those admitted can cope with the study of CCTU courses.

Academic Programmes

The courses presented to registered students of the University are all at undergraduate level, although it is involved, along with the Education Department of CCTV, in some 'open broadcasting' aimed at other levels; for example, the evening course on English (presented by Professor Chin lin). In the first two years of operation degree programmes in mechanical engineering and electronics were presented with courses as shown in Table 3.3. This table gives the number of television programmes transmitted for each course in each semester over the three years of the degree programme (English, presented in the Spring of 1980, for the 1979 intake, was by radio).

In addition to the current degree programmes the University wants to establish degrees in additional subjects such as Civil and Chemical Engineering, and possibly also in Arts, Social Science, Chinese Literature, Economics, and Industrial management.

As Table 3.3 indicates there are two semesters per year with a total of forty teaching weeks. A credit system is used based upon 3 credits for each hour of programming broadcast weekly: thus English counts as 33 credits. A total of no less than 200 credits are required for a degree certificate.

The degrees are intended to be comparable to those awarded by conventional 3 year colleges: there exists a central co-ordinating system within the Ministry of Education which lays down the syllabuses and monitors standards for all universities and colleges.

60

Table 3.3 : CCTU courses followed by the 1979 intake
(shown in terms of the number of programmes transmitted)

Course	1979 Spring	1979 Autumn	1980 Spring	1980 Autumn	1981 Spring	1981 Autumn	Degree Line*
English	4	4	3				ME/EE
Mathematics I	4	4					ME/EE
Mathematics II			4				EE
Mathematics III				2	2		EE
Inorganic Chemistry	4	3					ME/EE+
Organic Chemistry			3	2			−
Physics		4	4	4			ME/EE
Biology						4	−
Engineering Mechanics			4				ME
Strength of Materials				4			ME
Electric Circuits				5			EE
Applied Electro-Magnetic fields					3		EE
Electronics (Analog)					4	2	ME/EE
(Digital)						3	EE
Mechanisms					4		ME/EE
Machine Design						4	ME
BASIC and Digital Computers						5	Optional

* *ME = Mechanical Engineering; EE = Electronic Engineering*
+ *one semester only*

In addition to this national provision the LTUs can add their own courses. In the main these are taught through face-to-face methods, except in the case of places like Shanghai where the capacity exists to produce television programmes. (These are then transmitted on the local network.) It is hoped to further develop courses to meet local needs and conditions.

Media

As will already be evident the CCTU teaches through television, but also uses print and face-to-face tuition. Radio is only used in one part of the English course. (*Broadcasting* is used to refer to radio, and 'broadcasting' and television are produced and transmitted by two different branches of the Broadcasting Administration.)

Television provides the basic mode of instruction consisting largely of lectures written out on a black (green) board, as would be found in a conventional university. Although programmes are pre-recorded prior to transmission, little use is made of pre-prepared material, lecturers often writing and explaining what they need as they proceed. A 'lecture' typically goes on for 50 minutes and they are often given in doubles with a 5-15 minute break; the lecturer may, in some cases, carry on from where he or she left off before the break. When the 'blackboard lecture' format is used the result is sometimes difficult to view, with scrappy diagrams and cramped or untidy writing. Some programmes utilise a 'talking head' with graphics etc. presented on a separate camera. In essence, the programmes mirror in length and in style the lectures delivered at conventional universities in China.

Staff at the University are well aware of the shortcomings of these programmes, but the production pressures prevent elaborate programme preparation. The production facilities are also limited by the quality of the technical equipment, the back up facilities (such as graphic design) and the studio size. The potential is there for a more imaginative use of television, and examples exist of programmes using animated graphics of chemical processes, demonstrations of experiments, and the use of inserts of location filming of, for example, computer hardware.

The print component of the teaching package is largely made up of conventional textbooks. These books can be bought in the shops of national book retailers Xinhua Shu Dian. Three books, on linear algebra, computing, and machine design have been produced on a trial basis by the CCTU for their courses; the others are the same as those used in conventional institutions. However, all courses are supported by printed supplementary material. This material acts as a guide to the course, containing for example: the objectives; a review of content; and assignments (not used to assess students). The original idea was that this material was to guide the tutors but it is now also sent to students.

In view of the great pressure on television and its limitation (both in production and transmission) the University has recognised the need to develop its use of print as the main medium of instruction. Over the next few years it will be developing texts specifically for the distance learners. This will provide the pre-requisite for the development of a more imaginative use of television.

Assessment is entirely by examination at the end of each semester. Examinations are set centrally but organised locally. The LTUs mark the examinations in accordance with detailed criteria set by the CCTU.

The non-assessed assignments in the supplementary material provide one element in the student support, with tutors providing individual feedback on student answers. The LTU is responsible for the organisation of student support which includes face to face tuition and experimental work. The nature of the provision does, however, vary depending upon the location (a point discussed in the section on 'Student Support').

Course Design and Production

Courses are designed in outline by a group of teachers, including some from other universities. A course team then draws up a detailed plan for the whole course and individual programmes. This plan is agreed with the television director (production details only) and then approved by the Academic administration (controlled by academic staff). Thus all the main design decisions are in the hands of academics, even at the level of individual programmes. The television directors, employed by the Education Department of the CCTV, are mainly responsible for the technical production. This production is carried out in a CCTV studio where the facilities are very cramped; for example the studio control and recording are carried out from an Outside Broadcast van in an outbuilding adjacent to the main studio complex. The recording, formerly on two-inch tape, is now done on three-quarter-inch tape. CCTV hope to have a new studio building some time in the near future.

In addition to the difficult studio conditions, the CCTV Education Department has only 10 producers for some 30 hours of transmission. As mentioned earlier these production conditions account for the lack of preparation and the fact that programmes are recorded straight through without edits for such things as lecturers walking across camera to a new blackboard (with a black shadow effect being seen by viewers). Preparation time starts some three to six months before production and programmes are produced at least a month before transmission. Taking into account the considerable production constraints they do remarkably well in producing programmes. CCTU also has its own small studio, situated in a converted bunker. The equipment is only appropriate for a closed circuit operation, but they have in fact made some material for broadcast (for example, the animation referred to earlier). The limitations this kind of equipment puts on the staff will be reduced with new equipment to be delivered in 1982. When the CCTU moves into new premises (planned for 1986) they hope to have a studio. (At present their offices are housed in a wing of a secondary school.)

Obviously an issue for discussion within the University is its relationship to CCTV and the role of the University's own television production facilities. The possible role for the latter is the production of special inserts for broadcast programmes (with CCTV producing the bulk of the programme) or the production of experimental programmes which could be tested on groups of students. Alternatively, CCTU may do the bulk of the production of new courses, with appropriate help from CCTV.

As yet print is not a large part of the production operation. Several editors are responsible for the supplementary material and layout, and two graphic designers are responsible for the illustrations. Printing is done by government printers. When specially prepared teaching texts are eventually produced, the production process itself will have to be thought out.

Course Delivery

The CCTU's television programmes are transmitted in the morning and early afternoon between 8.30 a.m. and 4.10 p.m. (50 minutes for each subject with a 5 minute break between programmes), and networked nationally by microwave. It is the use of this microwave distribution which limits the amount of transmission time available to the University: the newspaper, *People's Daily*, uses it in the early morning for news distribution and collection, and general broadcasting occupies evening transmission. Other open broadcast educational programmes occur in the late afternoon and early evening.

Television programmes are viewed, by registered students, in groups at their work place. Reception in such a large country is of course variable and is exacerbated by the production limitations. (For example the 3:4 ratio - of the television screen - for presentation of material to camera is often ignored, resulting in a loss of information at the edges of the screen when received in places distant from Beijing.)

Distribution of conventional textbooks, which are made available by Xinhua Shu Dian, has often been delayed and limited in extent, with the result that many students have not been able to obtain the required books in time. Printed supplementary material is of course distributed by CCTU, being sent to the LTUs for reprinting and subsequent distribution to local district offices and study centres. On occasions CCTU has distributed directly to district offices and study centres, but with 100,000 copies of material this despatch operation proved to be overwhelming.

Student Support

A clear policy on the level and nature of student support is gradually being formulated, but it has to be flexible to allow for local conditions. Central policy covers the provision of television sets, print, tutors, experimental equipment, and classrooms. The autonomy of the LTUs would make the imposition of uniform policy impossible. Students will however all have access to a television set through group viewing, and a tutor for face-to-face teaching and assignment marking. There were 554 full-time and 14,804 part-time tutors in 1981, but there are reports of difficulties in students being allocated a tutor.

Although the LTUs administer and direct the provision of student support at a provincial level, it is clear that a considerable amount of organisation is devolved to the study centre level. The study centre is located in a work unit and is organised by the education section of, say, the factory. It is the variable conditions in the work units that determine whether, for example, students have access to experimental facilities. Because of the differences that exist at local levels it is not possible to give a general description of student support in all its aspects. Instead a description will be given of one study centre, Fung Tai, in the suburbs of Beijing; like so many things in Beijing it is unlikely to be 'typical', but it may nevertheless be regarded as an example of those study centres run by industrial organisations. Fung Tai study centre is located in a bridge factory (which is administered by the Ministry of Railways) with 4,000 workers and 120 technicians, and is fortunate in being able to use a vacated primary school. It has, therefore, the use of a number of classrooms and equips them with TV sets, blackboards and desks. The eleven teaching staff, five of whom are full-time, have a staffroom with a small reference library (5,000 books). Most of the students studying at the centre in 1981 came from the factory and were organised into two classes corresponding to the two intakes. They have classes six days per week with a total of 12-16 hours per week, i.e. about ten hours face-to-face tuition in addition to television programme viewing. Students study in the classrooms when not being taught by a tutor or watching television. The face-to-face teaching is used to explain difficult points in the television programmes and to answer student questions. In addition, some non CCTU courses are also taught in class.

There are about four hours per month devoted to experimental work and this is carried out in a school. This school is used by several study centres in the district, having been organised by the Beijing TVU district office. The study centre also gets assistance with experimental work from a local college, which in addition provides the part-time tutors.

It is only because Fang Tai is a large factory that these favourable facilities can be provided; smaller ones have to rely upon facilities and organisation provided at district level by the local office.

Student Progress

This is measured by examination pass rates which are very high, although this may be because tutors advise poor students against sitting an examination. The figures are incomplete, but in the examination at the end of the first semester in 1979, 80 percent of the 500,000 candidates passed. In Beijing 95 percent passed chemistry, and in Shanghai 96 percent passed all three courses (Mathematics, Chemistry and English). Of the 6,000 who took the examination for English in Xin Jiang, 72 percent passed. Similar kinds of figures have been recorded in various parts of China.

Organisational Structure

As has already been indicated, the basic system is of a central course design, production and assessment centre (the CCTU in Beijing) with

Figure 3.1 : A sketch of CCTU Tentative Working Structure

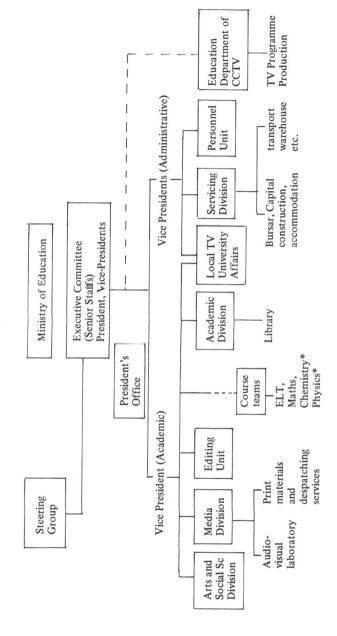

Note:

* *Course Teams of Electrical Engineering, Mechanical Engineering, English, and Biology are to be set up.*

the provincial LTUs being responsible for the organisation and operation of tuition. The centre does not therefore register students or control their learning environment.

The structure of the central unit, the CCTU, is shown in Figure 3.1. As the University is developing this can only be regarded as a tentative structure and it will have to change to meet the changing needs of the institution. For example, the Arts and Social Science Division exists as a separate unit at present, and this may change as courses in this area develop. The dotted line joining the Education Department of the CCTV to the structure indicates its special relationship within the organisation. Although it has a direct connection high up the hierarchy of the organisation, the directors of the Department have to mediate their relationship with the University at the programme making level.

Figure 3.2: Beijing T.V.U. Structure

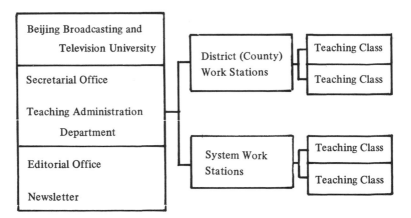

The general organisation of the LTUs is not clear, but again Beijing TVU can be used as an example. Figure 3.2 shows its structure. There are two kinds of study centres (or work stations as they are called): those organised by the area and district offices (for small work units); and those organised by particular industries (system work stations) such as, for example, the Bureau of Light Industry. (All industrial concerns are state controlled and administered by an appropriate Bureau.) There are 19 district and over forty system work stations (study centres), and these provide for 600 study groups.

The tasks undertaken by Beijing TVU are: admissions, supervision of tutorials, organisation of experiments, organisation of examinations, and the direction of local district offices. The district or system offices are responsible for the direct operation of student support. At the LTU level autonomy exists with, for example, the Beijing TVU Office being responsible for raising the pass level of the entrance examination above a minimum to regulate the number of students admitted, which is in turn determined by the local need and facilities available.

Costs

The budget, for which no figures are available, is administered by the State Council and the Ministry of Education. The funding for teachers, printing costs etcetera comes from the Ministry of Education, with the Broadcasting Bureau being responsible for television production costs. The LTUs fund all the support services and local costs, some of which will in turn be borne by work units. The work unit will also absorb the student's costs (about 200 yuan annually) so that he or she will not have to pay. However, the young school leavers have to pay 50 yuan (£15) per semester. It is usual for all benefits, such as housing, health care and education to be met by the work unit. Young school leavers are therefore at a disadvantage but should benefit when they eventually join the workforce as skilled workers.

Comments

As is evident from the above description, the University has made some remarkable strides in the first few years of its existence, by registering so many students, and by producing so many courses. Nevertheless, there are some problems to be faced.

The CCTU has reached the limit of the available transmission time for television, and it intends to cut the amount of television being transmitted per course in order to expand the course offering. This implies a change in role for television. This will not immediately relieve their production problems. Indeed, the change in role may increase these problems, particularly if it has to be reassessed for each of the existing courses. A pre-requisite for the change in role is the need to increase the teaching function of print, and this brings with it the need to design specially prepared printed material in those subject areas where no good conventional textbooks are available. Where these are available, the CCTU's policy is to produce guides to the textbooks.

The problem of the distribution of textbooks is likely to be overcome as courses are presented in successive years. Delayed distribution has been a particular problem during the initial presentation of the courses.

The provision of experimental work is another problem, particularly for an institution committed to science and technology. CCTU wants to increase the applied nature of its degrees - which represents a break with the long tradition of 'book learning'. The provision of home experimental kits directly to all students is not feasible and in any case is contrary to the 'group tuition' element in the University's organisation. Centres for experimental work will be necessary, and the University has plans to set up about 500. However, portable home experimental kits may be designed for use by students in rural areas.

At a more general, organisational, level the University must consider whether it can take on all the course material production operations, particularly television production. Here they face the issue found in all distance learning systems using television: the potential conflict between broadcasters and teachers. Arriving at a relationship between the two is fundamental to any multi-media system.

More fundamental is the question of whether CCTU can retain control over all parts of the operation. With a distance learning system of its dimensions this appears impractical, and this is made more so by the autonomy of the provincial education authorities. At present the University is a central materials production unit which produces distance learning materials for use in a variety of situations (including conventional face-to-face institutions), some of which are not under its control. However, if CCTU's degree is in any sense to be a nationally awarded degree, there must be some mechanism of quality control to ensure the degree's credibility.

Finally there is the issue of the nature of the student body. Currently the transmission restrictions mean that only full-time (or nearly full-time) students can do the courses, and this is a cause of complaint among students and their work units. The fact that the University serves a largely urban audience is another limitation. If it is to be an instrument of mass education it must reach the rural population. However, this would have enormous implications for the University. Such a vast number of students would require many changes in the distribution system and the support services. The addition of rural students may also require changes in the nature and indeed the level of courses. This represents an enormous challenge to the CCTU, but officials of the University are optimistic that steady progress will be made in reaching the rural population.

Reference

1. Abe, M. (1961) 'Spare-time education in Communist China'. The China Quarterly, 8, 149-159.

Chapter 4

THE UNIVERSIDAD ESTATAL A DISTANCIA, COSTA RICA

Greville Rumble

COUNTRY PROFILE

Geography

50,900 square kilometres divided into 5 geographical regions:

The intermontane *Central Valley* contains about 60 percent of the population and most of the major towns (San Jose, the capital with 0.54 million inhabitants, Alajuela, Heredia, Cartago).

The hot wet *Atlantic Coast* centred on the port of Limon. Main crop, bananas.

The humid *Northern Plain*, which is sparsely populated but now developing rapidly. Agricultural.

The hot dry plains of *Guanacaste* and northern Puntarenas province. Cattle and cereals.

The *Southern zone*. Bananas and palm oil.

Population

2.3 millions (1980 estimate). The population is culturally and racially homogeneous (97.7 percent white or *mestizo* descendancy), with the majority speaking Spanish. The most significant non-Spanish/*Mestizo* group is the largely English-speaking Afro-Caribbean population based on Limon, although young Afro-Caribbeans generally speak Spanish.

The birthrate has declined sharply (48 per 1,000 in 1960 down to 29.5 per 1,000 in 1975). 38 percent of the population are under 15 years old, 51 percent aged 15 to 49, and 11 percent over 50 (1980). 53 percent of the population were classified as rural in 1978; 33 percent of the population were classified as economically active in 1977, with 60 percent of the labour force being between 15 and 25 years old.

Economy

The country is dependent on agricultural exports, the most important being coffee, bananas and meat. 35 percent of the labour force is

72

employed in agriculture, 43 percent in service industries, 15 percent in manufacturing, and 7 percent in construction (1976).

Communications

Roads:	27,370 km. (1976).
Vehicles:	There are 74,000 cars and jeeps, 46,000 commercial vehicles, and 3,500 buses (1977). The bus is the usual form of transport for the majority of Costa Ricans.
Rail:	There are two passenger carrying lines from San Jose to Limon (Atlantic coast) and Puntarenas (Pacific coast).
Air:	Domestic services and air taxi services are available.
Telephones:	200,000 lines in 1981.
Television:	There are 5 channels. 82 percent of houses in the San Jose metropolitan area had sets in 1977, as did 69 percent of houses in the Central Valley, and more than 50 percent elsewhere.
Radio:	There are 5 non-commercial and 20 commercial stations. There is widespread ownership of receivers.
Newspapers:	There are two major dailies with more than 80,000 circulation.

EDUCATIONAL PROFILE

Primary and Secondary Education

There are four levels: Pre-school non compulsory education (1 year); a compulsory primary education comprising two 3-year cycles covering age range 6 to 11 years inclusive; a compulsory 3-year secondary cycle (ages 12 to 14) followed by a non-compulsory 2 or 3 year diversified cycle at secondary level in academic, technical, agricultural or other fields. This last leads to the *Bachillerato* title, which is a pre-requisite for entry to higher education.

Participation

The 1973 census showed that only 5 percent of the population had graduated from secondary school. Participation rates are high for

Latin America: 92 percent of children aged 6 to 12 attend primary school; 57 percent of children aged 13 to 15 attend the general secondary school cycle, and 33 percent of young adults aged 16 to 18 attend the diversified cycle (1978). The literacy rate was claimed to be 89.8 percent (1973) but there is evidence of functional illiteracy (30 percent of those aged over 10 in 1974).

Standards

There is criticism of the heavy emphasis on rote learning, poor classroom discipline, overloaded curriculum, the practice of automatically promoting children from the first to the second year of each three year cycle, and of lowering academic standards of the *bachillerato* leading to increased pressure for university places from ill-prepared students.

Higher Education

Higher education dates from 1940 (foundation of the University of Costa Rica). Pressure on places and a desire to innovate led to the foundation of the technologically orientated Technological Institute of Costa Rica (1971), the National University (1973), and the Universidad Estatal a Distancia (1977). The universities are autonomous, their planning being co-ordinated by the National Council of Rectors (CONARE) which was established in 1974 and has ministerial representation. A private university, the Autonomous University of Central America, with 2,456 students (1979) operates outside the system. There is a proposal for a second private university (University of San Jose) and a United Nations backed Peace University.

The State universities met about 50 percent of demand for places in 1978, (9,382 students were admitted out of 18,107 applicants to the State universities). The universities aim to satisfy social demand and meet the manpower needs of the nation. However, CONARE noted a tendency for the universities to overprovide educated manpower at professional levels and underprovide at the technical and lower professional levels (CONARE, 1979: 17). Another aim has been to democratise educational opportunities. The establishment of UNA and the ITCR was one response to these problems; a second was the establishment of University Centres in regions outside the Central Valley; and a third was the setting up of a distance teaching university.

THE UNIVERSIDAD ESTATAL A DISTANCIA (UNED)

Origins

In 1977 the Government decided to establish the Universidad Estatal a Distancia (UNED) as a fourth state-funded university. CONARE had initially suggested that the use of distance teaching methods should be evaluated through a five year pilot project (CONARE, 1975: VII-84 to VII-101) but this proposal was quietly shelved. CONARE's initial appraisal of the scheme suggested that the proposed university could meet the objectives of widening educational opportunities and alleviating social demand at a lower unit cost than that which could be achieved by expanding the conventional universities (CONARE, n.d.: 19-20). However, no detailed project appraisal was ever carried out.

UNED's early planners hoped that the University would:

1. Bring higher education to a greater number of the adult population who, for various reasons, could not take advantage of the traditional system and hence remained without an adequate university-based professional career preparation.
2. Provide a solution to the problems facing the agricultural and working population who have the ability to enter a university but who, for economic, social or geographic reasons could not enrol in the existing universities.
3. Accommodate an important part of the student population who year by year remained without a chance of registering in existing universities, and serve as a means of support to the existing university sector in terms of those students who, in spite of the fact that they have the required qualifications, remain outside the universities because of the shortage of places (Ministerio de Educación Pública, 1976).

The Students

Although demographic data on UNED's students is inadequate to answer all the questions one might ask, it is clear that the University is opening up educational opportunities to persons who would otherwise not have had a chance to enter the universities. Thus each year UNED receives a large number of applications following the announcement of the names of successful applicants to the conventional universities - a factor that suggests that UNED is regarded by some as an alternative (and second-choice) route to higher educational qualifications.

It is difficult to quantify the extent to which the University is either a second-choice institution or a genuine first-choice for those who have never contemplated entering a conventional university. Comparison between the province of origin of UNED and conventional university students suggests that UNED is opening up educational opportunities in areas outside the Central Valley, where all the conventional universities have their main campuses. This is particularly true for persons living in Guanacaste, Limon and Puntarenas provinces. For example, 12 percent of the total population lives in Puntarenas province along the Pacific seaboard. In 1979 the proportion of new students admitted to the State-financed conventional universities who came from Puntarenas Province was less than 5 percent of all admissions. Against this, 16 percent of UNED's first intake came from this Province.

Although the conventional universities have tried to meet local demands by establishing a number of University Centres in the country, the range of academic programmes offered at these centres is limited. UNED is thus able, through its use of distance teaching methods, to greatly increase the range of higher education courses available to persons living outside of the Central Valley.

Nevertheless, provision of educational opportunities does not necessarily imply that people will be able to make use of them. A major factor working against equal educational opportunities in Costa Rica is the cost of education, both direct (in terms of fees and other expenses) and indirect (in terms of lost earnings). This has particularly affected persons coming from the lower socio-economic classes. To show that it is widening educational opportunities, UNED must demonstrate that a significant proportion of its students come from disadvantaged classes.

Direct comparison between UNED and the conventional universities is difficult because the majority of UNED students are working (75 percent of new entrants in the second semester of 1979) or housewives (11.5 percent) and hence their status is dependent more on their own circumstances than on those of their parents. A further factor inhibiting direct comparisons is the fact that UNED's academic programmes are aimed at persons seeking professional qualifications. This orientation is reflected in the high proportion of students who come from the professional, managerial and administrative classes (75 percent of employed students in the first semester of 1979). In contrast, only 34 percent of the employed population works in these sectors, while only 17 percent of the fathers of a 1978 sample of University of Costa Rica students came from these sectors (Rumble, 1981: Tables 7.6 and 7.7). This bias towards the middle and upper classes is also reflected in the income of UNED's students. Only 7 percent of the students registered in the second semester of 1978 earned under 2,000 colones a month - that is, roughly the sum which would take them out of the lower classes. In contrast, 35 percent of the students registered in 1979 at the University of Costa Rica came from families with a monthly income of under 2,000 colones. This suggests that UNED is not providing increased educational opportunities for the economically deprived.

On the other hand, UNED seems to be attractive to persons who are older, working and married. The average age of UNED's students is higher than those of students in the conventional universities; a higher proportion are married; and, on average, more of them work than is the case in the conventional universities (although as many conventional university students in the age range 26 to 29 work as do UNED students). Table 4.1 gives details.

Table 4.1 Age, marital status and employment status of students in three Costa Rican universities.

Date Status	University of Costa Rica 1979 Registered students		National University 1978 Registered students		UNED 1979 Applicants for the second semester	
100% =		29,797		7,098		2,061
		%		%		%
Age: under	21	43.1	22	49.1	21	25.6
in range	21-25	37.5	22-26	26.7	21-26	32.5
over	25	19.4	26	24.2	26	40.7
Single		78.8		77.7		50.8
Married		19.3		19.4		44.0
Other		1.9		2.9		5.2
Employed		45.8(a)		40.4(a)		75.4
Not employed		} 54.2(a)		} 59.6(a)		11.5
Housewife						11.5
Other						1.6

Note: (a) Data-based on a small sample survey of students

UNED'S academic programmes

Initially UNED concentrated on developing a series of professionally orientated degree and diploma programmes *(carreras)*, of which thirteen are currently in existence, under development, or planned. In parallel, the University developed a number of Extension Courses. Students are also allowed to take individual degree and diploma level courses without registering on a *carrera* (the Free Studies Programme). Table 4.2 lists UNED's current and planned academic programmes. However, the extent to which UNED will be able to realise these plans has been called in question following the cuts in expenditure which have recently been imposed on the universities.

In addition to its own programmes, UNED has since 1980 been working in conjunction with the Ministry of Public Education on the development of course materials and the training of tutors for the Ministry's distance-teaching based secondary school programme for the *bachillerato* certificate. The original intention was that UNED would administer this programme, but in the present financial climate it was decided that it should be managed by the Ministry.

Table 4.2: UNED's current and planned academic programmes

Degree and diploma programmes
1. Basic Cycle (6 courses)
2. General Studies
3. Professional Studies (carreras) in:
   - 3.1   Educational Sciences for Primary School Teachers (Bachelor's Degree)
   - 3.2   Educational Administration (Bachelor's Degree)
   - 3.3   Business Administration (Diploma)
   - 3.4   Public Administration: Banking (Diploma)
   - 3.5   Administration of Co-operatives (Diploma)
   - 3.6   Farm Management (Bachelor's Degree)
   - 3.7   Public Service Administration (Master's Degree)
   - 3.8   Nursing (Diploma)
   - 3.9   Nutrition (Diploma)
   - 3.10   Health Service Administration (Bachelor's Degree)
   - 3.11   Development Promotion (Diploma)
   - 3.12   Child Social Services (Diploma)
   - 3.13   Agricultural Extension (Bachelor's Degree)

Extension Studies Programmes
1. Environmental Studies
2. Teaching of Geography
3. Professional education
4. Extension studies in health, family life, agriculture, crafts, etc.
5. Development of Scientific Interests

Free Studies Programme

The Course Structure

In the *carreras*, the basic unit of study is the course, each of which is equivalent to three credits. Each credit represents a theoretical 50 hours of student work over an 18 week semester. The planned course load of 4 courses per student per semester therefore implies a weekly student workload of 33.3 hours.

Students in the professional studies programme register on a particular *carrera*. They must have the secondary school leaving certificate *(bachillerato)* or a recognised equivalent. Most students are required to take the University's *Ciclo Básico* first, although students who have completed the first year of studies at the University of Costa Rica or the National University are granted exemption.

The *Ciclo Básico* consists of six courses, five of which count for credit (Spanish, Mathematics, Social Sciences (History), Science and Philosophy) and a sixth, on studying at a distance, which does not. Students taking a *carrera* leading to a diploma are required to take 20 courses (60 credits) at General and Professional Studies levels as well as the *Ciclo Básico*. Students at first degree level take about 37 courses (111 credits) at these levels, together with the *Ciclo Básico*. The main purpose of the *Ciclo Básico* is to introduce students to a wide cultural panorama and provide a basis of knowledge as a precursor to higher level studies. General Studies courses aim to widen students' horizons. While obligatory, they can be taken at any time following completion of the *Ciclo Básico*. At Professional Studies level there are a mix of obligatory and optional courses. Many courses are designated as prerequisites for higher level courses.

Students who proceed through the system at the planned rate of 4 or 5 courses per semester will graduate in 6 semesters (3 years) at diploma level and 10 semesters (5 years) at first degree level.

Media

The basic teaching medium is the printed course book of which there is normally one per course. Most of the books also have supplementary material which has been written as a result of the experience gained in teaching the course. Some of the courses have associated with them set books, which the students are expected to read.

Limited use is made of cassette-books - that is, a number of audio tapes with supporting printed materials which take the place of the basic course text. Television programmes are also produced in limited numbers and are intended to support the written course texts. Limited use of radio began during 1980.

Fortnightly tutorials take place at the University's Academic Centres, of which there are 22 throughout Costa Rica.

Course Design, Production and Distribution

The curriculum for each *carrera* and course is prepared by the Office of Curriculum Design in the Planning Vice-rectorate. Instructional design is undertaken by the Programme Co-ordinators in the Academic Vice-rectorate, who consult with various specialist staff.

The main course texts are written by external authors who are contracted by the full-time Academic Producers. The latter monitor the authors' progress and arrange for their work to be internally and externally assessed. A proportion of the authors (about 30 percent) have previously been involved in the curriculum design, in the sense that they have been consulted by the University's Curriculum Designers on the content to be included in a course. Supplementary materials are normally written by the Tutor Co-ordinators, who have direct experience of the problems encountered by students in the texts.

Texts are printed by the University's Press (Editorial UNED) which has its own full-time staff of designers, editors, and compositors. It publishes a number of books for the commercial market as well as producing the University's course texts, having an estimated annual production capacity of 200 books of 180 pages each.

Once printed, the course books are passed to UNED's Warehouse where they are stored and eventually dispatched to the various book-shops from which they can be purchased. Supplementary and other course materials and administrative notices are distributed through the University's Academic Centres.

So far as television is concerned, UNED uses the editing and studio facilities of two television companies, Channels 7 and 13. Total output is of the order of 80 programmes per year. The producers are full or part-time members of UNED's staff who liaise closely with the Tutor Co-ordinators and Academic Producers regarding content. The programmes, which are produced at marginal cost to the University, are transmitted on Channels 4,6,7,11 and 13. Total transmission is in the order of four hours per week (eight programmes). Video cassette playback machines have been installed in some of UNED's Academic Centres for students otherwise unable to view the programmes.

Radio is also used to a small extent. UNED has its own sound studio (commissioned in 1980) and at the end of 1980 it was broadcasting for a total of five hours a week on Radio Nacional and Radio Universidad.

Student Support Services

The fortnightly tutorials, which are not compulsory, are seen as part remedial and part supportive of the main teaching medium, the printed course texts. Students can also contact tutors by telephone at certain set hours. UNED uses the tutorials to obtain feedback on the problems which students encounter in their courses. Every other week the tutors meet with one of the University's full-time Tutor Co-ordinators - each of whom is responsible for the tutors on two or three courses. At these meetings, student learning problems are analysed and the results of the meetings are used to determine the content of television programmes, the need for supplementary printed materials, and the need for changes to the course texts when they are reprinted.

The tutors themselves are part-time employees. They are subject area specialists, responsible to the Tutor Co-ordinators. They work in a peripatetic manner, visiting the Academic Centres only to give the tutorial.

Assessment and Examination

During each 18 week semester, students are expected to complete a number of assignments (normally four per course) which are corrected by the tutor, and to attend mid-course and end-of-course examinations. The assignments count for 20 percent of the overall final grade and the examinations for 80 percent. Students have to obtain an overall Grade of 70 percent to pass the course. The assessment and examination materials are prepared by the Tutor Co-ordinators.

Student Administration

Persons interested in applying for entry to UNED have to buy a Matriculation Pack which contains information on the University, an application form, and a fees payment form. Students are required to pay a matriculation fee of 200 colones which entitles them subsequently to register on one course. This fee is paid directly into one of UNED's bank accounts. Proof of payment is then sent by the student together with his or her application form to UNED's Central Admissions Office. Students' applications are vetted against their academic qualifications to ensure that each applicant has the necessary minimum qualification for entry to the University (a high school *bachillerato* or its equivalent). UNED has to date been able to accept all applicants for entry. A list of accepted students is published in the national press. Students then attend one of the Academic Centres to register on one or more courses. At this stage, any additional course registration fees become due (100 colones for the second course and a further 150 for the third and fourth courses taken). Continuing students also attend the Academic Centres to pay their matriculation and course registration fees. Any student may withdraw from any course he has registered on during the first 22 days of the teaching period.

Student progress

None of the basic data is available in sufficient detail to enable one to evaluate with any degree of confidence the efficiency or effectiveness of the University, as measured by student progress. Drop-out is, however, a serious problem, as Table 4.3 shows.

Table 4.3: Student progress at UNED. Registered students by cohort

Semester		Cohort					Total
		1978/1	1978/2	1979/1	1979/2	1980/1	
number of students still registered	1978/1	1936					1936
	1978/2	n/a	n/a				1223
	1979/1	n/a	n/a	n/a			2986
	1979/2	410	287	678	1998		3373
	1980/1	503	349	363	888	4222	6325
% of cohort registered 1980/1		26.0	–	–	44.4	100.0	
Note: n/a = not available							

Source: UNED, Registry.

The causes of drop-out are complex, but two main reasons were cited by students who left the system in the first semester of 1979: 28 percent of those responding to a survey said that they dropped out because they could not reconcile the demands of their jobs with those of their study, while 30 percent said they could not find sufficient time to study. In addition, 13 percent deserted because they did not like studying at a distance, 3 percent left for reasons of ill-health, 4 percent because the *carreras* offered did not meet their needs, 4 percent for economic or financial reasons, and 4 percent for reasons of maladministration (UNED, 1980 a: 9-10). In another study, Pengelly (1979: 18) suggested that a number of inter-related factors combined "to create in the student's mind a lack of confidence both in themselves and in UNED". Pengelly identified, for example, an inability of students to organise their studies or judge their own progress, a lack of appreciation of what is expected of them, a general lack of study skills, the difficulty students have in obtaining accurate and reliable information and advice, and a general feeling of isolation, all of which factors combined to instil in students "a belief that the University does not really care about its students and their problems" (Pengelly, 1979: 21).

The 1979 survey on drop-out suggests that student workload is a particularly important factor in desertion. UNED's courses appear to be overloaded relative to the number of hours which its part-time students can devote to their studies. In theory a full-course load (12 credits) requires 33.3 hours of study per week over an 18 week semester. This theoretical workload stems in part from the standard definition of a credit adopted by CONARE (whereby a credit is equivalent to 45 hours work on the part of the student) and modified by UNED (to be equivalent to 50 hours work on the part of the student). In fact, UNED's students take on average 9.8 credits per semester, and work on average 11.1 hours per week (UNED, 1980b).

The actual weekly workload, then, is broadly comparable with those of students at the Universidad Nacional Abierta, Venezuela, and at the British Open University. Unfortunately, data is only available on those students who have successfully completed their courses. It is not known how much work is put in by the students who eventually drop-out, nor how much the official definition of workload per credit influences the course designers and authors.

Although drop-out and repetition is a serious problem in UNED, there is some evidence that this is also the case in conventional universities in Costa Rica - so much so that it is not uncommon for students to take twice as long as they theoretically should to complete their course. Fortunately the officials at UNED have accepted drop-out as a serious problem within the institution, and they are actively seeking ways to reducing it.

Organisational Structure

UNED's organisational structure is based on a small Rectorate and four Vice-rectorates (Administration, Planning, Academic and Research).

The Administrative Vice-rectorate provides a range of central services (financial control, accounts, transport, buildings maintenance, security, etc) as well as student administrative services (admissions, registration, records and welfare). It also oversees the production of UNED's course texts and the other books produced by Editorial UNED.

The Planning Vice-rectorate is largely concerned with drawing up the University's medium (one to five year) and short term (under a year) plans. Specialist offices formulate the five year University Plan, the building and accommodation plans, short-term project control schedules and the annual budget. A documentation and information centre is located in the Planning Vice-rectorate, as are offices concerned with institutional evaluation and statistical services. The Office of Curriculum Development is also located here.

The Academic Vice-rectorate is concerned with the design and development of printed and broadcast teaching materials, teaching (including the organisation of the academic centres), and the maintenance of academic standards.

This structure is subject to a number of weaknesses, most of which arise from the general failure to foster a sense of co-dependence between the various specialists involved. The rigid structuring of the organisation on a hierarchical basis results in the loss of that sense of mutual co-operation across functional areas which is so important in the design, production and teaching of multi-media distance courses. Particular weaknesses occur at the interfaces between the Office of Curriculum Design (in the Planning Vice-rectorate) and the authors and full-time Academic Producers (located in the Academic Vice-rectorate); between the Tutor Co-ordinators (who prepare the assessment materials) and the curriculum designers (who have specified the course objectives that are supposed to be tested); and between the authors and the Tutor

Co-ordinators, so that authors have very little awareness of the processes undertaken in the actual teaching of a course.

Governance

In UNED decision-making remains the preserve of the University Council which, with the exception of the Rector, is composed wholly of external lay members. The Council normally acts on the advice of the Rector and of the four Vice-rectors, who are in attendance at its meetings. The Rector also meets formally with his Vice-rectors on a weekly basis (Rectors' Council). It is here that the corporate management of the University is exercised. However, the usefulness of the Rectors' Council is reduced by its restricted membership and by the fact that only in very exceptional cases are non-members called upon to give their professional advice in person.

Below this level, the work of each Vice-rectorate is co-ordinated through the normally weekly meetings of the Vice-rectorate Councils, each of which is chaired by the appropriate Vice-rector and has as its members all the office heads in the Vice-rectorate. Persons from other Vice-rectorates do not normally attend such meetings. The whole emphasis of the structure is therefore hierarchical and departmental, culminating in the Rector and the University Council. A certain measure of cross-functional integration is provided by a number of standing committees and working groups, each of which work within well-defined terms of reference, and which draw their membership from any of the Vice-rectorates, as required. However, their effectiveness is limited because, firstly, the Rector and Vice-rectors do not normally attend such groups, which tends to lessen their importance; and secondly, it is clear that such committees are devoid of any power to take decisions, even at a relatively low level, since they must either report (as a committee) to the Rectors' Council or, as individual members, to the appropriate Vice-Rector. The concept of joint decision-making is an alien one. This lack of collective responsibility allows members who have failed to gain their way a ready opportunity to try to reverse a proposal by re-raising the issue outside of committee. It also means that there is a marked reluctance on the part of individuals to raise matters in committee, even where this might seem to be most appropriate.

The advantage of this structure is that it enables the officers to respond to problems quickly, but it effectively works against the complex interdependent nature of distance teaching systems.

Costs (see note 1)

UNED's 1980 budget anticipated expenditure of 55.3 million colones. Rumble (1981) showed that by 1985 costs are likely to rise to 137.5 million colones. About 32.4 percent of the increase is accounted for by the introduction of the proposed Secondary School *Bachillerato* programme. A further 18.2 percent covers the expansion of the broadcast element from the current 80 programmes per year to 240 per year (something which is now very unlikely to happen). 17.8 percent reflects an increase in student numbers, and 15.8 percent increases following on the planned growth in courses.

In spite of this overall increase in expenditure, Rumble shows that average student costs are likely to fall as student numbers increase (Table 4.4). These figures compare favourably with average student costs in conventional Costa Rican universities which in 1978 were as follows (at 1980 price levels): the University of Costa Rica, 11,110 colones; the National University, 17,360 colones; and the Technological Institute of Costa Rica, 37,240 colones. It is unlikely that the conventional universities have the same potential for economies of scale as UNED has. Indeed, as UNED increases student numbers, so its cost-efficiency as measured by average student costs is likely to improve dramatically.

Table 4.4 : Projected average student costs per annum, 1980-1985 (colones at 1980 price levels)

Year	1980	1981	1982	1983	1984	1985
Average cost per student	10,923	8,514	7,012	6,368	6,072	5,814

Conclusion

Although UNED has only been operating for four years, it has developed rapidly and is now playing a significant part in the overall provision of higher educational opportunities in Costa Rica. It is still too early to make definitive judgements on the success of the project. However, like all essentially healthy institutions, UNED is continually seeking ways of improving its systems in the light of experience. A few students have already succeeded in gaining a degree. A microcosm of the possibilities and problems of distance teaching, it is doing much to prove the potential worth of distance teaching methods at the higher educational level.

Note

1. During 1980 the value of the Costa Rican colon, which had been stable at 8.6 to the US dollar, began to float. Significant fluctuations occurred during late 1980 and 1981, with a general fall in the value of the colon, to as low as 40 to the dollar by December 1981. The collapse of the colon is having a drastic effect on local prices of imported goods. The economic situation is also affecting both UNED's costs and its plans. Indeed, during 1981 the University began to reappraise its plans and cut-back on budgets where possible.

References

1. CONARE (n.d.) 'La Universidad a Distancia'. San Jose: CONARE, Oficina de Planificación de la Educación Superior. Internal paper.
2. CONARE (1975) 'PLANES. Plan Nacional de Educación Superior. Versión preliminar 1976-1980'. San Jose: CONARE, OPES 1/75.
3. CONARE (1979) 'PLANES II. Plan Nacional de la Educación Superior 1981-1985. Documentos de Referencia 2. La Evolución del País y la Educación Post-secundaria'. San Jose: CONARE, OPES 33/79.
4. Ministerio de Educación Pública (1976) 'Proyecto de la Ley de la Universidad Estatal a Distancia'. San Jose: Ministerio de Educación Pública.
5. Pengelly, R.M. (1979) 'A report on an investigation into student progress and drop-out at UNED'. Milton Keynes: unpublished paper.
6. Rumble, G (1981) 'La Universidad Estatal a Distancia: una evaluación'. San Jose: Editorial UNED. In press.
7. UNED (1980a) 'Informe sobre la encuesta para conocer Factores que influyen en la desercion de los estudiantes de la UNED. Período de análisis 1979-1'. San Jose: UNED, Oficina de Bienestar Estudiantil. Internal paper.
8. UNED (1980b) 'La noción de crédito de CONARE y la dedicación académica UNED'. San Jose: UNED, Oficina de Investigación Institucional. Internal paper.

Chapter 5

THE FERNUNIVERSITÄT (FERNUNIVERSITÄT-GESAMTHOCHSCHULE-IN HAGEN), FEDERAL REPUBLIC OF GERMANY

Desmond Keegan

COUNTRY PROFILE

Geography

The Federal Republic of Germany consists of ten federal states plus West Berlin and has an area of 248,577 square kilometres.

Population

With a population of 61 millions, it is one of the most densely populated countries in Europe, but this population is unevenly distributed. There are thirty-one major cities each with over 200,000 inhabitants, yet 54 percent of the country is still farmland and 29 percent is wooded.

Constitution

Under its constitution, the Federal Republic of Germany is a democratic and federal republic, in which the legislative, executive and judiciary powers are separated.

Each state (*Land*) has its own parliament and administration. These parliaments have legislative powers in all matters not reserved by the constitution to the federal parliament. Education falls within state legislation.

Economy

The Federal Republic is one of the world's leading industrial nations and an important member of the European Community.

The major contributions to the G.N.P. come from industry and mining (47.8 percent); services (21.4 percent); commerce and transport (14.9 percent); and the public sector (13.2 percent). Agriculture contributes 2.7 percent. Factors which contribute to this economic achievement are technical expertise and management skills in industry; high education and training standards; and the industry of the population. To a large extent the benefits of this economic achievement have been distributed to the citizens.

The workforce numbers 25.6 millions (1980). This includes nearly two million foreign workers, the largest percentage being from Turkey.

By 1980 there were indications that the economic difficulties which have beset much of the western world since 1974 were beginning to affect the German economy. Inflation reached 6 percent and unemployment passed 1.7 million (7.3 percent) in 1981.

Communications

80 percent of German households have a family car and there are 471,000 kms of roadways; 6,700 kms of these are highclass motorways. The development of motor transport has not been allowed to dominate the railway system which maintains a national and international Intercity and Trans-Europe network. Internal shipping and air transport with eleven civil airports contribute to a comprehensive transport system.

Fifty percent of families have telephones and 90 percent television; 20 million newspapers are distributed daily and 50,000 books published per year. A comprehensive national computer information system (*Bildschirmtext*) is planned for 1984.

EDUCATIONAL PROFILE

The School System

Schooling in the Federal Republic is free and compulsory full-time from six to sixteen, and compulsory either full-time or part-time (for those who enter the workforce) from sixteen to eighteen. After four years at primary school (ages six to ten), the student attends one of four types of secondary school: *Gymnasium* (grammar school), *Realschule* (intermediate school), *Hauptschule* (lower secondary school) or *Gesamtschule* (comprehensive school). Only the first of these and one stream of the last lead to matriculation (*Abitur*). However, it is possible to progress to matriculation by studies at a series of technical colleges and colleges of higher education.

Higher Education

There are 243 institutions of higher education. Of these thirty-four are universities and ten are technical universities; there are seven comprehensive universities; eleven theological colleges; eleven colleges of education; 117 colleges of technology; twenty five institutes of art and music; six institutes of university status, and one distance teaching university, the Fernuniversität-Gesamthochschule-in Hagen.

German universities have traditionally been characterised by high academic standards, a concentration on pure research, restriction of entry to students aged twenty who have completed thirteen years (ages six to nineteen) academic study, lengthy study programmes of a body of knowledge rather than semester or annual credits, and a flexibility to move from one university to another during a degree programme. Not all these characteristics work in favour of a distance teaching university.

Within the framework of its charter, its financing by the state government ministry of education, and the influence of the Federal Ministry of Science in Bonn, a German university is an autonomous administrative entity. Although some erosion of university administrative autonomy has occurred in the last decade, the freedom to take decisions and make policy is very great.

Distance Education

200,000 students study annually at commercial correspondence schools. Television-based programmes (*Telekolleg*) are offered by a number of television stations at adult matriculation level, and radio-based programmes (*Funkkolleg*) at further education level by a number of radio stations.

The foundation of the German Institute of Distance Education *(Deutsches Institut für Fernstudien an der Universität Tübingen)* at Tübingen in the State of Baden-Wurtemberg in 1965 led to the involvement of state and federal government in planning for distance education. A plan to involve the existing German universities in a multi-media distance education project (*Fernstudium in Medienverbund*) was formulated in 1970. In the eyes of some it might have led to a German Open University.

In 1974 the Social Democratic Government of the State of North-

-Rhine Westphalia, fearing that complicated inter-government negotiations would delay the progress of distance education, announced the creation of the Fernuniversität and the appointment of Dr. Otto Peters as Foundation Vice-Chancellor.

THE FERNUNIVERSITÄT (FeU)

Origins and Development of the FeU

On 26 November 1974 the government of North-Rhine Westphalia granted the charter of the FeU to date from 1 December 1974.

The first staff were appointed in 1975 in the faculties of mathematics, education and economics. In a flurry of activity no fewer than seventy courses were prepared, printed and packaged for offering to the first enrolment in September of that year. 1,304 enrolments were received. The university occupied houses and apartments in Hagen.

The profile of courses available was extended in 1976 and 1977 and enrolments grew to 11,671 for the 1977 academic year.

By 1978 a fourth faculty, electrical engineering, was added; the network of more than thirty study centres was consolidated and the university's vice-chancellor was accepted as a full member of the *Westdeutsche Rektorenkonferenz* (the Vice-chancellors' committee of West German universities) - a sure sign that the university was coming of age.

In 1979 work began on the first of three stages of the new university buildings on the outskirts of Hagen, and the buildings were occupied the following year.

The election and first meeting of the university assembly (*Konvent*) in 1981 will bring to an end the introductory phase of the university. Student enrolments continued to increase with 20,991 new enrolments and 15,678 of previous cohorts enrolling, but the throughput of graduates (sixty-six to the end of 1981) began to be questioned. Financial pressure on the state government of North-Rhine Westphalia led in September 1981 to a government order to charge students for the printed material received as part of their course.

In November 1981 the government announced the postponement of the second and third phases of the new university buildings and discussed the relocation of half the university in unused buildings at the University of Bochum twenty kilometres away. The university reacted strongly, seeing in this move the threat of becoming a mixed institution (see chapter 1), thereby losing its character as a distance teaching university. The proposal was withdrawn and a modified second stage building approved.

Goals

The university was officially called *Fernuniversität - Gesamthochschule-in Hagen*. *Fernuniversität* means 'distance teaching university' and *Gesamthochschule* means 'comprehensive university', one which combines traditional university disciplines with the curricular areas of technical colleges. Thus the two terms largely overlap. *In Hagen* signifies that the university is situated in Hagen but has a wider mandate. The omission of the preposition *'in'* would signify that the university was identified with the city (as in 'Universität Hamburg').

The new university was given three goals:

1. To create additional capacity for academic study and thus contribute to the increase in capacity of the German university system.

2. To develop a system of academic continuing education.

3. To be engaged in the reform of university teaching by the development of new methodologies and media (*Handbuch*, 1979: 286).

In relation to these goals, firstly, FeU statistics for 1981 show no more than 8 percent of students could be regarded as recent matriculants. Secondly, continuing professional education in the Federal Republic, as in many countries, is provided by other means, and there never was much chance that a sizeable proportion of this market would be transferred to a distance teaching university. And thirdly, it is not clear that a distance teaching university is a suitable platform for launching a reform of lecturing in conventional universities.

As early as June 1977 (Peters, 1981: 180) the goals were modified, with the provision of extra places for school leavers relegated to third position. By then the FeU was already setting itself fresh informal goals which it set about achieving. Among these were: (1) to demonstrate that citizens in the Federal Republic would enrol in large numbers in a distance teaching university; (2) to attract students in employment;

(3) to produce printed learning materials that would not be criticised by other German academics; (4) to award qualifications that would be accepted as on a par with other German universities; and (5) to achieve a throughput of graduates per professor and group of lecturers at least equal to that achieved by a professor and equal group of lecturers in a conventional university.

Considerable progress has been made in achieving these informal goals.

Academic programmes

The FeU offers a number of integrated degree courses in mathematics, computer sciences, electrical engineering, and economics. There are courses leading to the master's degree in educational sciences and social sciences, and to the state qualifying examination for teachers in the senior departments of grammar and technical schools. Courses in law leading to the state examination are in preparation.

Degree courses are offered at two levels; the Diplom II is awarded at the end of from four to five years of full-time study, and is approximately equivalent to a masters programme at an English, American or Australian university. The Diplom I is awarded at the end of from three to four years of full-time study.

Table 5.1 Academic Programmes at the FeU

Faculty	Area	Awards
Mathematics and Computing	Mathematics	Diplom I Diplom II
	Computing	Diplom I Diplom II
Education and Social Sciences	State secondary teaching qualification	State Examination
	Educational Sciences	M.A.
	Social Sciences	M.A.
Economics and Law	Economics	Diplom I Diplom II
	Law	In preparation
Electrical Engineering	Electrical Engineering	Diplom I Diplom II

The Students

FeU enrols four types of students:

1. *Full-time students* require matriculation for entry. Their study goal is one of the academic awards referred to above; *Diplom, Magister* or teaching qualification. Full-time students study many subjects at a time for a minimum of three (Diplom I) or four (Diplom II) years. The programme requires a minimum of forty hours study per week, and conceivably may need sixty hours per week. Enrolment as a full-time student is not recommended for someone who is working full or part-time.

2. *Part-time students* are normally in employment or are housewives. They requires matriculation for entry and study for the same degrees as the full-time students. The number of subjects taken at the same time is reduced, and the study programmes take twice as long as for the full-time student. A typical course leading to Diplom II would take a minimum of twenty hours study per week for eight years.

3. *Auditing students* do not require matriculation and cannot study for an academic award. They select courses for their continuing professional or personal education. On completion of the study they receive a certificate of participation.

4. *Conventional university students* enrolled at another German university can enrol at the Fernuniversität (1) to do background study, (2) to vary their programme at their own university by studying a subject not available there, and (3) to get additional study material to help them succeed at their own university.

The pattern of enrolments is presented schematically in Table 5.2, while Table 5.3 provides information on the number of students in each category who were enrolled in 1981.

Table 5.2 Schematic presentation of patterns of enrolment at FeU.

Student status	Require Matriculation	Award of Degree?	Length of Programme	Minimum study per wk 1981	Fees
Full-time	Yes	Yes	3-4 years	40	DM 20 (services)
Part-time	Yes	Yes	6-8 years	20	DM 20 (services)
Auditing	No	No	—	Depends on choice of subjects	DM 35
Conventional university students	Yes, must be enrolled elsewhere	Yes; of another university	—	—	—

Source: adapted from Fernuniversität - Gesamthochschule (1981) Personal und Kursverzeichnis. Hagen: FeU. p. 27.

Table 5.3 Student enrolments by faculty and category, 1981.

Faculty	Year	Full-time	Part-time	Auditing	Other universities	Total
Mathematics and Computing	New 1981	316	1096	1198	766	3376
	Re-enrolled 1975-1980	241	1319	1714	1485	4759
Education and Soc Sci	New 1981	227	634	1918	892	3671
	Re-enrolled 1975-1980	235	1446	1800	1356	4837
Business and Law	New 1981	634	2179	2443	1656	6912
	Re-enrolled 1975-1980	939	3984	3391	2251	10565
Electrical Engineering	New 1981	154	561	570	334	1619
	Re-enrolled 1975-1980	15	486	202	127	830
					Total	36,569

Source: compiled from Fernuniversität-Gesamthochschule, Studenten Statistik 1975-1981. Ausgewählte Daten zur Entwicklung der Studentenschaft. Hagen: FeU.

In 1981, 75 percent of students were male and 25 percent female. 40 percent of the auditing students (5280) and 3 percent of the other university students did not have matriculation or equivalent. Age groups were represented as follows: 18-24 years: 25 percent; 25-31 years: 42 percent; 32-38 years: 18 percent; 39-45 years: 8 percent; over 45 years : 5 percent. Only 577 of the 36,569 students were in the age group 18-24 years and were studying full time.

21 percent of students were studying for the Diplom I; 12 percent for the full Diplom II; 4 percent for the *Magister Artium* (M.A.); 5 percent for teaching qualifications and 58 percent were not studying for a university qualification.

50 percent of students resided in the State of North-Rhine West-phalia, 48 percent in other states of the Federal Republic of Germany, and 2 percent in Austria, Switzerland or further afield (a total of forty countries). 86 percent of students are in employment, and research carried out at the university's Central Institute for Distance Education Research (*Zentrales Institut für Fernstudienforschung* - ZIFF) has shown that the students' minimum average working week is thirty-five hours.

From these statistical data it can be seen that the University has to a large extent been successful in the challenge it set itself of attracting working adults to enrol in distance programmes at university level. It is an enrolment that is quite foreign to the traditional academic concept of German universities. It is also clear that the university has set these students an enormous study programme: a minimum of twenty hours per week for eight years side-by-side with a minimum of thirty-five hours per week in employment.

Needless to say there are dropouts. The figures quoted are all for provisional enrolment, that is, students who sign the application form and are sent learning materials by the university. The university does not keep official records of effective enrolments: that is, students who actually work or send in assignments for correction, but from the data quoted in Table 5.3 a comparison can be made between new enrolments in 1981 and the relatively small numbers of those who survive from the 1975-1980 cohorts.

The admission of students auditing courses is one of the ways that the university carries out its mandate in continuing professional educa-tion. With fees until 1981 kept at a minimum (35 DM), and the right of any German citizen to audit a course at any German university, it is clear that this is an attractive form of enrolment. However, the university has so far never tried to define a precise study goal for such students and it is difficult to assess their performance. To audit a course at a conventional university one has at least to travel to attend; at the FeU one can stay at home and the links of the student to the university are tenuous. A court decision has made it clear that a student auditing a course has the right to the full course, so that a student must receive full mailings of material for every course chosen even if he or she has dropped out.

A German university student has the right to transfer to another university during his course of study and to enrol for the same programme at more than one university. Again the FeU is obliged (and wishes) to be comparable to other German universities even though the legal provisions are hardly designed for a distance teaching university. At the time of the founding of FeU in 1975 the balance of students transferring was very much against North-Rhine Westphalia; students went from the Ruhr to places like Tübingen and Heidelberg. The FeU contributed to reducing the balance. Seemingly a large number of the 8,867 1981 enrollees who are enrolled at another university (24.2 percent of the FeU's population) wish to have the University's learning materials but do not wish to participate in the activities of the University.

Factors such as these will come more into consideration in the years from 1982 when the question of the University's success in producing graduates comes into focus. For the present the University argues that a normal study programme takes a minimum of eight years and the sixty-six graduates (sixty-five in Business and one in Mathematics) by the end of 1981 are really ahead of the normal graduation pattern.

Media

The distance teaching universities are sometimes referred to as 'universities of the air'. As the FeU exists in a country that is a world leader in communications technology, it is important to study the use made of this technology at the FeU and its choice of medium for learning materials.

In 1981 the FeU offered 1,200 courses. All 1,200 were print-based. Forty use supplementary audio cassettes and fifteen have optional video-tapes. No course is computer-based, though off-line connections and commenting on students' assignments in the LOTSE and CMA systems is widespread. The university does not broadcast on radio or television and there are no plans for it to do so in the near future. Little use is made of telephone tuition.

German academic traditions place great importance on the professor's published research and the autonomy of his teaching. At conventional universities students study extensively from printed texts for four years full-time for a *Diplom* or at least eight years full-time for a doctorate. Thus the choice of print based course materials by the FeU faculties has some roots in university tradition.

The debate on educational technology and the construction of media taxonomies was eagerly pursued in the Federal Republic in the late 1960s and the early 1970s. That debate is now closed and the inherent superiority of print-based materials over other audio-visual media generally accepted.

The appointment of a number of young and relatively inexperienced staff to the FeU may also have contributed to the conservative approach to choice of medium, as academic reputations are based on printed not audio-visual materials. Even the external authors, mostly professors from other German universities, did not experiment with the new media.

Course development

In distance teaching universities there are two major administrative subsystems: the course development subsystem and the student support services subsystem (the structures that support the student once the learning materials have been developed and dispatched).

Keegan (1980: 15) has suggested that in a distance teaching university the teaching becomes institutionalised; that the lecturer's personality and relationship to students is lost; and that both content and form of teaching are influenced by persons other than the lecturer. This is only partly true of the FeU. In the German university tradition, teaching is closely linked to the chair of the individual professor and this tradition is reflected in FeU courses.

The basic principle of course development at the FeU is the desire of the faculty to present a rounded offering and the desire of the individual professor to teach his or her specialities. The initiative for a new course comes therefore from an individual professor who wins support for the development from his faculty. There is no upper limit to the number of courses that can be offered and the range of offerings by the faculty is limited only by staffing.

Once faculty approval has been won, the responsibility for development rests with the professor who proposed the course. In the FeU's early days many courses were contracted out to well-known professors at conventional universities. The amount of development done in-house by the full-time professorial staff varies from department to department. The general goal is to have 50 percent of the course written by external authors, attracting well-known experts in this way. In respect of materials developed in-house, the professor writes the learning materials, then usually passes them to his lecturers for comment.

The materials are then analysed by the Centre for Development of Distance Study Materials (*Zentrum für Fernstudienentwicklung* - ZFE) from the viewpoint of didactic structure. The ZFE advises and supports the faculties in the development of learning materials, develops and evaluates media for use in learning materials, and monitors the material's production process. It has qualified academics in each faculty area in addition to technical production staff. It presents a report on the draft materials to the professor who decides whether or not to modify his text. The materials go also to the Central Institute for Distance Education Research (ZIFF) (which carries out pure and applied research on distance education, and sponsors doctoral-level distance education research projects), for analysis to see if the materials agree with distance education principles.

When the faculty is satisfied that the text meets the University's formal requirements, the materials are sent for printing. The FeU uses an A4, single column, portrait format with a generous 6 centimetre margin on the right hand side of the page. This is used for captions. There is extensive use of line drawing, but photographs and colour printing occur rarely. This was originally for didactic reasons, but now financial considerations have more weight.

When the materials have been completed and the academic year begins, a comprehensive evaluation process is undertaken by the ZFE. This evaluation report is presented to the author who decides whether he will modify his text in the light of the evaluation.

Printed materials are produced by a number of printing companies in Hagen and surrounding towns and then stored for dispatch at the FeU. Dispatch is a highly computerized process, with learning materials being distributed in batches at various pre-determined times in the academic year, without reference to student progress. Audio and video materials are produced within the university by the Centre for Development of Distance Study Materials (ZFE).

The process described produces distance learning materials of a demanding and academically rigorous nature. The materials have been scrutinised by the other German universities and found to be of as high or higher standard than the teaching of the same subject in conventional systems.

Assessment and examination

The courses run for one teaching year of about twenty-eight weeks. The subject matter of each course is so arranged that some twenty hours of study time comprise one unit. In this way a student taking four courses receives fourteen units for each course, that is altogether fifty-six study units in one teaching year. Part-time students receive correspondingly less.

In most faculties a student concludes the study of one unit by sending in an assignment for marking. A small part of the correction may be dealt with in the form of computer marking. At the end of the course there is a supervised terminal test. The marks given for this test are stated according to the system of assessment normally in use in German universities.

The importance given to assignments varies from one faculty to another. In general they are required for authorisation to sit for the examination; rarely do they count towards assessment. There are fixed cut-off dates for the submission of all assignments, whether tutor-marked or computer-marked. On reception, assignments are normally batched and then given to demonstrators (*Wissenschaftliche Hilfskräfte*) to be marked. These demonstrators are usually post-graduate students and their work is monitored by the full-time lecturers.

The university's impressive computer facilities are used extensively by the Faculty of Economics for analysing and commenting on student assignments. In the LOTSE (Wilmersdoerfer, 1978) system the computer scans students' accounting answers for errors and then prints out individual letters to students on their performance from banks of pre-composed responses. A more advanced system (CMA) has been introduced recently to sensitise the computer still more to individual students' performances.

Student support services

The debate in the distance education literature on the weighting of student support services in a distance teaching university remains unresolved. There are those who claim that an excellent teaching package is all that is needed and that student support services, especially of a face-to-face kind, are peripheral or even a watering down of the purity of distance teaching.

On the other hand some claim that no true university education can take place without a meeting of minds and that the normal means for achieving this form of academic socialisation is face-to-face contact on the university campus.

It is not an idle debate as the economic implications are as important as the academic ones. The traditional claims for the cost-effectiveness of distance teaching universities vis-a-vis conventional ones is based on the first premise. The mass production of learning materials without diminution of quality and the ability to increase rapidly the number of students without a parallel increase of costs, because the costs in a distance system are not volume specific, are arguments that have frequently been used in favour of the foundation of distance teaching universities. It is clear that if one builds compulsory face-to-face sessions into a distance system, the cost structure changes and costs approach those of a conventional university since, for each increase in student numbers, costs increase.

The FeU tends to emphasise the quality of the learning materials and to play down the role of student support services.

If a student has a problem with the course materials or with an assignment he can, in theory, telephone, write to or even call to see the professor or his lecturers (*Wissenschaftliche Mitarbeiter*) in Hagen. Few do. A larger (but still very small) number seek help from the nearest study centre. Little real teaching is done on the basis of the assignments submitted by the students.

The FeU has 28 study centres in the state of North-Rhine Westphalia, eight in the rest of the Federal Republic and two in Austria. A study centre is usually an office plus the use of a number of classrooms in a municipal or educational building. The network of 28 in North-Rhine Westphalia ensures that no student is more than 40 kilometres from one. Some municipalities that realise that they are too small ever to have a university presence, like Lüdenscheid, have made the FeU warmly welcome.

The average study centre has a secretary and is open from 15.00 to 20.00 Mondays to Fridays. It has a team of mentors who represent the faculties in their region, provide regular tutorials, and are available to advise students. Some library facilities are provided either at the study centre or the municipal library. The mentor's role is a delicate one as he cannot infringe on the teaching rights of the professor and is unaware of the progress of students as the grades on assignments are confidential and are not communicated to him.

There has been considerable difficulty establishing study centres outside North-Rhine Westphalia, especially in those states with Christian Democrat governments which were not in favour of the foundation of the FeU. This has tended to undermine the working of the study centre system as there are persons in the FeU administration who require that whatever facilities are available to some students should be available to all.

It is difficult to generalise for all faculties but in general the emphasis on the role of face-to-face sessions tends to be focused on the later stage of the study programme. On the whole face-to-face sessions, even compulsory weekend courses and seminars, are introduced in the second half of the students' programme (years five to eight for a part-time student).

The computerised systems of the University have been extended to the university's counselling of prospective enrollees. On the completion of an optional questionnaire sent to them by the university counselling office, the computer (STEB) is programmed to respond individually on problems of choice of subjects, future study difficulties, difficulties in adaption to distance study and financial problems.

Organisation and decision-making

The decision making structures of the University are represented schematically in Figure 5.1.

The foundation vice-chancellor (Gründungsrektor) is the official representative of the university, chairman of the central committee and of the Senate, and responsible for the good organisation of the FeU.

The central committee (Rektorat) is composed of the foundation vice-chancellor, the four pro-vice-chancellors and the secretary of the university. It is the leading executive body, responsible for all matters

Figure 5.1   Organisational and decision making structure of the FeU.

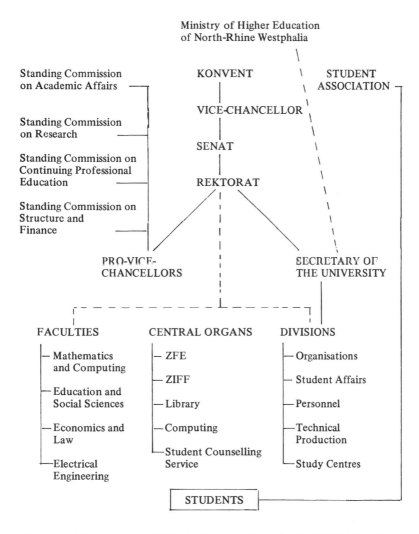

Source: Adapted from Fritsch, H. and Schuch, A. (1979) Studieren an der Fernuniversität. Hagen: FeU.

that are not officially assigned in the university charter to other bodies. The secretary of the university (*Kanzler*) plays an important role because he is the normal link to the ministry in Düsseldorf and because of his influence in financial matters. He has veto rights in this committee in all financial matters.

The senate (Senat) is composed of the foundation vice-chancellor as chairman, eight professors including the four pro-vice-chancellors, three lecturers (*Wissenschaftliche Mitarbeiter*), three students, two administrative staff and the secretary of the university. It is the major policy making body.

The assembly (Konvent) is composed of sixteen professors, eight lecturers, eight students, and eight administrative staff. The assembly draws up the university statutes and contributes to policy.

In addition there are four standing commissions: for research; academic matters; continuing education; structure, organisation, and finances.

The organisational structure of the University comprises also the academic departments (the faculties), the central institutions, and the administrative divisions.

The faculties are responsible for curricula, research and tuition, and they organise the courses of study and conduct examinations. There are, at present, four faculties:
*   The Faculty of Mathematics and Computing, which has sixteen professorships.
*   The Faculty of Education and Social Sciences, which has fifteen professorships, and whose departments include educational theory, educational sociology, adult education, empirical sociology, philosophy, politics, psychology, communications theory, theory of music.
*   The Faculty of Economics and Law, which has eleven professorships in Economics and six in Law. Law is a sub-faculty, striving to achieve full faculty status.
*   The Faculty of Electrical Engineering, which has five professorships in theoretical, automative, constructional, computer and information aspects of electrical engineering..

The central institutions are the ZFE, ZIFF, the Library, computing centre and student counselling service.

The *Centre for Development of Distance Study Materials (ZFE)* advises and supports the faculties in the development of learning materials, develops and evaluates media for use in learning materials and monitors the production process for materials. It evaluates and reports on existing courses.

The *Central Institute for Distance Education Research (ZIFF)* carries out pure and applied research on distance education methodology and sponsors doctoral research in distance education. The Centre has two professors of its own and shares three professors with the Faculty of Education and Social Sciences.

There are five administrative divisions (organisation, student affairs, personnel, technical production and study centres).

Within the University structure the autonomy of the faculty in academic matters and even of the individual professor is extensive. The 1949 German constitution characterises as a basic right the freedom of a university professor to teach and research what he thinks fit. Within this context it would appear that there have been two major influences on the evolution of administrative policy at the Fernuniversität: (1) the desire to be seen as similar to a "normal" German university; and (2) juridicial decisions or test cases.

Snowden and Daniel (1980: 86) and Rumble (1981: 182) have argued that special administrative structures are needed for distance teaching universities. The argument does not hold true for the Fernuniversität. There is a clear organisational drive to establish structures and procedures as similar to those of a "normal" university as possible.

The frequent recourse to juridicial decisions to settle points of university administration and test cases is a feature of German academic life. Such decisions of the courts hamper the administrative flexibility of the university management, especially when the law courts hand down a decision which is more suitable for implementation in a conventional than in a distance teaching university.

Conclusion

In the seven years since its foundation in 1975 the FeU has established itself as one of the universities of the state of North-Rhine Westphalia, and has attracted enrolments from all over Germany. Despite financial difficulties in the closing months of 1981 and an inherent fragility evidenced in the threat of the move to Bochum (and the slowing down and abandonment of the building programmes) it appears to be a permanent feature of the Federal Republic's university scene. Another challenge may lie ahead as the number of candidates for conventional universities is forecast to fall from 1988 onwards, although it is not clear to what degree this will affect the FeU.

The University has chosen a structure which seeks in many ways to diminish the administrative and academic differences between distance teaching universities and their conventional counterparts. This may be attributed to a young experimental university seeking to establish itself in a hostile academic climate.

Although dependent on the model of the British Open University for many of its administrative procedures, it has diverged from that model extensively in its academic approach. It is sometimes claimed that the University of South Africa (UNISA) in Pretoria is a closer didactic model. Both UNISA and the FeU are centralised organisations; rely on printed materials to the virtual exclusion of audio-visual; reject the large course team approach for course development; emphasise the learning package rather than student support services (although UNISA tends to place more emphasis than the FeU on correspondence tuition in response to the students' assignments); and teach extensively at Master's level and beyond. Especially in Mathematics, joint research programmes have been undertaken by the FeU and UNISA, whereas academic contacts with the British Open University are rare.

References

1. Fernuniversität-Gesamthochschule (1981) 'Personal und Kursverzeichnis' Hagen: FeU.
2. Fritsch, H. & Schuch, A. (1979) 'Studieren an der Fernuniversität'. Hagen: FeU.
3. 'Handbuch Hochschulen in Nordrhein - Westfalen' (1979). Düsseldorf: Der Minister für Wissenschaft und Forschung des Landes Nordrhein-Westfalen.
4. Keegan, D. (1980) 'On the nature of distance education'. ZIFF Papiere 33 Hagen: FeU, ZIFF.
5. Peters, O. (1981) 'Die Fernuniversität im Fünften Jahr'. Köln: Verlagsges Schulfernsehen.
6. Rumble, G. (1981) 'Organisation and Decision-making'. In Kaye, A. and Rumble, G. (eds.) 'Distance teaching for higher and adult education'. London: Croom Helm.
7. Snowden, B. and Daniel, J. (1980) 'The economics and management of small distance teaching universities'. Distance Education, 1, 1, 68-91.
8. Wilmersdoerfer, H. (ed.) (1978) 'CMA-Schlussbericht'. Hagen: FeU, ZIFF.

Chapter 6

EVERYMAN'S UNIVERSITY
(HA'UNIVERSITA HA'PETUCHAH)
ISRAEL

David Seligman

COUNTRY PROFILE

Geography

20,700 square kilometres comprising a coastal plain rising to the Hills of Judea and then falling away to the West Bank of the river Jordan, the Dead Sea, and the Judean Desert. Galilee (in the north) and the coastal plain are cultivated, while the Negev (in the south) is desert.

Population

3.7 millions (1980 estimate). The population is made up of 3.1 million Israeli Jews, 590,000 Israeli Arabs, and 50,000 from other groups. The post-1967 administered territories of the West Bank and the Gaza have a population of 1.1 million Arabs.

61 percent of the population occupies 11 percent of the area (the coastal strip between Haifa and Ashdod). The Negev, with 65 percent of the landspace, is largely desert and has less than 7 percent of the population. Less than 3 percent of the population live in the Kibbutzim (collective farms).

Economy

Israel is largely self-sufficient in foodstuffs. Agriculture is a major source of export earnings. Natural resources are limited, although there are extensive deposits of chemicals and some copper. Water resources are limited and carefully controlled.

There is a thriving industry based on imported raw materials. Exports of finished products include diamonds, textiles, chemicals, fertilizers, tyres, electrical equipment, cement and pharmaceuticals. There is, however, an unfavourable balance of trade. High inflation and full employment have been facts of life in recent years.

Communications

There is an efficient bus service over the whole country. Major centres are linked by rail. There are many private cars; an internal air service; a reasonably good postal system; and a fully automatic telephone system.

There is one television channel transmitting mainly in monochrome, but increasing the number of colour transmissions. Radio is broadcast on several channels. Broadcasting is under the control of the Israel Broadcasting Authority (*Reshut Hashidur*). Educational broadcasts are transmitted on the national channels. Schools Educational TV programmes, vocational programmes and some Everyman's University programmes are produced by the Instructional Television Centre. The army has its own radio programme.

EDUCATIONAL PROFILE

Structure

The Ministry of Education is responsible for educational planning up to the higher education level. The National Council for Higher Education is supposed to regulate university growth and development, but in practice the universities have been virtually autonomous. However, a central body to allocate funds to the universities has recently been established which might make more rational development planning possible.

The education system is centralised with the Ministry having wide responsibilities covering curricula, educational experiments, administration of examinations, appointment of teachers to elementary schools and so on. Local authority responsibility is largely restricted to construction and maintenance of buildings, supply of equipment, and the provision of auxiliary services.

Schools

The majority of Israeli women have full-time jobs so that the percentage of children aged 3 and 4 attending nursery school is high. At age 5 one year pre-primary education is compulsory.

The primary/elementary schools take children from the age of 6 to 14. At age 13 an examination (*Seker*) provides an indication of the type of secondary education the child will attend. Junior High Schools (*Hativat Benaim*) are gradually being introduced which will take children from age 11 to 15.

There are three secondary strands: Academic, Vocational, and Agricultural. Children who successfully complete the *Seker* go on to the academic stream and pupils are also received from the Junior High Schools. At age 17/18 the School Leaving Certificate Examination (*Bagrut*) is taken in about 6 subjects. The results of *Bagrut* determine university entrance. There is a wide variety of vocational schools preparing students for work in trades and business. In addition to the full-time vocational schools there are a number of schools offering evening classes to children who have left school at the age of 15. Most of the agricultural schools are boarding schools.

There is separate provision for religious education within the State system. The religious schools are under the direction of a Religious Education Department in the Ministry of Education. They offer basically the same curriculum as the State Schools but with a higher proportion of religious subjects. 24.9 percent of children attend elementary and secondary religious schools.

On the establishment of the State the Kibbutz school system became part of the ordinary state system. Kibbutz children are expected to stay at school until age 18. Originally the system disapproved examinations but there has been a change in attitude and some Kibbutz children now take the *Bagrut* examination.

In Arab areas instruction is in Arabic and the curriculum does not include Bible Studies and Hebrew Literature. Under the Mandate Arab education, but not Jewish, was the responsibility of the British, and a separate 'system' developed. In 1947, 60 percent of boys and 20 percent of girls attended elementary schools. Now almost all the boys and 80 percent of the girls attend full-time education. Secondary schools have been built and an Arab Teacher Training College established.

Higher Education

There are 7 traditional universities in Israel. Six of them have under-graduate and postgraduate students; the seventh, the Weizmann Institute, is a research institution where only postgraduate work is undertaken. The total number of students at the 7 institutions is 50,000, and more than one-fifth of them are postgraduates. It is currently the policy in all the universities to increase the number of postgraduate students while attempting to maintain undergraduate numbers at something like their present level.

Educational Broadcasting and Technology

The Instructional Television Centre (*Hamerkaz Letelevizia Limudit*) was initially funded by the Rothschild Foundation. It now operates within the Ministry of Education. The broadcasts it has produced for schools, over a range of subject areas, have been well received. It is planning to expand its operation into adult education and co-operation for production with Everyman's University. Transmission is via the broadcasting authority's single TV channel. A second channel is planned.

Educational radio programmes are produced and transmitted by the Israel Broadcasting Authority in co-operation with the Ministry of Education.

The Centre for Educational Technology (*Hamerkaz Letechnologia Chinuchit*), also funded by the Rothschild Foundation, is now linked closely with Everyman's University. It is doing some interesting experimental work and has several successful programmes in computer assisted learning.

EVERYMAN'S UNIVERSITY (EU)

Origins

The Israel Ministry of Education and Culture and the Council for Higher Education set up a Committee on Post-Secondary Education in May 1970. Amongst its recommendations it was suggested that an 'Open University' experimental programme be established. In early 1971 the Rothschild Foundation reached a similar conclusion. On 15 September 1972 the Schramm Commission issued its final report *An "Everyman's University" for Israel* (Schramm *et al.*, 1972). In August 1973 the Cabinet unanimously approved the establishment of the University;

the authorisation from the Council for Higher Education came in October, and it was incorporated in April 1974. In October 1976 the first cohort of students was enrolled. Everyman's University received formal recognition as an Institution of Higher Learning with the right to award a degree in July 1980.

The University's objectives are listed as:

1. To provide access to higher education at home to all those unable to study within existing educational frameworks, without disrupting their normal occupations;
2. To assist elementary and junior high school teachers to study towards an academic degree;
3. To provide those who left their studies at an early age with a second chance to acquire higher education;
4. To help raise the general educational level of the population.

Students

Entry is open in that no formal entry qualification is required. Basic literacy is of course necessary and there are some preparatory courses for those who need them.

Table 6.1 provides basic demographic data on students registered on each of the University's four academic programmes in the eighth semester. The figures demonstrate considerable variation in the characteristics of students on the various programmes.

The Programmes of Study

Four programmes of study are available:

1. *Pre-academic courses* are provided in English and Mathematics at high school level, and are intended as a preparation for the academic degree programme, although some students go on to complete their *Bagrut* (Matriculation) examinations.

2. The Academic *Degree Programme* which provides a B.A. There will be 200 courses available by 1983. The curriculum is drawn up by the University itself and the courses written either solely by internal course teams or with the help of external academic consultants. The courses fall into five categories: Mathematics, Exact Sciences, Life Sciences, Humanities and Social Science.

111

Table 6.1 : Characteristics of Everyman's University students registered in the eighth semester.

Programme	Pre-academic	Academic	Adult Education	Vocational
100% =	635	7185	892	576
	%	%	%	%
Sex				
Male	46.1	44.9	32.5	96.7
Female	53.9	55.1	67.5	3.3
Age				
Under 21	10.6	14.4	5.3	9.1
21 to 26	28.9	27.8	31.5	24.1
27 to 35	31.4	27.8	35.6	42.2
Over 35	29.1	30.2	27.6	24.6
Number of years of previous education				
8 or less	4.4	2.0	3.3	3.8
9 or 10	16.4	5.8	5.5	12.9
11 or 12	53.6	53.9	39.8	47.4
13 or more	25.6	38.3	51.4	35.9
Occupation				
Office work/ management	15.0	14.9	17.3	5.5
Armed forces	15.3	18.8	12.7	18.6
Education	15.8	17.1	18.3	9.1
Health sector	6.8	6.0	11.5	5.7
Technological	13.1	10.7	9.6	44.4
Housewives	7.5	5.0	4.5	0.2
Students /others in work/ unemployed	26.5	27.5	26.1	17.0

Source: Everyman's University, President's Report, 1979/80.

3. *Adult Education* courses in fields like public health, environmental studies, spoken and literary Arabic, and special interest courses.

4. *Vocational* courses that are planned in conjunction with the Ministry of Labour. These include courses for electronic technicians, accounting, and technical drafting which have been developed on the curriculum provided by the Ministry of Labour which recognises the certification given.

The medium of instruction is Hebrew. However, students, especially in the advanced academic courses, are expected to have a working knowledge of English.

Media and Course Structure

Each course normally runs for an 18 week semester. There are two such semesters in each year, one starting in September and the second in

February. In addition, there is an intensive 10 week summer semester. The bulk of the teaching is through *correspondence materials* which are produced at a high quality level in A4 format with many pictures and diagrams.

Television programmes are available for 35 courses, each of which have from 6 to 12 programmes. About five hours per week is available on the country's single TV Channel but transmission times are not always convenient for all students. *Video cassettes* of programmes are available and can be seen at study centres. Some programmes are specially produced either by the Centre for Educational Technology, with whom the University shares a building, or by the Instructional Television Centre, which is in the building next door. Many existing films from other sources are adapted to meet course needs.

Radio programmes are essentially for enrichment and follow a more general broadcasting format. They are prepared by the academics in conjunction with a producer from the Israel Broadcasting Authority. At present transmission is limited to 6½ hours per week.

Audio Cassettes of radio programmes are available at study centres. Cassettes are also sent as part of the package of materials for some courses, e.g. English, Arabic, Maths, Electronics, Music.

Home Experiment Kits are provided for use on science and technology courses, and special teaching aids, including a mini-computer, are provided for students on mathematics courses.

Set Books, which are a compulsory component of courses, are always carefully considered as they can be very expensive, in short supply and in languages other than Hebrew. To overcome these problems, some books have been translated, and sets of books are kept in study centre libraries which are also prepared to expand their collections on special subjects.

There are 36 *Study Centres* throughout the country. Students are allocated to these according to course and where possible by the area in which the student lives. The part-time tutors, who usually have full-time academic posts in other institutions, provide face-to-face tuition, giving about six sessions per course. Sometimes day schools are held at the Centres as well. The Centres are usually based on existing academic institutions where facilities such as laboratories and libraries are used by the EU students.

Course Development

The Academic Advisory Committee decides on the overall course profile of the University. Proposals for courses are checked against this profile to see how well they fit the master plan. The courses can be proposed by central academics, or any other academic who has worked for the University. A final decision to proceed or not with a course is made by the President of the University.

Texts are written by central academics or by external consultants. At the first draft stage material is sent for internal and external reading and suggestions are made for improvement, re-writing and suitability. These suggestions are then considered and implemented by the text author. Academic control of course materials, once the course has been approved by the Academic Advisory Committee and the President, lies with the Course Team, the Vice-President for Academic Affairs and the Director of Course Development. Because of the large number of outside contributors, it is important that this control is at a senior level and diplomatically handled.

Discussion on the use of illustrations, graphics, and editing, will have been proceeding during the draft stages.

It is intended that *Developmental Testing* be carried out where possible but this will depend on the time available and the pressure to meet deadlines. So far very little developmental testing has taken place but feedback after actual student use is taken into account for any necessary corrections.

The final rewrite and editing of the text is carried out by the course assistant and editor. Finally, after editing by the central core Course Team and approval from the Director of Course Development, the text is sent for printing and goes through all the print production stages.

During the first draft stage of the text, discussions concerning other components of the teaching package take place. If suitable television programmes are not available then plans are made to produce them. Similarly the need for radio programmes is considered as is the necessity of home experimental kits.

Course Production and Distribution

After the final draft of the printed text has been passed it is photoset and with graphics and layout prepared in-house, the camera-ready copy is sent to an outside printer. Liaison with the printer is carried out by the Publishing Office.

Television programmes are either (1) bought and used as they stand (usually a commentary, in Hebrew, is added), or (2) specially produced, often with the help of the Centre for Educational Technology or in collaboration with the Instructional Television Centre.

Radio programmes are made in conjunction with a producer from the Israel Broadcasting Authority.

Home Study Kits are designed to meet the requirements of some courses and are assembled and maintained by a central unit of the University.

Materials are sent to the students in one mailing. For courses not ready at the beginning of the semester, additional mailings are possible.

Broadcasts, radio and TV, are transmitted at scheduled times. Video and audio cassettes of all programmes are available for use at selected Study Centres.

Student Administration

Courses are advertised in the national press and through the wide distribution of handbills giving basic information about courses.

On enquiry, prospective students are sent a Course Handbook and Application Form. Entry is 'open' but students are told that it is advisable that they should have reached the academic equivalent of eleventh grade for the Academic Degree Programme. A student registering for the first time is allowed to take one course only. In subsequent semesters, he may take two or exceptionally three courses.

A student is not placed on computer file until registration is complete, i.e. the application form has been correctly filled in and the registration fee paid.

The only limits on the number of students allowed to register for a course are practical ones, e.g. where there is a limited number of study kits or where no additional tutorial and study centre arrangements can be made.

Student Support Services

Students are usually allocated to a Study Centre of their own choice. There are 36 such centres scattered all over the country. Because of lack of facilities at some centres (e.g. laboratory space) not all courses can be tutored at all centres. Where this is the case, or where there are insufficient students to make up a group, students are allocated elsewhere. Groups vary in size depending on the nature of the course.

Study Centres are hired from the local municipality or from another institution. They vary considerably as to facilities but have as many resources as possible to help the student. They are open on certain days of the week at given times. The library, which usually has most of the relevant course materials, is opened an hour before tutorials begin to allow students to borrow books and use reference sources. Self-help groups are allowed to use centre premises, and video and audio cassettes are also available.

To enable students who are in need of personal assistance or who are unable to take advantage of Study Centre Tutorials there is a system of telephone tuition. This operates in two ways: (1) Telephone numbers for central academic staff on each course are made available, enabling students to obtain help with course materials, and (2) a list of tutors who can be contacted at specific dates and times is published in the Study Guide.

Assessment and Examination

The assessment model used is a combination of continuous assessment throughout the semester and examination at the end of the course. The weighting between the two components is 60 percent - exam, 40 percent - continuous assessment. Assignments, of which there are usually between 8 and 10 per course, vary in weighting, but students are informed of this in the study guide. Students must do a minimum of 50 percent of the assignments set in order to be considered for credit. This can vary from course to course, e.g. Philosophy stipulates that all are necessary. If students have met the specified requirements but not completed all assignments then the weighting placed on the examination will be higher to make up the 100 percent assessment. Students are warned if they have not completed enough assignments to enable them to be awarded a credit. Both Tutor Marked and Computer Marked Assignments are used. The ratio between the number of Computer Marked Assignments (CMAs) and Tutor Marked Assignments (TMAs) tends to be approximately 6 CMA / 4 TMA. It is recommended that 1 CMA is used per 2 text units and 1 TMA per 3 units. Some courses have

116

compulsory assignments and students are not awarded a credit if these are not completed.

Students have to return completed assignments by a certain specified date. Late submission of assignments is allowed if there is good reason for this - for example, illness or army reserve service.

There can be delays of 5 or 6 weeks from the time of submission before students are notified of CMA grades. This poor turnround time can seriously disadvantage students needing feedback on their performance as the courses only last 18 weeks. Tutors are asked to mark all TMAs within 2 weeks of the cut-off date and return the grading form giving the individual question scores, the overall grade for the assignment, and comments on the student's piece of work and progress. A computer printout is produced showing the marks awarded by each tutor, giving the average for each tutor and the overall average. This printout is sent to the person in charge of the particular course and to the Examinations section. Each tutor's marking is monitored and the academic responsible assesses both the marking and the advice given to the student. Tutors who prove unsatisfactory are not reappointed.

Prior to the examination students are informed of their current total number of assignments submitted and those who have not yet done the required number have to complete them so as to be eligible to take the examination. Following the marking of the examination, students are informed of their grade and of their overall course result (which also takes into account continuous assessment).

Statistics are produced after marking is completed, and it is possible that a course will be entirely remarked. There is no formal check on standards across the three alternative exam papers used for each course at the end of any one semester. No outside examiners are involved in the awarding of results or the review of the course's assessment and student performance, nor is there any formal mechanism for notifying and highlighting 'mishaps' which may have occurred through the year which could affect students' performance (for example: late arrival of material or very poor tutors). The vetting of the examination papers by an external academic (Academic Advisory Committee) is seen as being adequate in safeguarding standards and fairness.

In some courses compulsory assignments are set which must have been attempted before a student will be credited for the course. The Biology and Science courses also have compulsory laboratory sessions and compulsory meetings/tutorials. In the case of these compulsory elements, students can be allowed to fulfil the requirement in the following semester when taking another course. In the case of compulsory CMAs and TMAs, extra time is allowed for their completion but these cannot be left until the next semester.

Student Progress

The figures given in Table 6.2 show the proportion of initially registered students in each of the four academic programmes who (1) cancelled their registration, (2) abandoned their studies, (3) studied for the whole academic term, and (4) were eligible to sit the examination. It also shows the proportion of students who (1) sat the final examination and (2) were awarded credit, as a percentage of those who studied during the semester and the number of students who were awarded credit as a percentage of those who sat the examination. Cancellation of registration took place prior to the due date for the payment of the first instalment of fees. Abandonment of registration occurred where students did not pay the second instalment of fees. Students who paid both instalments could postpone their studies (and hence the examination) to the following term. (Recently students have been required to make a single payment of fees, with implications for the concept of abandonment of studies.)

Organisation and Administration

Approximately 250 full-time staff are employed at Everyman's. This includes some 25 academic staff; 100 course assistants and editors; and 30 typists and graphic artists. The remainder are administrative, data processing, library and audio visual staff. There are in addition, course writers on contracts, and about 360 part-time tutors.

The University is managed by the President, two Vice-Presidents and three Directors of specific areas: (1) Course Development (which includes media services); (2) Course Maintenance and Tuition; and (3) Student Administration.

There are also support services: Library, Personnel, Finance, Purchasing, and Public Relations.

The supreme authority of the University is Council which determines University policy, supervises the implementation of its decisions and administers the affairs and assets of the University. The academic

Table 6.2 : Student progress in the seventh semester at Everyman's University (provisional figures)

Programme	Pre-academic	Academic degree	Adult Education	Voca-tional
Total students registered	387	6942	420	680
= 100% =	%	%	%	%
As a percentage of total registrations				
(1) Registrations cancelled or postponed	8.3	10.2	9.3	5.6
(2) Study abandoned	20.2	9.4	9.0	10.1
(3) Studied during the whole academic term	71.6	80.4	81.7	84.3
(4) Eligible for final examinations	19.4	57.6	20.0	54.0
As a percentage of those who studied				
(1) Number of students who sat the final examination	32.5*	52.4*	24.8*	57.4*
(2) Number of students awarded credit	28.2*	43.9*	23.6*	44.7*
As a percentage of those who sat the examination				
(1) Number of students awarded credit	86.7*	83.8*	95.3*	77.8*

Notes:

* indicates that these figures are provisional but indicates the minimum level of awards made. The number of students gaining credit could increase marginally (by up to 2 percentage points) following the results of the third and fourth examination sittings.

Source: Everyman's University, President's Report, 1979/80.

authority is the Academic Committee composed of professors from universities throughout Israel and members of EU's academic staff.

The Academic Advisory Committee concerns itself mainly with policy, with the development of a profile of courses and the maintaining of academic standards. This committee is not a governing or direct policy-making body, but acts in an advisory capacity. Sub-committees of this body represent each Field of Study.

Resources

EU's buildings are located in the suburbs of North Tel-Aviv; one of the buildings is shared by the Centre for Educational Technology (CET). The latter building was originally planned for CET but as the two organisations work closely together (and were initially financed by the Rothschild Foundation) there seemed to be no initial problems in adapting the building to accommodate both. Academic and administrative office space is available; there is also a library, laboratories, computerized photo-typesetting and reprographic facilities, and large committee rooms. CET has a video outside broadcasting unit that has been used to produce programmes for EU. The Instructional Television Centre is built next to the CET/EU buildings. Tel-Aviv University, which has extensive university facilities, is across the road.

Financial control is the responsibility of the President. The costs for the first five years of Everyman's operation were met mainly by the Rothschild Foundation. Since then the University's budget is largely met by the Government, through the Council for Higher Education Grants Committee.

Capital investment in buildings, equipment and furnishings has amounted to about 4 million dollars (at today's prices). Annual recurrent expenditure in 1980/81 was about 6.1 million dollars, of which about 51 percent went on course development and publication costs, 37 percent on student and course delivery costs, and 12 percent on overhead operating costs. Students paid a fee of 55 dollars per course credit, a fee level which was about 60 percent of the level charged at other Israeli universities. The cost to the student of a degree (18 credits) was therefore 900 dollars.

Conclusion

Everyman's University has clearly been a successful institution. Academically it is undoubtedly fulfilling an important role and the variety of courses presented is adding considerably to the range of provision available to adults in the vocational and academic areas of need. As in other countries though, it does not seem to be reaching that part of society which traditionally does not continue into higher education, or which could be considered disadvantaged.

It might be that it takes more than an institution alone to change established habits and attitudes, and that what is required is a restructuring of the education system, especially at the secondary level, which would affect fundamental attitudes to further training and education for adults. However, it is important to remember that the extended provision is there, and now that Everyman's University is academically established in the framework of Israeli education it can look forward to satisfying the social objectives which lay behind its establishment.

Reference

1. Schramm, W., Hawkridge, D. and Howe, H. (1972) 'An "Everyman's University" for Israel'. Jerusalem: Hanadiv.

Chapter 7

THE ALLAMA IQBAL OPEN UNIVERSITY, PAKISTAN

Alec Fleming

COUNTRY PROFILE

Geography

796,096 square kilometres, with four political/geographical regions:

The Punjab. 47 million people. The eastern agricultural and industrial province, producing most of the country's rice, wheat, cotton and sugar-cane. Chief cities: Lahore, Rawalpindi, Faisalabad (Lyallpur), Multan. The small *Federal area* in the north of the province contains Islamabad (200,000), the capital city, built in the late 1960s/70s.

Sind 18.9 millions, lies in the south, between the Punjab and the Arabian Sea. Chief cities: Karachi (6 millions), the national port, and Hyderabad. Much of the province is arid and uncultivated.

Baluchistan, the largest province, has the smallest population (4.3 millions). It borders and ethnically overlaps with Iran. It is mountainous, remote and pastoral. Chief city, Quetta.

Northwest Frontier Province (NWFP) 10.8 millions. It lies against Afghanistan, the Karakorams and Kashmir. It is tribal territory, with the Pathan city of Peshawar, its chief city, close to the Khyber Pass. *Azad (free) Kashmir, Jammu* and the small agency territories of *Hunza* and *Gilgit* lie up beyond NWFP and the Punjab, to the north-east. Across the border is the disputed Kashmir territory occupied by India.

Population

83.8 millions (1981) and increasing at 3 percent per annum. About 70 percent rural; some 50 percent under 16 years. Estimated labour force 24 millions, also growing at 3 percent per annum. There is high under/unemployment. 95 percent is Muslim. The principal language is Urdu, but provincial languages have a strong presence; English is the common official language. There is a high illiteracy rate (over 70 percent) especially among women.

Economy

Agriculture provides some 32 percent of GDP, 35 percent of exports and employs over 56 percent of the labour force. 13 percent of the workforce is in manufacturing, etc; 10 percent each in commerce and services; construction and communications have 4 percent each. Textiles are important in manufacturing and export. Manpower is also an important export, with over 700,000 working abroad. Approximately 50 percent of export earnings are spent on oil imports. Estimated per capital gross income is 250 US dollars.

Communications

Roads:	96,000 km.; 35,000 first-class. Principal load-carriers are six-wheeled Bedford lorries. Donkeys, camels and ox-carts are used throughout the country for local carrying. Rural travel is by private bus; in towns by bus, minivan, taxi, tonga (horse and cart), with bicycles very common.
Rail:	Government-run 10,500 km. system.
Air:	There is a well-used network of internal air-routes, with international airports at Islamabad and Karachi.
Television:	Pakistan Television Corporation, Islamabad, plus 5 regional stations. 6-7 hours' daily transmission on one channel. 800,000 receivers (1980-81).
Radio:	Pakistan Broadcasting Corporation, Islamabad, plus eight local stations, usually 2-channel, with broadcasting in Urdu and local languages. 1.5 million licences (1981), but undoubtedly many more sets.
Telephones:	350,000 (1981)
Post Offices:	12,000
Newspapers:	112 dailies, 318 weeklies and bi-weeklies.

EDUCATIONAL PROFILE

Administration

The Federal Ministry controls broad policy, curricula, books and standards. Provincial departments fund and administer education at all levels, although the University Grants Commission (UGC) is a national co-ordinating body for higher education.

Structure

Apart from religious instruction, pre-school education is practically non-existent. After the age of 5 there are three levels - primary, secondary and higher, with five stages: primary 5 - 10; secondary middle 10-12; secondary high 13-15; higher secondary 15-17. Education is free up to class 10 (14 years), but not compulsory. After class 12 (16 years) matriculation is taken (5 basic subjects, 1 vocational/commercial). Vocational/technical training is available from class 9 and elementary teacher-training can begin from age 15. There is a growing private sector: mosque schools have been established following government initiative.

Participation

Rounded percentages of age groups (1978/79)

Primary	6.5 millions	55 percent
Middle	1.4 million	23 percent
Secondary	0.6 million	14 percent

Nearly three times more boys than girls attend primary school, and nearly four times more at middle and secondary. Drop-out in the early stages is very high.

Standards

Classes are generally large, facilities inadequate, curricula/teaching are highly formalised. Primary instruction is usually in the local mother tongue; middle and secondary instruction in Urdu. Children are automatically promoted from class to class, up to Class VIII, thereafter by annual examinations.

Higher Education

There are nineteen universities, with an enrolment of 62,048 (0.3 percent of age group) in 1980-81. Each university is autonomous, although funding for the last two to three years has been by the Federal government, and curricula/degree structures are theoretically validated by the UGC. In addition, vice-chancellors (who have a four year term) are appointed by the chancellor of the university concerned, who is usually the governor of the province. The Chancellor of the AIOU is the President of Pakistan and the Pro-Chancellor is the Federal Minister of Education. There are very active student bodies, often mirroring national political groupings.

All provincial universities give instruction at honours and post-graduate level only; university ordinary bachelors' degrees are taken externally at degree colleges. Medical and specialist engineering degrees are taken only at universities and some specialist colleges. Such graduates are in high demand, particularly abroad; but for arts graduates, jobs are not plentiful. There is an extensive private student system permitting home study.

Teacher training

Initial training is broadly of two kinds - for primary or secondary teachers. Primary teachers require a one-year Primary Teacher's Certificate for post-matric students, or a one-year Certificate of Teaching for holders of the Intermediate pre-degree Certificate. Both are followed by one year's in-school supervision.

Secondary teachers require a one-year B.Ed. post-graduate degree or an M.Ed./M.A.

THE ALLAMA IQBAL OPEN UNIVERSITY (AIOU)

Foundation, Structure and Purpose

The AIOU was formally established in 1974, following the passing of the People's Open University Act. Its origins lay in the Education Policy (1972-80) document, which stated:

"A People's Open University will therefore be established to provide part-time educational facilities through correspondence courses, tutorials, seminars, workshops, laboratories, television and radio broadcasts and other mass communication media . . . " (Federal Ministry of education, Education Policy (1972-80), Section 7.10).

125

The main objectives of the University, given in the Act which followed, are as follows:

1. To provide facilities to people who cannot leave their homes and jobs.
2. To provide such facilities to the masses for their educational uplift.
3. To provide facilities for the training of teachers.
4. To provide for instruction in such branches of learning, technology or vocations as it may deem fit, and to make provision for research and for the advancement and dissemination of knowledge in such a manner as it may determine.
5. To hold examinations and to award and confer degrees, diplomas, certificates and other academic distinctions to and on persons who have been admitted to and have passed its examinations under the prescribed conditions.

These very broad and ambitious objectives were translated into statements of position and intent by the second Vice-Chancellor:

The People's Open University ... is entrusted with the task of serving the whole country and all categories of people ... its clientele are the masses. It rejects the elitist view that only a small selected class of people can benefit from higher education ... that for any real learning to take place people have to be secluded behind walls of educational institutions and pursue a rigidly structured curriculum. The University is not designed to replace the formal education system, nor can it do so. It will complement and supplement existing educational institutions. (However) Education for skilled labour, technicians and other occupations in business, industry and agriculture has mostly been ignored by the formal educational system. The People's Open University will give high priority to the occupational education of farmers, industrial workers and craftsmen. (Zaki, 1975)

Initial course plans were drawn up on an ambitious scale, and fairly high and immediate student enrolment was envisaged. Actual development can be viewed generally as occurring in three phases: the initial development stage; a second stage of re-thinking, systematisation and progress; and the present, third stage of consolidation and planned development. In fact, during the University's first four years, five distance-learning courses or programmes were actually presented; four of these were very successful and continue still in amended form:

PTOC (Primary Teachers' Orientation Course), Elementary Arabic, Vegetable Growing, and the M.A. courses in Education Planning and Management. In addition, an Integrated Functional Education Project was completed and is now being copied in other locations. The current (1981) position in each programme area is outlined below.

1. Teacher Education. Responsibility for this lies with the University's Institute of Education. In producing courses, it draws heavily on the subject departments in the University. Current and projected courses in this area are summarised in Table 7.1.

Table 7.1 : Summary of Current and Projected Courses in Teacher Education.

Title and Target Audience		Length	First Presentation & Cycles so far	Potential Audience	Enrolled To Date
PTC	Primary Teachers' Certificate for serving untrained teachers, includes teaching practice. Compulsory nomination by District Education Officers.	22 weeks	1980 (4)	10,000	2,644
PTOC	Primary Teachers' Orientation Course - for serving teachers. Compulsory enrolment, no extra salary. Two bi-annual cycles one for summer-closure schools, one for winter.	18 wks	1976 (8)	155,000	59,304
CT	Certificate of Teaching. Higher grade primary and middle-school qualification. 7½ credits, students take 2½-4	9 wks each	1982	10,000	—
STOC (CT)	Science Teachers' Orientation Course for middle-school teachers.	9 wks	1982	3,000	—
ATOC	Arabic Teachers' Orientation Course.	9 wks	1982	—	—
M.A.	8-credit degree in Educational Planning and Management. Participants nominated by provincial departments.	18 wks each credit	1976	—	1,150
PGDE	Post-graduate Diploma in English. Special 2-credit course for Punjab lecturers.	18 wks each	1981	2,000?	263

Note to Table 7.1

Education is also available for study at Intermediate level in the General Education Programme and a B.A. level course is planned.

The *Primary Teachers' Orientation Course* resulted from a direct request from Provincial Education Ministers for assistance in introducing a new primary curriculum. There are over 160,000 teachers in more than 58,000 primary schools. It was hoped that, by an enrolment of 40-50,000 students per annum, the entire teaching force would be covered within three years. However, such coverage has not proved feasible, the largest cycle numbering 15,000. Up to 1982 nearly 60,000 teachers had taken the course; i.e. nearly 40 percent of the primary total, and the PTOC is the AIOU's most successful course in terms of enrolment. However, at least a further nine annual presentations would be needed to cover the entire primary teaching force and, as a sizeable number of teachers entering since 1974 will have been familiarised with the new curriculum in their initial training, it has been decided to run down the course by gradually adopting voluntary enrolment.

2. Functional Education, i.e. helping individuals to acquire and extend knowledge and skills for direct use in their work and their homes, with the associated aim of assisting with community development. Relatively few courses have been produced in this area, partly because of staffing problems, but mainly because of the extra demands of preparing such courses, although thinking may have been to some extent bound by the actual concepts of distance-teaching and individualised learning - as opposed to providing resource packs and encouraging group learning.

To date, five non-assessed courses have been produced. These are aimed at a double audience: literate farmers (and in some cases house-holders), and Field Assistants and other workers (Table 7.2).

3. General Education   Table 7.3 lists the currently available and immediately projected General Education courses, many of which are of an applied kind.

In all subjects for Intermediate level and above, students must have matriculated. The only exceptions are Arabic and electrical courses; for the former the AIOU's own elementary course is accepted. For the latter, non-matriculates are accepted, but if successful they obtain a certificate of course completion only. It was originally planned to offer courses at three levels: Foundation, Intermediate and B.A. The first was seen as a bridging device for those students who had dropped out of the conventional system after obtaining matriculation. Five

Table 7.2 : Current and Projected Courses in Functional Education

TITLE	TARGET AUDIENCE	ENROL-MENT	FIRST PRE-SENTED	ENROL-MENT TO DATE
Vegetable Growing (2 versions) winter and summer	Urban and semi-urban householders. Free supply of seeds	Bi-annually	1977	5,946
Soil Problems	Literate farmers/ small holders, and Field Assistants	Annually	1979	1,015
Plant Protection		Annually	1979	1,240
Poultry Farming	Literate rural and urban householders	Bi-annually	1980	2,015
Tractor Repair and Maintenance	Rural tractor owners and literate mechanics	Annually	1981	364
Sheep and Goat Husbandry	Literate farmers/ small holders and	In preparation for 1983		
Farm Machinery	Field Assistants	In preparation for 1983		
Principles and Methods of Agri-cultural Extension	Agricultural Field Staff	In preparation		
Home Management	Rural women	In preparation		
Farm Management	Rural women	In preparation		
Principles and Methods for Women Extension Workers	Women Field Staff	In preparation		

Table 7.3 : General Education Course List

Note: Figures are total enrolments since inception. Other courses are
1981/82 introductions and no figures are available.

Elementary
Functional Arabic   8727

Intermediate (i.e., post-Matric, pre-degree)

Arabic	1561	Education	997
Urdu	7426	General Science	2253
Daftari Urdu		Food & Nutrition	3027
(Official) (½)	5407	Rural Development (½)	1950
Iqbaliat (*)	3063	Electrical Wiring (½)	7434
Pakistan Studies (E)	2355	Book-keeping and	
English	5237	Accountancy	306

New courses launched in October, 1981
Electrician (½)
Economics

Projected Intermediate courses for 1982

Arabic Teachers' Orientation	Islamiat (c) (½)
Course	Pakistan Studies (c) (½)
Statistics	Islamiat (E)
Economics II	Child Care and Development
Banking	

B.A. courses

Economics	3870	Urdu	2543
Economics of Pakistan	341	Iqbaliat	901
Business English	4042	History of Islamic World (1940-1980)	383
Pakistan Studies (E)	1623	Sociology	379
Accountancy	215	Literature of Pakistan	203
Export Marketing & Management I	1058	Pakistan Studies (c) (½)	1170
Islamiat (c) (½)	1194		

Projected B.A. courses

Arabic	Social Work
Auditing	Social Development
Education	Export Marketing & Management II
Business Mathematics & Statistics	Urdu Adab

concerned with the life, works and philosophy of Allama Iqbal.
½ = a half course
c = compulsory, by Presidential Decree.
E = elective.

foundation courses in Urdu, English, Basic Sciences, Social Sciences and Mathematics were offered in February 1977 on a pilot scale, with an enrolment of two hundred for each course. The actual enrolments ranged from 51 for Social Science to 173 for English. The drop-out rate was exceedingly high, over 75 percent for all courses, and the pass rate very low. The programme had in fact been put at risk very soon after its start when, in May 1977, all educational establishments were temporarily closed. This prevented the operation of the University's study centres in local schools and colleges, and also created a climate of uncertainty throughout the country. It was felt, however, that apart from deficiencies in the actual courses and poor publicity, students themselves were uncertain about the status of the courses and were reluctant to take them if they would not lead to a publicly-validated qualification. It was decided, therefore, to re-start the General Education programme at the Intermediate level, which was a known and nationally recognised certificate. A list of thirty-two new courses was drawn up - all for presentation six months later. Six Intermediate courses were in fact presented in April, 1979. These attracted over 6,000 enrolments - a quite massive response compared to the Foundation course numbers. However, this achievement, and the later one in October 1979 of producing two B.A. courses, also locked the University into the commitment to produce, as rapidly as possible, enough Intermediate and B.A. degree courses to enable students to actually obtain those qualifications without a break in their studies. This, together with other factors, accounts for the comparative over-development of the General Education area.

Critics of the University have maintained that it should not be offering conventional subjects for a conventional degree qualification, which is likely to be sought by already privileged students who are well catered for by the "private student" system, whereby students with the necessary entry qualifications may register for a degree at their provincial university. Under this scheme attendance at lectures is not required and indeed is not possible: candidates simply register for and take the examinations when they are ready, relying on libraries and "bazaar texts" to prepare themselves. The failure/drop out rate is very high and it has been suggested that the system should be abolished and private students diverted to the AIOU. This would have some important effects: first, it would make the AIOU programme even more viable and cost-effective; secondly, it would probably improve the quality of study of private students and give them greater flexibility of subject choice. However, such an influx may well increase the pressure already felt by the University to offer traditional subjects, and the large numbers would put a considerable strain on the AIOU, both centrally and regionally. The loss of the income derived by provincial universities from these candidates may be a further factor in the delayed implementation of the proposal.

One of the characteristics of the General Education area until recently was in fact its *ad hoc* structure, courses being produced without any logical sequence or pattern. A coherent course structure is now being built up through the introduction of the following optional "majoring areas": (1) Business Studies, (2) Social Sciences, (3) Language and Literature, (4) Islamic Studies, (5) Technical/Vocational Studies, and (6) Home Economics.

4. Research and Development. The R and D programme, which is directed by the University's Institute of Education, has divided itself into two broad areas: Non-formal Education, and Research and Statistics. The non-formal education programme has itself two main strands of development. First, the *Integrated Functional Education Project* (IFE), the first phase of which has consisted of two 18-month village projects with an emphasis on literacy and work skills, together with the development of community consciousness and self-help. A third project has been under way in Sind since 1977. Despite difficulties with this, a further five projects across the country have been financed with assistance from UNICEF. Second, the *Functional Educational Project in Rural Areas* (FEPRA), which is financed jointly by the UK Overseas Development Administration and the Government of Pakistan and which is to be on a larger scale than IFE, involving about 50 villages, and also wider in scope. As well as literacy, vocational and community skills, the project will be attempting to develop group use of existing AIOU Functional courses, as opposed to individual study. It will also foster the close involvement of other agencies and institutions.

Current and Future Programme Development

Overall the number of courses increased dramatically during 1979 and 1980, from four courses to twenty-seven. By April 1981 the number had increased to 37, and by October 1981 to 49. During 1982 the number is expected to reach 60, and by 1983/4 to be over 100. These courses are not perfect and some are lacking in a learner-centred approach, but given the logistical and other problems involved, this is a quite remarkable achievement.

Nevertheless, it is clear that a main thrust of the University's activities was intended to be towards basic literacy, vocational and community programmes, particularly for rural areas. Development on the scale optimistically expected for such programmes has not occurred, although the basis laid down through the projects in Integrated Functional Education is providing a foundation for FEPRA, which will now be part of a wider programme in Social Development. This should open up opportunities at the sub-degree, functional level, particularly for women. The Home Economics Department has been expanded to include Women's Studies and the University's first woman full professor has been appointed with a special responsibility for developing women's education. The establishment of a national research cell for women's education, to be located at the AIOU, has been proposed, together with a programme of multi-level courses in social education. These developments will be complemented by projects to develop local study centres to act as community focal points and as servicing centres for groups in remoter areas.

The second broad strategy proposed for the current period of development is to concentrate course production upon agricultural and commercial areas, and within these to produce clusters of courses on related topics. The basis for this already exists at the Functional, Intermediate and B.A. levels (see Tables 7.2 and 7.3).

Media and Methods

All certificated courses (i.e., in Teacher and General Education), whether half or full, last twenty weeks. Full courses have 18 units and half courses 9, each unit requiring 8-10 hours of work. The last two weeks of each course constitute the examination period. Unassessed courses (e.g., in agriculture) last for nine weeks.

The teaching units or materials consist of printed books, with diagrams and supplementary material where required (e.g., glossaries, handbooks), plus radio and television broadcasts where appropriate. Courses in the General Education programme have 5 or 10 radio programmes, including an introductory one, plus 2-6 television programmes, where appropriate. For certified courses, tutorial support is provided at study centres and through assignments; non-credit courses generally have no tutorial support. General Education courses have 1½ hour evening tutorials provided fortnightly. Courses involving practical skills (e.g. Electrician's) have compulsory tutorials for both the practice and testing of these. Functional Education courses consist of one or two printed and heavily illustrated books, 10 radio programmes, and 2-5 television programmes, but generally have no tutorials.

Course Planning, Approval and Writing

Future course planning and the formulation of departmental course profiles have only recently emerged as activities, principally in the Institute of Education. The University is now trying to follow a general timetable for course approval and production, although the present planned time-scales are in many cases still far too short, and have to be extended by sheer force of circumstances. Responsibility for the co-ordination of production lies with the Course Progress Co-ordinator. His remit is a very broad one and includes not only checking on the progress of current courses, but also responsibility for printing and publicity, and for the Student Enquiry Service.

The usual course production procedure is that once a proposal has been approved, a course writing team is assembled and briefed. Most of the members of the course writing team are likely to be external authors, some living perhaps hundreds of miles away from the University. The content of units is discussed, deadlines are set and the "team" disperses, each with his or her unit-writing task. The deadlines are usually for a whole course or its first and second halves, meaning that 9 or 18 units are handed over at a time. This method has very serious and practical drawbacks: (1) discontinuity, duplication and imbalance can easily occur; (2) the system does not permit adequate review, discussion and editing of drafts, leading to content over-load; (3) illustrating and editing bottlenecks are created; and (4) there is very little time for textual correction and revision. The use of an evolutionary or build-up process, and even a basic course team structure, is still at an elementary stage in most departments. In addition, external authors may have neither the time nor motivation to develop techniques for writing distance learning materials.

Once a set of drafts is received, they are scrutinised by the course co-ordinator, a central and often senior academic who acts as the academic chairman and administrator for the course, and any on-campus course team members. Revisions may be requested of the writer and a fresh deadline given. For some courses the whole team is called together again and all the units are reviewed over a two or three day session. Sometimes, also, there is a course editor, who is one of the course team, and most units also are seen by external reviewers, particularly where very specialist topics are involved. Drafts are next passed to editors and illustrators.

The Design Section of the University's Institute of Educational Technology advises on printed unit layouts and on special illustrative needs. Work at this stage suffers from equipment and scheduling problems, together with staff shortages, although individual standards are high.

The Editing Cell has lacked professional staff for both Urdu and English texts and is consequently under much pressure. A Social Sciences professor is in overall charge, with one full-time staff member, plus an ad hoc team of other faculty members.

Draft units are finally despatched by the Course Progress Co-ordinator to the printers.

Course Production

The lack of a fully effective production system has compounded existing problems caused by over-ambitious course programmes, unrealistic target dates, and late deliveries by the printers. Even where acceptable manuscripts have been handed over to the printers in good time, long delays have occurred, leading to the postponement or interruption of a course. However, it is hoped that the University will have its own press by 1983, and this should solve some of the problems it faces.

There is a further complication: that of language. Virtually all courses are presented in Urdu. However, Urdu printed from type-face is not always readable by some groups who have learned to read from calligraphed texts. All Functional courses must therefore be sent to a calligrapher, who may take up to three months (or more) to produce a hand-written set of units. Virtually all printed units are from drafts in Urdu, handwritten by the author, since Urdu typewriters are not common and are relatively laborious to use. This fact alone discourages the production of successive drafts, inhibits the simultaneous reading of

135

units by course team members, reviewers, editors and others, and therefore prolongs the preparation process. An early decision was to present B.A. texts in English, partly on the grounds that teaching in degree colleges is theoretically all in English and partly because it would assist students' facility in the language, particularly useful if they hoped to proceed further than B.A. level in their studies. This policy has now been abandoned following student complaints about the difficulty of using such texts unassisted. The M.A. in Educational Planning and Management presents all its texts in English, and Intermediate Science is available in both languages.

Radio and television production are the responsibility of the Institute of Educational Technology. Four to five radio programmes are produced each week, from scripts prepared by course team members in collaboration with producers, of whom there are four. Production problems in the past have stemmed from improvised and quite inadequate studio facilities. One or two television programmes are produced each week at Pakistan Television Corporation from AIOU scripts. The Institute's director is the only member of the University's staff experienced in TV production. Overall in broadcasting there have been management and production-scheduling problems, and the quality of both radio and television programmes has not been high. However, the recent completion of the new studio complex, the first buildings in the development plan will, no doubt, bring improvements in both aspects, particularly after the staff training modules have been completed. Installation of radio equipment (UK funded), and TV equipment (UNDP pilot studio), is expected by spring 1982. This will provide studios of a fully professional standard.

Materials Distribution

Mailing is done entirely by hand in one large room by a group of workers in a circle around a large table, who perform a conveyor belt routine of accumulating a set of books, putting them in an envelope, tying with string, sticking on a label with brush and paste, and piling the envelopes ready for the campus post office, which applies postage stamps. Mailing is now fairly continuous and about 1,000 packets of books per day are despatched.

Radio programmes are transmitted by the Pakistan Broadcasting Corporation (PBC). The chief transmitting problem is that the PBC

1000kw transmitter in Islamabad is operating at half-strength, on economy grounds, so that national coverage is not possible. Tapes of programmes are therefore sent by domestic airline to regional PBC stations: local broadcast times cannot be guaranteed.

Television programmes are transmitted by the Pakistan Television Corporation (PTC). Recently PTC has increased its fee for producing and transmitting AIOU TV programmes from 16,000 Rupees (£800) to 26,200 Rupees (£1,310) per half hour programme, an overall increase of nearly 64 percent. As a result, only six courses in the April 1981 semester continued with a TV component, and that was in each case subjected to stringent review. For the October 1981 semester, however, 29 new programmes are scheduled for first presentation courses. Access to television is in fact estimated to be very low: 6 percent nationally and only 1.2 percent in rural areas and small towns (Rafe ul Zaman, 1980).

Student Administration

Because of its wide range of courses, the AIOU has students from very varying backgrounds. Those taking teacher education courses are teachers or educational administrators, who are nominated by their provinces and receive their courses at no cost to themselves or their sponsoring authorities. The same is true of most students taking Functional courses in agriculture. Other students taking these courses pay a fee of 10 Rupees per half course - a deliberately low fee. General Education course students pay 30-35 Rupees per half course and 60-70 Rupees per full course. There is also a special technical course fee of 50 Rupees. Students in literacy and other projects pay no fees at all. The Functional and General Education courses are advertised in national and regional press about 6-8 weeks prior to the start of the courses. Posters and leaflets have also been employed. Application forms must be obtained from a branch of The National Bank of Pakistan. Completed forms and a bank draft for the fee must then be sent to Islamabad or a regional office. Students are registered by hand. Address labels have to date been produced by a hired computer. However, the University is about to set up its own computer based system for admissions, student and tutor records, and fee accounting, using recently purchased equipment.

It is known that, particularly in urban areas, some students are "moonlighting" in that they are already full-time students at other institutions and are using the AIOU courses as reinforcement material. Some, too, are private (i.e., non-attending) students at provincial universities, and the AIOU courses are providing or adding to basic text book study.

The University functions largely on a double semester basis i.e., the shorter Functional courses are presented in January and July, and Teacher Training and General Education courses are presented in April and October. Each of these latter semesters is 20 weeks long (18 study weeks, plus 2 examination weeks), leaving a theoretical six-week "turn-round" period (1) for examination marking, the computation and publication of course results, and (2) for publicity, enrolment and organisation for the next semester. It has been largely the case, in fact, that examination results have not been known to students before they enrolled for, and often not before they have started, their next course. Indeed, notification of some course results is a year behind, which may raise questions about the appropriateness of the semester system.

Student Support Services

AIOU has ten regional offices, as follows: Peshawar, Gilgit, Faisalabad, Quetta, Mirpur, Rawalpindi, Lahore, Multan, Hyderabad, and Karachi.

Nominations for teachers' courses and Functional courses are made through the regional offices and they also receive many of the applications for the General Education courses. Examinations are also arranged by regions. Additionally, the Regional Directors are important channels for student and tutor feedback and for liaison with local authorities and agencies and other institutions. Their task is a very difficult one, however, given the enormous areas of some regions and their geographical nature. They have no supporting full time academic or counselling staff, and tend either to be office bound or to spend many hours driving to distant parts of their regions. Proposals for the appointment of part-time Senior Tutors and for the further development of regional services have yet to be implemented.

The University has 103 study centres which are located in local colleges and schools. For PTOC and PTC some centres change from cycle to cycle, according to the distribution of students. For most General Education courses, the centres are regular ones, at least in towns and cities. Rural areas are generally poorly served, mainly because of scattered student populations and transport difficulties.

In the General Education programme, separate tutorial groups must sometimes be provided for women, partly because of sex-segregation conventions, but partly because some women are not permitted or encouraged to be away from their homes after dark, meaning that mid-afternoon tutorial sessions have to be arranged.

An attempt is being made to solve some of the rural problems by the establishment, through specific projects, of model study centres, each equipped with a range of audio-visual equipment, including a television set. At the same time, such projects, using part-time staff, will try to evolve local student support systems with a particular emphasis on the study needs of women. This aspect of regional development is directly related to the increased emphasis on social need programmes. Both these aspects, study centre equipment and tutorial support, have implications not only for AIOU development programmes, but for those of other local agencies and for community self-help initiatives in education and training.

Tutors are appointed by Regional Directors, who also set up study centres and arrange the tutorials. Tutors are usually college lecturers and graduate secondary school teachers. Their training or guidance consists of briefing sessions at the beginning of each semester and tutor guides to their courses, plus a general booklet on teaching by correspondence. There is a scheme for monitoring tutors' work, although it is only barely implemented, and their marking is not always checked either for grading or teaching comments.

Assessment and Examination

In the Teacher and General Education programmes a half or full credit is awarded to students successfully completing their courses. Six full credits are required for the award of an Intermediate Certificate and eight for a B.A. degree. Students may study up to two full credits in each six-monthly semester. They are not obliged to register every semester and at present may spend as many years as they wish obtaining their qualification. Teachers obtaining a Primary Teacher's Orientation Course Certificate may count it as one credit towards an Intermediate Certificate.

The assessment system for General Education and Teacher Education is as follows:

* 50 percent Continuous Assessment (2-4 assignments)
* 50 percent 3-hour final examination
* A pass level of 40 percent must be obtained in each of these two component areas.

In the Functional Education programme, there are no assignments or examinations. A course completion certificate is issued to those satisfactorily completing a questionnaire about the course. There has been a proposal that Field Assistants and other workers taking a group of, say, five half courses might be awarded a diploma. This would introduce assessment, but it would be limited to those functionaries.

Course Enrolments

Total course enrolments in each of the academic years 1975/6 to 1980/1 are given in Table 7.4. Table 7.5 provides information on course enrolments by academic programme in the academic year 1980/1. Other data on enrolments to date is provided in Tables 7.1 to 7.3 inclusive.

Table 7.4: Course Enrolments, 1975/6 to 1980/1

Academic Year	Course Enrolments	% Difference on previous year
1975-76	976	
1976-77	6,787	+ 595
1977-78	23,611	+ 248
1978-79	32,091	+ 36
1979-80	45,018	+ 40
1980-81	41,013	– 10
	152,496	

Table 7.5 : Course Enrolments, 1980/81

	Number of Course Enrolments	As a percentage of total enrolments
General Education:		%
Intermediate	19,603 a	48.2
B.A.	7,263	17.8
Sub-total	26,956	65.9
Teacher Education:	6,036 b	14.8
Functional Education:	6,414	15.7
Research & Devt.	1,607	3.5
Grand total	41,013	

Notes

(a) Includes 2,472 on shorthand and typing courses. These face-to-face classes at regional centres were taken over by the AIOU from another agency by government order. Some 9,000 students have obtained certificates.

(b) Includes 253 in the post-graduate Diploma in English Language Training.

Educational Effectiveness and Student Progress

Testing the effectiveness of non-assessed courses is very difficult, although useful starts with questionnaires have been made with the agricultural courses. The conventional evaluation of effectiveness for assessed courses comes from the final course results. For the PTOC, the assessment results have varied considerably (Table 7.6). Further figures are not currently available. The overall pass rate is therefore beginning to reach half. Lack of financial or promotional incentive has been suggested for the non-participation rate - most of those who do not come forward for the examination do not do the assignments either - and there is little monitoring of participation or performance by District Education Officers.

The Allama Iqbal Open University, Pakistan

Table 7.6 : PTOC Course Results

	Percentage successful
1st cycle (examination only)	48% of those enrolled: 5426 93% of those sitting: 2593
2nd cycle (assignments and examinations)	17% of those enrolled: 14,501 96% of those sitting: 8,007
3rd cycle (assignments and examinations)	47.6% of those enrolled: 7,559 94% of those sitting: 4370
4th cycle	22.8% of those enrolled
5th cycle	21.6% of those enrolled

In the General Education programme (Table 7.7), some of the results are very poor indeed e.g. English, General Studies, Rural Development and Daftari Urdu. For the last two courses, however, most of the students were compulsorily nominated and may be already qualified at Intermediate level (and beyond), and may simply not trouble to do the assignments or the examination. Some students may also be enrolling simply to assist with their studies as full-time or private students, while others may be interested solely in the subject matter; e.g., English, Arabic or Electrical Wiring. Moreover, if the figures are adjusted by including only those who actually participated in the courses by doing both the assignments and the examinations, the results alter quite dramatically, as Table 7.7 indicates. There is no disguising the fact, however, that there is a serious drop-out problem because some courses are perhaps too difficult or not well-prepared; because some students

142

are perhaps ill-prepared, poorly motivated, or poorly supported; or perhaps because they find it difficult to adapt to a new system of learning that makes heavy demands on their qualities of application and self-discipline. The reasons are likely to be many and varied. The University is giving attention to this very urgent problem, and it is clearly essential for it to seek both for reasons and for remedies where these are possible.

Table 7.7: General Education Programme Course Results 1979

	APRIL		OCTOBER	
	"real pass"	Adjusted	"real pass"	adjusted
Elementary Arabic	34.3	100.0	24.8	93.7
Urdu	35.0	95.9	35.0	84.1
Daftari Urdu	12.0	77.1	16.6	75.0
Iqbaliat	31.0	92.2	37.9	83.4
English	0.5	46.6	6.2	37.4
Rural Development	9.0	100.0	19.0	94.3
Food & Nutrition	24.0	74.5	25.2	50.1
Electrical Wiring	--	–	37.7	85.2
General Science	--	–	3.9	37.5

Organisational structure and staffing

The organisational structure of the University is based on the three areas of academic, service and operational, and administrative departments. There are ten academic departments (Agricultural Sciences, Basic Sciences, Social Sciences, Home Economics and Women's Studies, Industrial Education, the Institute of Education, the Institute of Arabic and Islamic Studies, English, Urdu and Oriental Languages, and Iqbaliat). The service and operational area encompasses the Library, the Institute of Educational Technology, the Course Progress Office, Regional Services, the Editing and Translation Unit, Mailing Services and the Research and Statistics Unit. The Administration combines the Registrar's Department, Admissions, Examinations, Accounts and Project Development (buildings and equipment). Including the Vice-Chancellor there are about twenty senior administrative staff, some thirty senior operational and servicing staff (including Regional Directors), and nearly fifty academic staff. There are two staffing difficulties. First is understaffing, to which is linked the protracted process of actually selecting and appointing staff. This has been very serious for some departments (e.g., Industrial Education, in which the head of department was for three years the only person responsible for technical courses and who also constituted the Home Economics Department). The second problem is directly related to the first. To obtain staff, several departments have resorted to deputation, a fairly common procedure whereby individuals are seconded from their permanent institutions to serve at the AIOU for, usually, two or three years. In some instances these periods have been extended to four or five years; in others, individuals have returned to their parent institutions very abruptly, leaving a vacancy which may be unfilled for some months.

All the service departments and the administration, whose work is essential to the functioning of the University, have difficulties too. These are largely centred round problems of planning and manpower allocation; procedures and organisation, and the control and supervision of work tasks. These problems frequently have crucial consequences for the making and presentation of courses; for the organisation of tutorial and other services, and for relationships with students.

Saudi Arabian consultants have made a major contribution to the teaching of Arabic, while the UK has funded, since 1976, an advisory team whose successive members have come mainly from the UKOU.

Finance and economic effectiveness

There have been three financial development plans. The final one, providing for the comprehensive development of the University, was initiated in 1976 and finally approved in November, 1978. The total development cost was set at R153.9 millions (approximately £7.5 millions at 1978 prices). This sum included a foreign aid component of R48.2 millions (£2.5 millions approximately) and provided for land acquisition and buildings. It also covered the production and distribution of study materials, including broadcasts, and the purchase of printing, audio-visual and scientific equipment, as well as books, office equipment, furniture and vehicles.

In January/February 1979, an Evaluation Mission from the UK Overseas Development Administration visited the AIOU in connection with the phasing of further aid support. In its section on economic effectiveness, the Mission's report (Collister, 1980) discussed first the potential effect of the AIOU in helping to solve some of Pakistan's problems of skilled manpower. It pointed to the major contribution the University could make to the national economy by training technicians and discussed specific courses (e.g., Electrical Wiring and the Electrician's course). It also pointed out that several courses in the General Education Programme have a strong in-service or employment-related bias, citing the B.A. Business English, B.A. Accountancy, Intermediate Book-Keeping and Accountancy, and the Arabic, Urdu and English courses.

A full comparison of the cost effectiveness of the AIOU Intermediate and BA courses, with corresponding costs in the country's conventional system, was not possible at that time, nor was it feasible to carry out a cost-benefit analysis, e.g., by forecasting graduates' potential earnings. From its enquiry, however, the Mission was of the view that, taking into account amortization of capital costs, salaries and other recurrent expenditure, together with student numbers, the AIOU would progressively show considerable cost advantages over other conventional institutions. The report stresses that, in conventional education, costs (e.g., classrooms, teachers) increase pro-rata to increases in student numbers. By contrast, AIOU per capita costs *decrease* as student numbers grow, in that capital and recurrent costs (e.g., salaries, broadcasts) remain virtually the same irrespective of student numbers.

Two important additional points were made:

1. AIOU courses can result in a more efficient and more intensive use of existing educational buildings and facilities in the country

2. *Foregone earnings*, if possible to calculate, would be an important factor in any comparison. It was certainly the case that, in the Functional, Teacher Education and General Education programmes, students were able to take courses directly relevant to their work performance and personal prospects while still continuing with their jobs, without loss of earnings, and without their employers losing their services (especially in teaching).

Conclusions

The AIOU has already demonstrated that it can attract enrolments of very considerable size: e.g., the Primary Teachers' Orientation Course (with a five-year total of 59,304 students) and the General Education programme (with over 26,000 course enrolments in 1980-81 alone). It has also shown that it can provide programmes of a very wide range, from basic literacy projects through to post-graduate work. The basis of an effective course-production system has been laid and the framework for a regional support service exists. It is slowly establishing itself not only as an institution which is innovative in both its areas of concern and in its methods, but also as a wide national resource and co-ordinating focus in the field of adult and community education.

It would be surprising, however, if it were without problems as an institution. Some of these are obviously external and derive from the very reasons for the University's existence: the enormous variety and degree of needs, themselves related to the economic, geographical and social characteristics of Pakistan itself. Others are external in another sense; e.g., problems of communications, and printing. Many of the problems are internal and are capable of solution. A sizeable array of courses is now available, and more deliberately structured programmes are emerging. Emphasis is being particularly directed towards the need for functional and social education and towards women's courses. A second and essential need is for the enhancement of the educational quality of the course materials and improvement of the actual course production process. A third priority is the development of a more effective local study-centre network, especially in the context of social and women's education. This in turn could lead to more collaborative work with voluntary and government agencies, at national and local level, extending and mutually reinforcing the skills and resources that each has to offer.

If there can be improvement and development of this kind, achievement by the AIOU of the objectives set for it in 1974 may be brought immeasurably closer. It is already an institution of much educational and social significance, both within and beyond Pakistan; its potential significance is even greater.

References
1. Allama Iqbal Open University (1979) 'Five Year Report'. Islamabad: AIOU
2. Allama Iqbal Open University (1981) 'Summary of Enrolment Statistics 1975-80'. Islamabad: Research and Statistics Unit, AIOU Institute of Education.
3. Collister, P. et al. (1980) 'Mid-term Review of ODA's aid to Allama Iqbal Open University, Pakistan'. London: Overseas Development Administration.
4. ul Zaman, Rafe (1980). Paper by the Director of Educational Television, PTC.
5. Zaki, W.M. (1975) 'Education of the People'. Islamabad: The People's Open University.

Chapter 8

THE UNIVERSIDAD NACIONAL
DE EDUCACION A DISTANCIA, SPAIN

Arthur James

COUNTRY PROFILE

Geography

504,792 square kilometres, including the Canary and Balearic Islands. Three quarters of Spain is high plateau and mountainous, with two-thirds of the population living in the coastal plains of the north-west from Galicia to the Basque Provinces, and in the east from Barcelona to Valencia and Almería. One third of the population of the central area (3.2 millions) live in the capital, Madrid. Barcelona is the largest city with 3.5 million people, and there are 36 cities with over 100,000 people.

Population

37.4 millions (mid-1979 estimate), of which 13.2 millions (35.2 percent) are actively employed, and 1.6 millions (12 percent) unemployed. Castilian is spoken by three quarters of the population. Basque is spoken in the rural districts of Vizcaya, Guipúzcoa, and Alava; Catalan in Provence; and Galician (akin to Portuguese) in the north-west of the Peninsula. Shortages of various skilled craftsmen and technicians have a greater effect on the economy than any shortage of high level manpower. In the long term the education system must not only expand its output, but also reorientate priorities to meet the planned or expected demands of growing sectors of the economy. More emphasis should be given to modern professions that have been evolving in recent times such as electronics, engineering, marketing, business administration, systems analysis, and urban planning (Horowitz, 1974: 85).

Economy

Spain has one of the fastest growing economies in Europe and in the early 1970s was in the process of transformation from an underdeveloped to a developed country with strong industrial growth. However, agriculture is still an important sector with 7.9 percent of the Gross Domestic Product and 18 percent of the labour force. Except for hydroelectricity, Spain is poorly endowed for power resources, and is dependent upon crude oil imports for 66 percent of its total energy requirements. There is significant foreign investment in a number of sectors of the economy.

Politics

With its shifting political, economic and social patterns, Spain presently is highly volatile. Forty years of dictatorship under Francisco Franco (died 1975) have given way to a democratic monarchy under King Juan Carlos (November 22, 1975), with subsequent changes in the Constitution, free general and municipal elections, and a shift from centralism to greater regional autonomy.

Communications

Rail:	13,351 kilometres (1977)
Roads:	145,997 kilometres (1977) of which 56,106 kilometres are macadamised. The mountainous nature of the country has been an obstacle to the creation of good road and railway communications
Cars:	8,952,628 (1978)
Air:	Mostly state controlled (Iberia)
Telephone:	11.1 millions (1979)
Television:	9.6 millions (1978) TV Española: 2 programmes.
Radio:	Radio Nacional de España: 4 programmes on medium and FM; 4 regional programmes
Newspapers:	167 dailies with a total circulation of around 5.7 million copies (1977)

EDUCATIONAL PROFILE

Structure

Preschool education, which is voluntary, exists for children aged 2 to 6. This is followed by compulsory primary education for children aged

6 to 14. Secondary education from age 14 to 17 is non-compulsory and divided between a three year *academic* programme, leading to the *Bachillerato* certificate, and a two or three year *technical* course. Students aged 17 to 18 intending to go on to university must take a pre-university orientation course (*Curso de Orientación Universitaria* COU), although mature students (aged over 25) are excused this requirement.

Statistics (1977/8) (INE, 1980: 15-19)

Enrolments *	Preschool	1,008,796
	Primary	5,579,662
	Secondary	1,385, 300
	Tertiary	649,525
		8,623,283

*Excludes 299,600 who do not fit into the pattern, such as special education, art, nursing, and commercial studies.

One third of primary school and two thirds of secondary schools are still private.

The school year runs from September to June; the university year runs from October to June.

Higher Education

Development since the 1950s has been marked by a rapid expansion of the system from 54,000 students in 1949/50. Six new universities have been founded since 1970 to meet the increasing demand that has itself been generated in part by a population increase, in part by rising educational standards, and in part by the new attitude of regarding higher education as a basic right rather than a privilege. The number of universities is now 33, including 4 private ones. As a part of this changing climate, Spanish universities have since 1970 been required to admit persons over 25 who have not obtained the normal entry requirements (*Bachillerato* plus a pass in the COU). Mature students are now admitted provided they pass an examination of aptitude, capability, and character.

Spain's universities have since 1845 been subject to centralised government control. Legally, the governance of universities is centralised. Curriculum and practice are imposed on the universities and it is the State itself which confers degrees. For historic reasons university level education tends to be geared to professional training, which the name for degree courses, *carreras*, suggests. A government bureau supervises, directs, inspects and co-ordinates activities. However, increased autonomy is expected to be given to the universities in the near future under a proposed Law of University Autonomy now before Parliament (the *Cortes*), and likely to be passed in 1982.

The 1970 General Law of Education aimed at far-reaching reforms in all areas of education (Moncada, 1972; MEC, 1973) to meet the demands engendered by the rapid economic, technological, social and intellectual changes which Spain is now experiencing. Distance (off-campus) education was specifically mentioned as one way in which people could acquire qualifications at any level, irrespective of age and status. These political aims have now found concrete expression in (1) the Centro Nacional de Educación Básica a Distancia (CENEBAD) founded in 1979, which grants the Certificate of Elementary Education; (2) the Instituto Nacional de Bachillerato a Distancia (INBAD), founded in 1975, which also provides the Curso de Orientación Universitaria; and (3) the Universidad Nacional de Educación a Distancia (UNED) which offers opportunities at the tertiary level.

Spain's higher education is not without its problems. Sharp increases in student numbers have not been matched by increases in physical plant, the number of trained university teachers and provision of teaching and research facilities (Villanueva, 1980:53). Villanueva, while noting the increased input of students, notes the low level of output: ". . . the university 'boom' of recent years in Spain was produced by the numbers of students, not by the numbers of graduates" (Villanueva, 1980: 56). Fifty to seventy percent of registered students drop out, especially in the first and second years, with perhaps only 15 percent successfully completing their studies and obtaining the title of *Licenciado* (INE, 1980: 30-31).

UNIVERSIDAD NACIONAL DE EDUCACION A DISTANCIA (UNED)

Origins

UNED's origins lie in the far-reaching reforms incorporated in the 1970 General Law of Education, approved by the *Cortes* on 4 August

1970. Like distance teaching universities in other countries, it aims to give a second chance of higher education to those who, for various reasons, had lost the first.

UNED developed very rapidly. Initial planning began in 1968. A formal planning committee was established on 6 May 1971; the University's charter was granted on 18 August 1972; a Rector (Manuel Jesús García Garrido) was appointed on 15 September 1972 with a brief to have UNED functioning by 1 February 1973; initial courses were approved by the Ministry of Education and Science on 14 December 1972, and the first group of 11,400 students on Admissions, Law and Letters courses were enrolled on 6 February 1973.

Apart from its method, UNED is equivalent in every way to conventional universities in Spain. Its degrees are of equal status; like the conventional universities, it offers discipline-based *carreras* with fixed programmes of courses, without electives; and students are able to transfer credit between UNED and other universities.

UNED was established with three groups of students in mind: those unable to begin or to complete higher education; those living in remote areas; and those ambitious for more qualifications. This includes the so-called "free students" who matriculate in a traditional university but who, for some reason or another, cannot attend class and hence must study independently as best they can. The failure rate of these external students is understandably high, and, until the coming of UNED, little was done to help them.

The Students

UNED's students tend to be older than those in traditional Spanish universities; nearly all work full time; most are married; and they come mainly from the professional and mid-executive ranks, with the majority having some form of academic qualification (UNED, 1981a: 38-66).

Around 63 percent are between 26 and 40 years of age. This proportion has varied only a point or two over the years and is constant across all faculties except Law. Here 18 percent are over 40 compared with 11 percent in the other faculties. Women tend to be younger than men students. However, only 30 percent of students are female compared with 40 percent in traditional universities (INE, 1980: 39). Two thirds of the men are married, but less than half (46 percent) of the women are.

Sixty five percent of the students are public servants (teachers or administrators), middle management, or workshop managers; 13 percent come from the professions. Hardly any are drawn from the "working class", which is to be expected because of the bar imposed by entrance qualifications. Seven in ten work in enterprises that employ more than 100 workers, and this confirms the view that UNED's students come largely from the urban and industrial sector of Spain's society.

If one takes 'equivalent' professional and technical qualifications into account, about 47 percent of UNED's students can be assumed to be studying for a second *carrera*. Of the remainder, about a half satisfy university matriculation requirements, with the balance (27 percent of all students) being unqualified and taking the University's Admissions course.

In a survey, the three most common reasons given by students as a reason for studying were to improve professional knowledge, improve job prospects, and broaden cultural knowledge. Thirteen percent were studying purely as a hobby and 24 percent to obtain a university degree (UNED, 1977a). About 30 percent expected to be promoted as a result of their studies.

The majority (99 percent) of students live in Spain. About one percent are resident in other countries, mostly in Western Europe. Within Spain, the relative distribution of students appears to be affected by the degree of industrialisation and urbanisation, the location of good regional study centres and the existence of a local conventional university.

Academic Programmes

UNED offers three academic programmes: (1) an admissions course; (2) a number of degree courses (*carreras*); and (3) in-service training courses. Table 8.1 lists these programmes of study and indicates the proportion of the 1979/80 student population in each of them.

There are six faculties. One of these administers the Admissions Course. The other five administer, through their departments, a total of eleven *carreras*. To obtain the degree of *Licenciado* the student must follow two cycles of five *cursos*, each *curso* consisting of five or six subjects called *asignaturas*. The first cycle of three *cursos* is of a general nature, the second cycle of two *cursos* is more specialised. A student will need to take 25-30 *asignaturas* for a degree.

Table 8.1:   UNED's Academic Programmes

Programme of Study (and faculty/carrera)	Number of asignaturas	Number of Students as a percentage of the total (1979/80)	
		by Faculty	by Department
Total number of students in 1979/80 = 100% =		51,146 %	51,146 %
1. Admissions Course	7	22.8	22.8
2. Degree Courses (Carreras)			
Law	25	19.5	19.5
Philosophy and Letters		23.9	
Geography and History	26		7.3
Philology	29		3.4
Philosophy & Educational Science	31		7.8
Psychology	5		5.4
Economics and Business Administration		10.4	
Economics	30		5.7
Business Administration	31		4.7
Science		5.6	
Physics	21		1.9
Mathematics	23		2.3
Chemistry	23		1.5
Industrial Engineering	29	2.4	2.4
3. Inservice Training		15.4	
Teachers of Business Studies	8		3.7
Elementary School Teachers			11.7
		100.0	100.0

In the traditional university, which follows the same plan, a *curso* equates with a year's study. UNED is different in that students complete a *curso* when they can. In fact the average student takes about 3-4 *asignaturas* a year.

There is a third cycle for doctorate studies. UNED has so far awarded seven or eight doctorates. These consist of four or five *asignaturas* and a thesis.

UNED has no age bar, but harmonises with traditional universities in its matriculation requirement of *Bachillerato* plus the COU for people under 25, or, for those over 25, a special admissions examination. However, while conventional universities set their own tests, UNED has from the start recognised that a mature student will need to recover the rhythm and habits of study of his secondary school days, will need to fill in gaps in his knowledge and will need to become tuned to the different ways of learning at a distance. Accordingly UNED developed its own Admissions Course to help these mature students pass the admissions examination. Modelled on the academic regime of the undergraduate degree programme, the Admissions Course lasts eight months and covers four *asignaturas*. All students follow a common core of subjects in Spanish language and Geography and History, and, according to their choice of *carrera*, two specialised *asignaturas*. Someone interested in Industrial Engineering, for instance, would study, in addition to the two core subjects, Special Maths and Physics. The whole course costs 10-12,000 pesetas (£56-£67) plus textbooks, and most students manage it in a year, mainly because for them the ground is familiar.

None of the conventional universities had an admissions course, and in the mid-1970s UNED's results seemed to more than justify the innovative step it had taken in providing such a course. Half the students who presented themselves for examination were successful compared with only 10-25 percent elsewhere. But today the numbers have dropped to 39 percent; figures for other universities are not known. About one in seven of the present undergraduates were formerly Admissions students, but students in the Armed Forces are known to use the qualification for promotion only, and do not proceed to a degree.

UNED now offers (1981) three programmes for in-service training. One is for teachers of Business Administration, qualified already by a Diploma gained after the first cycle, who enter the second cycle of studies and who complete eight *asignaturas* for a *Licenciado*. The second is for teachers of Elementary Education, to bring them up to a new standard of training. However, because of its duration it does not count towards the award of a *Licenciado*. In 1980/81 the University introduced the third - an eight month training programme, consisting of four *asignaturas*, for nurses who qualified under an old scheme, to bring them to the level of a new scheme which confers on them a Diploma of *Asistente Técnico Sanitario* (ATS). UNED is thought by the Government to be particularly suited to this sort of work since nurses are scattered nationwide, and the course has enrolled about 8,000 students.

The increase in UNED's undergraduate student population (from

11,400 in 1973 to 45,146 in 1979/80) has been in part due to the University's expanding programme of *cursos* and *asignaturas*, which, with the exception of Psychology (which only began in 1979/80), is now complete. However, if UNED is to keep its initiative, it will need to broaden the spectrum of its studies. It seems likely that a Faculty of Politics and Sociology will be added next, as this is an area which, with the exception of the University of Madrid, is not covered by Spanish universities. A proposal to introduce practically orientated diploma level courses in Telecommunications, Agricultural Engineering and Agricultural Business Administration is also being discussed. Such courses would be less theoretical than the degree courses, and would correspond to the first cycle of university-level education.

Media and Instructional Methods

Four main components are used in the teaching system: (1) printed materials, (2) audio-visual materials (radio, cassettes, transparencies); (3) tutor-marked assignments, self-tests, and twice-yearly formal exams for the assessment of student study difficulties, progress, and status; and (4) opportunities for individual and group tuition, counselling, and enrichment activities (seminars, lectures, etcetera) at provincial centres.

The aims are to try to break with the usual textbook/narrative presentation form; to make learning experiences auto-didactic; to vary the media so as to try to sustain motivation; and to avoid the isolation of home-based study by offering opportunities for students and tutors to meet regularly.

The study materials consist of printed course texts (*unidades didacticas*), radiophonic guides, and audio-cassettes. Each *asignatura* consists of six printed (A4) units, usually bound separately. Each contains six sections with a key theme, idea, or concept around which the subject matter is orchestrated, so that each *asignatura* has about 36 organising themes. The first of the six units always contains the scheme or synoptic view of the *asignatura*. Material is keyed to published text books, of which there are usually one or two per *asignatura*.

Students are recommended to gain a general grasp of the theme, to study carefully the writer's instructions about key ideas, to consult and study the various questions posed, to supplement and consolidate his or her understanding using the materials and explanations which

155

the writer feels necessary to fill in gaps, and, finally, to work through the self-correction exercises at the end of each theme, for which answers are provided. Exercises can also be construed as diagnostic, since students are urged to refer back to material they have not understood.

With some exceptions, the majority of units are considered acceptable by some 77 percent of the students; only nine percent think they are poor (UNED, 1981a: 82). This is an improvement since the last questionnaire three years earlier (UNED, 1977a) when only 50 percent thought them satisfactory.

In the early days of planning the intention was to have a fully multimedia distance teaching system using both radio and television as well as print and tuition. However, by the time UNED came into being in 1973 it was clear that, within the context of the overall expansion of the education system arising from the implementation of the 1970 Law, this would be prohibitively expensive and so television is not used, although some 30 video cassettes have been produced.

There is limited radio transmission (15 hours a week) on Radio 3, from 8 to 10.30 each evening except Saturdays. Three hours is given over to the Admissions Course, with the rest being divided amongst the faculties in relation to the number of students on a particular *carrera*. The problems that stem from the rigidity and frugality of open air transmission on radio are leading UNED to make greater use of audio cassettes, with their advantages of flexibility. Some 3,000 audio cassettes are now available - an average of about ten per *asignatura*.

More students now are listening to broadcasts than before: figures show an increase from 28 percent in 1976 to 51 percent (UNED, 1981a: 87). Nevertheless a large proportion of students (41 percent) never listen, although this is a dramatic improvement over the previous figure of 71 percent (UNED, 1977: 239). Of those who listen, almost all (91 percent) thought the broadcasts were both good and interesting (UNED, 1981a:90).

Course Design

A proposal for part or all of a *carrera* is prepared by members of a Department for scrutiny by the Faculty Dean. If approved it is sent to members of the Junta de Gobierno (UNED's governing body), then forwarded by the Rector to the Minister for Universities and Research (a Bureau of the Ministry of Education and Science), and finally, assuming approval, to the Consejo de Ministro (advisory body). A citation is then printed in the State Bulletin and funds are released for UNED staff to expedite the plan. This procedure usually takes just over a year and once approval is granted the plan cannot be changed in any way without repeating it.

Members of the department then apportion responsibilities for developing the various *asignaturas* or the *cursos*. A budget of 240,000 pesetas (£1,350) per *asignatura* is set aside for its writing. The person directing the writing can delegate the whole or part of the task to an outside consultant, or he can do it himself, claiming the fee or a proportion of it as extra pay. Sales outside of the university are high and there have been problems over copyright. There is a proposal to pay a fee of 400,000 pesetas (£2,250) per *asignatura* with UNED holding the copyright.

To start with the *asignaturas* were normally written by members of UNED's central staff but now most of them are written by professors from other universities, working under the supervision of faculty staff. The change stems from the need to increase the number of *asignaturas* rapidly without unduly increasing the numbers of tenured staff.

It has been alleged that this trend has generated problems for UNED staff, who must administer the teaching of others' materials, in that professors from traditional universities tend to write in text-book rather than in self-instructional form so that the didactic unit is just a study guide. This occurs in spite of the fact that unit writers are given a detailed guide of instructions and principles for writing material, compiling tests, and preparing audio-cassettes which has been prepared by the University's Institute of Educational Science (UNED, 1976b).

Course Production and Distribution

Printed materials are produced by commercial printers, assembled and stored in the large central warehouse and delivered to the 52 provincial centres prior to the start of the academic year. Information on numbers required is obtained from returns of student enrolments. Students collect the whole of their year's work from either provincial centres or selected book shops. At some centres with large numbers of students this can result in long queues forming. However, this is preferable to the system used before 1979 when units were posted to students at intervals and UNED's image suffered because only a third were delivered on

157

time. Now 80 percent of the students receive them in time (UNED, 1981a: 85).

UNED produces in its own studios 15 minute length radio programmes for broadcasting through Radio Nacional de España and cassettes for use by students in their own home.

Student Support Services

Since 1976 UNED's central headquarters has provided a limited telephone tutorial service (code named CONSULTEL) which began as a pilot experiment (Roldán Ruiz, 1977). It is available to students taking the Admissions Course and the second cycle of courses in the *carrera* in Business Administration, and is later to be extended to students on high population courses. Students with a learning problem can call a Madrid number from anywhere in Spain between seven and nine o'clock in the evening (live operator) or at any other time (automatic answering machine). Students are instructed to provide the following information in serial order: name, *asignatura*, town, personal telephone number, and a brief statement of the problem. This business-like procedure minimises the length of the call to 30 to 60 seconds per student. To conserve resources, replies, made between 7 and 9 o'clock, must necessarily be brief. In fact they last on average ten minutes depending on the problem. Apart from the initiating call there is no cost to the student.

Most of the student support services are provided by centres (*Centros Asociados*) (UNED, 1976c) which have increased in number from 11 in 1974 to 52 in 1980/81. The centres have a median enrolment of 650 students within a range from 7,000 in Madrid province to only 60 in Almadén (Ciudad Real). The number of teacher-tutors in the centres range from 166 to 3, with a median of 30, and student-tutor ratios range from 138 to 4 with a median of 24. There were 1,696 teacher-tutors in 1980.

Students attend the centres for tutoring and advice from their teacher-tutors and to sit course examinations. The centres have libraries, study rooms, laboratories, lecture theatres and offices. They are seen as cultural as well as teaching centres.

Centres near conventional universities can draw on their staff for tutors who also have the time to attend briefing and training courses. However, centres which are far away from conventional universities may have to make do with tutors working in non-academic jobs and who cannot attend training sessions lasting for more than a couple of days.

UNED was envisaged from the start as a decentralised university in which centres would be autonomous in their funding and policies. Such autonomy, it was hoped, would foster the support of local groups and ensure their acceptance of responsibility for the centre, as well as the greater efficiency of the teaching system. Thus centres could be established through the initiative of corporations or public and private agencies where there were sufficient students. Agencies which wished to promote and sponsor a centre made a formal request to the Council of UNED with the offer to underwrite all expenses (including buildings, heating and lighting, equipment, materials and the salaries of all personnel, including the teacher-tutors). In 1979/80 nearly half the cost of running UNED (46 percent) was born by sponsors.

Principal sponsors to date have been local governments and town halls, savings banks (which are also charitable organisations), the armed forces, *universidades laborales* (technical colleges) and commercial and industrial enterprises. Centres in organisations such as the Chrysler car company, Radiotelevisión de España and the Ministry of Finance are for their own staffs only. Other centres are open to anyone.

To start with there was a tendency to accept centres which were not prepared to offer the full range of facilities. Today higher standards are imposed and UNED has also set aside 30.5 million pesetas (£170,000) to support the weaker centres. However, there are still a number of centres which do not provide a service for all *carreras*. Students of Physics, Chemistry, Industrial Engineering and Mathematics are catered for in only 26 to 30 of the centres. This lack of support, allied to the intrinsic difficulties of scientific subjects, explains why numbers in these subjects have scarcely increased over the years. Of 45,146 admissions and undergraduate students who enrolled in 1979/80, only 7 percent lacked the effective support of a centre.

Regular attendance has doubled in percentage terms since 1976, and while this is mainly for examinations and enrolment, attendance at classes, meetings and consultations has increased so that centres are playing a greater part in the development of students. The presence of a centre, the image it creates, and the facilities it has influence the number of student applications. Ironically this creates imbalances in the geographical distribution of applicants so that only 30 percent of them

159

now live more than 50 kilometres from a centre. There is still scope for centres in rural and semi-rural areas and at present 14 provinces out of the 50 have no centres at all.

Physical distance from an UNED centre undoubtedly influences attendance, but the phenomenon of "mental distancing" is also apparent from the attendance figures. Regular attendance is greater among women with 37 percent than among men, with 28 percent. This relatively low attendance is surprising, since in the eyes of students the greatest problems with learning at a distance are the lack of communication between themselves and other students and tutors, the lack of a university ambience and a general loneliness. The fact that the majority of students have positive attitudes about the general aims of centres and their functioning, and that they believe that centres are working efficaciously towards benefitting their cultural development, suggests that a key factor in the poor level of attendance is lack of time.

UNED's teacher-tutors work part-time in the centres. They arrange appointments with students, answer queries by letter, telephone, or face-to-face, mark the assignments and send monthly reports on the progress of students to the various faculties. They also arrange lectures, seminars, and other activities which can make their centre a "mini-university". According to a 1976 survey of tutors (UNED, 1977b), the majority of tutors are men (84 percent), nearly half are under 40 (42 percent), and almost all (92 percent) have another job. The number of tutors has doubled since this survey, however, and so the proportions may have changed.

While most of their time is spent on correcting assignments and completing the teaching of subject matter, about two thirds of the tutors see their major function as guiding, counselling, and giving students psychological support in their studies. There is therefore a gap between what they are doing and what they feel they should be doing. In spite of this 71 percent of the tutors were optimistic about UNED's future, while only 20 percent were pessimistic (UNED, 1977b: 17).

Marking the assignments is particularly important. As well as giving a grade, the tutor adds comments, fills in gaps with further explanations and makes suggestions. Such "instructional dialogues" are of summary importance, not only because they are at the base of the tutorial function, but also because for most students it is the only point of contact they have with their tutors. It is therefore surprising to learn that on average 38 percent of students still receive back assignments without comment (UNED, 1981a: 78). Overall, this suggests that the tutor's work load is too heavy, or that briefing from central head-quarters is either inadequate or ignored. Nevertheless, 78 percent of the students think their teacher-tutor is doing a good job, and 50 percent of those who receive comments on their assignments think they are helpful.

Assessment and Evaluation

Assessment and evaluation is of four kinds: course work, examinations, recommended activities, and overall evaluation.

UNED's students write their assignments in specially-produced booklets of which there are four keyed to units 1,2,4, and 5 of their *asignaturas*. These contain a number of objective-type tests (say 10), 4 or 5 questions requiring short written answers and key terms to be defined. The back page is left for students to ask questions about any problem associated with content or method. Students send these assignment booklets by registered post, in specially-coded envelopes, to their teacher-tutor who is required to correct, comment and return them within a given period of time.

There are no assignment booklets for units 3 and 6. After these units students must attend a *Centro Asociado* for a formal test on the first or second half of the course work, as appropriate. These exams take place in February and June, although students who fail have a further opportunity to sit the examination in September. Marks are averaged over the two exams. The first exam is partly diagnostic: staff are able to tell students where they went wrong and what to do about it. Results for the four course-work assignments are entered on a student's personal record card using the five-point numerical scale common to all Spanish universities. Students must complete the four assignments before sitting the formal examinations although this condition may be waived where there is good reason.

Supplementary to the assignments and the examinations are non-obligatory "recommended activities". These give students a chance to expand their personal interests in, and preferences for, a particular subject area.

The final event is the assessment of the student's whole performance in course work, examinations and supplementary activities. Course examiners have some degree of discretion in giving weight to continuous assessment and supplementary activities but at least 80 percent of the overall grade must relate to the student's performance in examinations. This is because, outside the examination room, students have opportunities to submit work that is not entirely their own.

Both the assignments and the self-tests are viewed by the majority of students as a necessary and useful part of the learning process. Assignments are thought to be useful by 64 percent of students and self-tests by 82 percent. Only 12 percent and 3 percent respectively think they are a waste of time (UNED, 1981a: 80-1). The fact that a third of the students think that assignments are of little or no use, however, raises the question of what the response would be were course work to be given more weight in the overall assessment.

Student Administration

UNED does not specifically advertise for students. Instead it relies on increasing public awareness of the University and its activities to attract applicants.

Would-be students can obtain an envelope of registration forms and cards from a *Centro Asociado* or certain other offices. Applicants must register at their local provincial centre. For undergraduate courses, the charge is about 3,000 pesetas (£17) for each *asignatura* and its associated assignment booklets; text-books are of course extra. Students can take up to 10 *asignaturas* a year.

On admission a student opts for a particular *carrera* (or for the Admissions Course). Once he has chosen his programme he must follow the prescribed *cursos* and *asignaturas*; there are no electives. Generally, formal curricula are standard across the universities, although the greater autonomy envisaged for the universities will no doubt stimulate change. At present, however, a student in, say, Law in UNED would tend to study the same subject matter as campus students in the universities of Madrid, Salamanca, or Barcelona.

Until 1976 UNED's academic calendar differed from the traditional universities in running from 1 February to 30 September of the same year, a pattern directly modelled on that of the United Kingdom Open University (García Garrido, 1976:84). This did not work well, and so today a student has a similar calendar to one in the traditional university. This makes student transfer in and out of UNED easier.

Student Progress

The results given below are drawn from an analysis of student success rates on 268 *asignaturas* presented in 10 *carreras* during the four academic years 1977-1980. The total number of *asignaturas* presented was 1014, with 453,540 student registrations on them. Data for the Admissions Course are presented separately. A detailed analysis of results which includes comparisons with the United Kingdom Open University is given by James (1982).

Averaged over years and *carreras*, 44.3 percent of the students presented themselves for their *asignatura* examinations, and of these 63.1 percent were successful, giving a final pass rate of 28.0 percent per *asignatura*. It can be seen that giving up the study of a particular *asignatura* (not synonymous with dropout from the system) had more weight than examination failure in determining this pass rate. However, these figures hide wide variations in each of the *carreras*, with Science based students having an overall pass rate of 22.5 percent compared with 30.8 percent in non-science based *carreras*. These pass rates were much the same for each of the four years.

More serious, perhaps, for UNED's future is the reduction in the proportion of Admissions Course students who pass. In 1973, 39 percent of enrolled students passed, but the proportion has declined to only 13-14 percent in the three years up to and including the 1979-80 session. This result is difficult to explain but it may be that the quality of applicants has declined.

By the end of 1979, 982 people had applied for their degree of *Licenciado* (UNED, 1981b: 10). It is likely that there are some who are eligible to apply who have not yet done so. This figure may not appear large, but it should be taken in context: only about 15 percent of conventional university students succeed, and they can take up to eight years to do so.

It is difficult to estimate the numbers of students who drop out. McIntosh and Morrison (1974) of the British Open University point to the problem of knowing who has abandoned study and who has merely dropped out temporarily. At UNED the average appears to be about 48 percent a year (UNED, 1981a: 98), and this includes Admissions and the in-service course for teachers of Business Administration; excluding these the rate drops down to 37 percent. The fact that 50-70 percent of students in conventional universities drop out within one or two years (Villanueva, 1980: 56) means that UNED compares very favourably.

UNED staff point out that the University is giving people a chance to take subjects at a tertiary level and is helping to raise the general cultural life of their country. They also point to the number of UNED dropouts who intend taking up studies at traditional universities and who transfer their UNED credits. This suggests that UNED is opening up opportunities to people who might otherwise have had no chance of higher education. Two surveys, one in 1976, the other in 1979, confirm these views. More than two thirds of students (69 percent) now think that UNED facilitates access to a university education as compared with only 45 percent in 1976; and 66 percent as against 57 percent in 1976 believe that UNED is playing a very good part in the university life of Spain (1981a: 67-71).

Organisation and Administration

The Spanish Ministry of Education, through its Secretary of State for Universities and Research, still has legal authority over the university system. It is assisted by the National Board of the Universities (Junta Nacional de Universidades) whose membership consists of the chief executives of the universities (Rectors) and the presidents of the Boards of Trustees (Patronatos). The Minister presides at meetings. The National Board must be consulted on all matters affecting the universities, particularly on expansion and planning. Its permanent council is called the Board of Rectors (Consejo de Rectores). UNED is part of this system.

UNED's organisation is detailed in "Organización de la UNED" (UNED, 1976a) There are nine divisions: (1) the Board of Trustees (Patronato), (2) the Governing Board (Junta de Gobierno); (3) the Faculties (of which there are six, counting Admissions); (4) the faculty departments, of which there are 12; (5) the Permanent Education Division, connected with in-service courses; (6) the Provincial Centres (*Centros Asociados*); (7) the Institute of Educational Science; (8) the Management of economic and administrative affairs; and (9) the Secretary General, who, with the Management, supports and co-ordinates all the activities of UNED.

Apart from some details due to its special nature, UNED's organisation is very similar to that of the traditional universities in Spain.

164

The *Junta de Gobierno* is a small governing body or cabinet which consists of department heads who convene as a whole or in committees to discuss academic matters. It generally meets once a month. Faculties themselves also have juntas.

The faculty departments, each under the control of a full professor (*Catedrático*), are assigned a variety of functions: (1) to decide contractual arrangements for teaching staff; (2) to prepare and revise course materials; (3) to produce assessment tests; (4) to correct examination scripts; (5) to make contact with tutors in the *Centros Asociados*, with the aim of co-ordinating effort; and (6) to answer students' queries by means of letters, telephone and face-to-face contact.

All universities have a department called the Instituto de Ciencias de la Educación, whose function is to improve teaching and carry out operational research (MEC, 1974). UNED's Institute has responsibility for briefing and training the staff in the *Centros Asociados*; improving teaching methods through the compilations of manuals on the preparation of course materials, counselling, and study methods; and for an integrated programme of research projects aimed as seeing whether the University is fulfilling its social purpose.

Resources

UNED's budget for 1980 was 1,089 million pesetas. Direct government funding contributed 42 percent, the remainder coming from student fees (25.3 percent), sales of books and materials (12.7 percent), a supplement for in-service training of teachers (12 percent), and a balance brought forward from 1979 (8 percent). In addition the government paid the salaries of tenured staff direct (100 million pesetas) and other agencies met the costs of the Centros Asociados (772 million pesetas). The total 'system' cost in 1980 was therefore 1,961 million pesetas (£4.29 millions). The average cost per student was about £240.

Conclusion

It can be said, with a certain degree of confidence, that UNED is fulfilling the social purpose which was assigned to it. A typical student is an adult who has been employed for several years, having left the family and social background of his birth and attained a higher social and occupational status than that reached by his parents.

There are still problems. There is a lack of centres in some areas while not all of them are able to provide for the full range of subjects. The autonomy of the centres, valuable in some respects, has resulted in variable standards.

However, there is an increasing belief that UNED is playing a valuable role in university education and reaching a different audience from that attending the conventional universities. There has been an increase in the numbers of *Centros Asociados* and a doubling of their attendance, a vast improvement in the distribution of teaching materials and an increased use of audio-cassettes. Above all, both staff and students believe in UNED's future.

References

1. García Garrido, M.J. (1976) 'La Universidad Nacional de Educación a Distancia' Barcelona: Ediciones CEAC.
2. Horowitz, M.A. (1974) 'Manpower and Education in Franco Spain'. Hamden, Connecticut: Archon Books.
3. INE (1980) 'Estadísticas de la Enseñanza en España'. Madrid: Ministerio de Económicas, Instituto Nacional de Estadísticas.
4. James, A. (1982) 'Una comparación de las estratégicas de evaluación y de los resultados de la Uned de España y la Open de Inglaterra'. Universidad y Sociedad. In press. (Also available in English in mimeograph.)
5. McIntosh, N. and Morrison, V. (1974). 'Student demand, progress, and withdrawal: the Open University's first four years'. Higher Education Review, 7, 37-60.
6. MEC (1973) 'Ley General de Educación y Disposiciones Complementarias'. Madrid: MEC.
7. MEC (1974) 'Instituto Nacional de Ciencias de la Educación'. Madrid: Ministerio de Educación y Ciencia.
8. Moncada, A. (1972) 'Directions of development in higher education in Spain'. In 'Worldbook of Education', 297-309. London: Kogan Page.
9. Roldán Ruiz, J.A. (1977) 'La Consulta Telefónica y la Enseñanza a Distancia'. Proyecto CONSULTEL, Teleenseñanza Números 21/26. Madrid: FUNDESCO.
10. UNED (1976a) 'Organización de la UNED'. Madrid : Ministerio de Educación y Ciencias (MEC).
11. UNED (1976b) 'Criterios Metodológicos de la UNED'. Madrid: MEC
12. UNED (1976c) 'Centros Asociados de la UNED'. Madrid: MEC.
13. UNED (1977a) '76/77 Encuesta Profesores-Tutores'. Madrid: MEC.
14. UNED (1977b) 'La UNED Vista por sus Alumnos'. Madrid: MEC.
15. UNED (1979) 'Guía del Curso, 1980/81'. Madrid: MEC.
16. UNED (1981a) 'La UNED y sus Alumnos: Curso 1979/80'. Madrid: MEC.
17. UNED (1981b) 'Los Primeros Licenciados de la UNED'. Madrid: MEC.
18. Villanueva, J.R. (1980) 'Present and future in higher education in Spain'. Higher Education in Europe, 2, 5, 51-57.

Chapter 9

THE OPEN UNIVERSITY, UNITED KINGDOM

Keith Harry

COUNTRY PROFILE

Geography

244,108 square kilometres.

There is considerable variation in terrain and the climate is generally mild and temperate.

Population

55.9 millions (1980 estimate), of whom 91 percent live in urban areas. London, the capital, has 20 percent of the urban population and there are 17 other cities with a population of more than half a million.

In mid-1979, 21 percent of the population was under 15, 64 percent between 15 and 64, and 15 percent 65 or over. The birthrate declined during the 1970s (17.8 per 1000 in 1966 to 11.6 in 1977), but there was an increase to 13 per 1000 in 1979.

The working population numbers nearly 50 percent of the total population. Currently unemployment stands at close to 3 millions. There are distinct regional cultural differences. English is the dominant language, but the Welsh language was spoken by 21 percent of the population of Wales in 1971, and Gaelic is spoken widely in north Scotland and the Hebrides. Immigrant population languages include Punjabi, Gujarati, Bengali, Urdu. Commonwealth immigrants are only the latest in a succession of small-scale immigrations.

Economy

Manufacturing industry accounts for 28 percent of total domestic output, and services for 62 percent. The nation is one of the largest importers of agricultural products, raw materials and semi-manufactures, and is amongst the largest exporters of aerospace products, electrical equipment, finished textiles and many types of machinery. Another growing export is oil. Production industries (quarrying, mining, construction, manufacturing, electricity, gas and water) account for 54 percent of total employment, and agriculture for only 2.5 percent, although more than half the country's food is home-produced.

Communications

Total road mileage in the United Kingdom in 1979 was 224,568. Licensed vehicles at the end of 1980 numbered 19,210,000.
British Rail has 27,592 miles of track (1979).
There are extensive internal air services with 171 airports.
In 1980 there were 18.3 million combined radio and television licenses. Approximately two-thirds of television sets receive colour transmission. In 1981 the British Broadcasting Corporation (BBC) operated two television channels, while a third was operated by the Independent Broadcasting Authority (IBA). A fourth channel, which will begin transmission in 1982, has been allocated to the IBA. The BBC has four radio channels, provides national radio services for Northern Ireland, Scotland and Wales, and operates 22 local radio stations. 33 independent local radio companies operated in 1981 and 11 more are planned for 1982-83.
26.7 million telephones, 17.6 million exchange connections, 86,000 telex connections and 67,000 data transmission modems had been installed by 1981.
The Post Office delivers to 22 million addresses every working day. Its sorting operations are in process of being mechanised.
Ten morning national daily papers and seven national Sunday newspapers are currently published. A great number of morning, evening, Sunday and other weekly newspapers are also published through the country. Newspaper circulation totalled 33.5 million in 1980.

EDUCATIONAL PROFILE

Structure of Pre-school, Primary and Secondary Education

Pre-school education is optional.

Primary schooling is compulsory from the age of 5. Different systems operate in different areas. At 7 children may progress to a junior school then to secondary school at 11. A more recent development has been the establishment of first schools for pupils of age 5 to 8 or 10 and middle schools covering various age ranges between 9 and 14. In Scotland, primary schools take children from 5 to 12, normally having infant classes for children under 7.

Secondary schooling is compulsory to age 16. Over 80 percent of the secondary school population attend comprehensive schools which take pupils from the local district without reference to ability or aptitude. Various systems are in operation, including the provision of sixth-form colleges in some areas for 16-18 year olds. Some selective grammar schools and secondary modern schools still remain. Secondary education in Scotland is almost completely organised according to the comprehensive principle, but is largely selective in Northern Ireland. Fee-paying pupils are admitted to independent schools.

Higher Education

The post-war expansion of higher education saw the number of universities increased from 17 in 1945 to 45. Expansion has now ceased and in 1981 the Universities' funding body, the University Grants Committee, has recommended extensive cuts in provision in many institutions. Steep increases in tuition fees for overseas students have reduced the number of such students. In 1980-81 there were 258,175 full-time university students in Britain, including 48,439 postgraduates. The universities are funded by the Government and through income from student fees, the actual distribution of funds being undertaken by the autonomous University Grants Committee. However, certain institutions, including the Open University, are funded directly from the Department of Education and Science (DES).

Higher education is also provided on advanced courses at polytechnics and other establishments of higher and further education. There are 30 polytechnics in England and Wales, one in Northern Ireland and 14 equivalent Scottish institutions. Over 600 other colleges maintained or assisted from public funds, offer courses leading to recognised qualifications; they include Institutions of Higher Education in England and Wales, into which former Colleges of Education (for teacher training) have been assimilated. In 1978/9 approximately 852,000 full-time and sandwich course students (including 296,000 at universities) followed advanced courses, and a further 332,000 took non-advanced courses, many of them studying for recognised vocational and educational qualifications. In addition, some 3.6 million adults study part-time, including 640,000 released by their employers for further study during working hours.

Adult education in the UK is generally taken to mean courses of post-school education outside the main areas of higher, professional and technical education. Courses are provided by Local Education Authorities, certain residential colleges, extra-mural departments of universities, and various voluntary and statutory bodies.

THE OPEN UNIVERSITY (OU)

Origins

The Robbins report on Higher Education (1963) stated that there was an untapped pool of adults in the United Kingdom who could benefit from a university education but had 'missed out' earlier in their lives. In the same year, Harold Wilson, then Leader of the Opposition, in a speech delivered in Glasgow, described his idea of a 'University of the Air', a home study university which could employ radio and television as an integral part of its teaching system, and whose principal purpose would be to increase the numbers of graduate teachers and qualified scientists and technologists. In the early 1960s only 6-7 percent of school leavers each year progressed to any form of higher education (including teacher training and technical education), a proportion which compared unfavourably with other developed countries. The need for more higher education was amply illustrated by the enrolment figures in the University of London External Degree programme, which had 20,000 United Kingdom students, of whom 7,000 studied by correspondence. A further half a million people were also studying correspondence courses provided by a variety of other institutions.

In 1964, Harold Wilson, the new Prime Minister, asked Jennie Lee, a junior minister in the Department of Education and Science, to take special responsibility for the University of the Air project. Committed to the establishment of a University with high academic standards, she gained Government commitment to the project. In 1967 the Government established a Planning Committee. Its terms of reference were

"To work at a comprehensive plan for an Open University, as outlined in the White Paper . . . , and to prepare a draft Charter and Statutes". The Planning Committee Report was published in 1969, providing a blue-print for the University. A Royal Charter was granted in June 1969, establishing the Open University as an independent and autonomous institution authorised to confer its own degrees.

The idea of the Open University was initially greeted with considerable scepticism and even hostility, but the developing institution has achieved credibility in the academic world, and has survived a decade of political change and national economic crisis.

Programmes of Activity

The OU's activities can best be considered in terms of a number of *programmes*. The three teaching programmes, for undergraduates, postgraduates, and associate students, are described more fully below. In addition to these, the University has a research programme; an institutional research and development programme; a small programme of international activities; and, through a subsidiary company (Open University Educational Enterprises Ltd.) a marketing progamme (related to the marketing of the University's teaching materials).

The Undergraduate Programme:
student characteristics, course profile and student progress

The OU's undergraduate programme leads to a general degree recognised as equivalent to a degree from any other British university and designated a Bachelor of Arts (B.A.) degree.

No formal educational qualifications are required for admission to the undergraduate programme; the only requirements are that applicants must be at least 21 years of age and resident in the United Kingdom. Exceptions are made in the case of British service personnel stationed overseas, and special arrangements are made for handicapped people and for residents in institutions. The Open University is therefore not in direct competition with conventional universities for students; a pilot project was undertaken at the request of the DES for 18-21 year olds, but the relatively small number of applicants and their relatively poor results indicated that this is not a priority area for university level education at a distance (Woodley and McIntosh 1980).

In the first years of the University, teachers represented the largest occupation group amongst applicants, but their numbers have declined (from 30.2 percent of applicants for 1972 courses to 13.8 percent for 1982) as teaching has become increasingly a graduate profession. Housewives now form the largest group (17.8 percent for 1982), and 45 percent of applicants for 1982 courses were from women, a higher proportion than are enrolled in conventional universities. A continuing trend is the increasing proportion of applicants in the 31-40 age group (35.3 percent for 1982).

Although the Planning Committee Report did not specify that 'working class' applicants (i.e. workers in manual and routine non-manual occupations) should be regarded as a specific target group, the Open University has been commonly regarded as having a special responsibility in this area. The first Vice-Chancellor stated his view that it was inevitable and in the long term beneficial for the University that its early students should in the main be highly motivated and already relatively well-educated members of the middle classes. The survival of the University and the attainment of credibility was dependent on low drop-out rates (Perry, 1976: 143-144).

The numbers of applicants from manual and routine non-manual occupations have increased (from 22.2 percent in 1972 to 30.5 percent for 1982 courses), as have those from adults with no formal educational qualifications (9.3 percent in 1974 to 11.1 percent for 1982 courses). The proportionate increases in applications from manual and routine non-manual workers and from adults without formal educational qualifications, groups which together represent the educationally relatively disadvantaged sector of society, have been very gradual. Woodley (1979:10) demonstrates that, given adequate support, students from educationally disadvantaged groups can successfully complete degree level studies and need not swell the drop-out figures. Unfortunately, students from this area may well be affected by steep fee increases which have been imposed on the University.

Unlike most degrees in other English universities, the OU degree is obtained through gaining credits, six for a B.A. degree and 8 for a B.A. Honours degree. A credit is awarded on completion of a one-year course (the 34 week academic year runs from February to November) on the basis of continuous assessment, a 3-hour final examination, and the fulfilment of certain summer school and fee requirements. Not all courses are full-credit courses; some are offered as half-credit courses, theoretically requiring half the amount of work over the same period of time.

A full-credit course is based on 32 weekly units of work, each of which will require between 12 and 15 hours of study. A student may obtain a maximum of two credits per year. The minimum period of study for a B.A. is 3 years and for a B.A. (Hons.) 4 years; in practice most students take at least 6 years and 8 years respectively, unless they are able to claim credit exemptions.

The four levels of OU courses are foundation, second, third and fourth. All students must complete a foundation course, a broadly-based introductory course which assumes no prior knowledge of the subject. Foundation courses are offered by the Faculties of Arts, Social Sciences, Mathematics, Science and Technology, but not by Educational Studies, whose courses begin at second level. After foundation level, students can make up their own programme of study. Second level courses generally present a wide choice of subject matter, whereas third and fourth level courses, of honours standard, are more specialized. A student seeking to obtain a B.A. (Honours) degree must include at least two credits at third or fourth level amongst his eight credits.

The 134 courses available in the 1982 undergraduate programme are produced by the faculties, either individually or by two or more in co-operation. Many lower level courses are multi-disciplinary. All students receive a booklet entitled *Undergraduate Courses* which examines the various considerations involved in choosing courses and describes in detail the individual courses available. Leaflets are also available which give information about vocational and professional areas where OU degrees and course credits are recognised as qualifications comparable to those offered by other United Kingdom educational institutions.

It is the University's policy to offer a broad range of academic subjects in its undergraduate programme, while recognising the constraints of its policies of open entry and home-based study. There are some subjects which can not be taught (e.g. Medicine and Veterinary Science) while others (such as Law) are excluded because there is already adequate provision for their study on a part-time basis. The University does not teach Modern Languages at present but is considering this possibility. Despite constraints, it has succeeded in offering courses drawn from approximately thirty disciplines ranging from literature, history and music to biology, chemistry and electronics.

A total of 45,882 applications were received for 24,600 places on 1982 undergraduate courses, but only 6,000 of the original applicants were left without a place due to many offers being declined. This is almost certainly the result of the recent fee increases. Since the University opened, over half a million applications have been received, and 160,428 students have finally registered. The total number of students enrolled on undergraduate courses in 1981 was 59,968.

Some 5,750 students graduated from the Open University in 1981 and, in addition, 2,000 people who gained the B.A. degree in previous years qualified for the B.A. Honours degrees. The total number of graduates from the University is now 45,000. Of those students who enrolled for 1971 courses, 56 percent have obtained B.A. Ordinary degrees, and 12 percent have become Honours graduates. In comparison with many distance teaching ventures, the OU has been very successful in preventing excessive drop-out. 'Unqualified' students, that is, those not possessing the normal minimum qualifications for entry to a British university, do less well than qualified students - but nevertheless by 1978 four out of ten of the unqualified students who entered in 1971 had graduated (McIntosh *et al.,* 1980:55). The OU's success has demonstrated that large numbers of people can successfully study at a distance. Keegan (1980:52) and Sewart (1981:12) both suggest that this success stems from the fact that the OU has balanced the development of high quality learning materials with the provision of comprehensive student support services.

The Postgraduate Programme:
student characteristics, programme characteristics, and student progress

The first taught OU postgraduate course is the BPhil in advanced educational and social research methods, to be piloted in 1982. With this exception, the degrees of BPhil, MPhil and PhD are awarded on completion of a programme of research or advanced study and submission of a dissertation or thesis.

In 1981 the University had a total of 694 registered postgraduate students, of whom 127 were full-time students supported by grant-awarding bodies and based on the Milton Keynes campus and at the Oxford Research Unit. 95 were part-time internal students employed by the OU. The remainder were part-time external students working independently in their own time and at their own expense, and are supervised jointly by Open University academics and by external supervisors appointed by the University. At present it is possible to admit only about 15 students per faculty per year to the part-time external higher degree programme.

The vast majority of external postgraduate students registered on 1 October 1980 were male (75.5 percent). 32.8 percent were aged 26 to 35, and 33.2 percent were aged 36 to 45. Half of them (50.9 percent) were lecturers or teachers, 12.6 percent were qualified scientists and engineers, and 13 percent were administrators and managers. Two out of three of them (66 percent) had a university first degree, and 19.6 percent had a higher degree. By the end of 1981, 24 part-time external students had been awarded a BPhil degree, 25 had been awarded an MPhil, and 32 a PhD.

The Associate Student Programme: student characteristics, course profile, and student progress

The associate student programme is designed for adults who wish to extend their knowledge of their own career or to acquire knowledge of a new field without embarking on a full degree programme. Courses specially created by the Centre for Continuing Education are available together with individual courses drawn from the undergraduate programme and packs devised from parts of existing OU course materials.

The associate student programme is likely to be an area of considerable expansion during the 1980s. Proposals being considered in 1981 include the production of updating materials for scientists and technologists, doctors, veterinary surgeons, dairy farmers, and members of a number of paramedical professions. The programme provides courses in the following areas:

1. Community education courses. These are short courses (8-14 weeks) not designed to be at degree level and not involving the full range of support services offered to other students. Seven courses are available in 1982 in the areas of parent, health, employment and consumer education.

2. In-service teacher training courses. The University's first diploma course, for the Diploma in Reading Development, has been produced in this area, together with school-focused courses and self-study packs for teachers.

175

3. Health and social welfare courses. Three courses have so far been produced, parts of which are also available as self-study packs.
4. Technological updating materials. Two self-study packs on microprocessors are available.
5. Management education. The first materials from this area should be available in 1983.
6. Courses drawn from the undergraduate programme.
7. Courses in historical, cultural and political subjects created from existing OU course materials.

In 1981 around 20,000 students enrolled in the associate student programme. The characteristics of the associate student population vary from course to course, and differ significantly from the undergraduate population. In 1980, 49.5 percent of the students on full-length courses in the programme were male; 38.7 percent were lecturers and teachers, 16.9 percent were in the professions and arts, 10.1 percent were housewives, 7.4 percent were technical personnel, 5.1 percent were qualified scientists and engineers, and 5.1 percent were clerical and office staff. 23.4 percent did not have the qualifications normally required for entry to a university, 20.6 percent had a Teachers Certificate or its equivalent, and 35.8 percent had a University degree or postgraduate diploma.

Many associate student courses carry credit which may count towards a B.A. degree if the student later registers in the undergraduate programme. Students who complete the course work and pass a final examination receive a Course Certificate, and a Letter of Course Completion is sent to students who completed the course satisfactorily but did not sit (or failed) the examination.

Media and Methods

The *printed main text* is the principal teaching medium in most OU undergraduate and associate courses. A number of fourth level courses require students to undertake a project or are based principally on set books supported by direct contact with academic staff. The student also receives printed supplementary materials which may consist of broadcast notes to accompany radio and television programmes, offprints, computer-marked and tutor-marked assignments and other information which needs to be revised regularly and is therefore not suitable for inclusion in the main texts, which are normally produced for use over a period of at least four years. The students are required to buy certain specified *set books*, which may be 'readers' compiled specially for the course, and receive a list of recommended reading which may be borrowed from public libraries.

OU main texts are large-format (297x210 mm) paperback books usually of around 100 pages, printed to a high standard and illustrated with photographs and diagrams. They are closely integrated with additional reading materials, with assignments, and with radio and television programmes to form *units of work*, each requiring one week of study. The main texts contain self-assessment questions to help the student determine his progress.

Printed materials created by the Centre for Continuing Education frequently differ from those produced for undergraduate courses. For example, the parent education courses in the community education area are based on a series of booklets, colourfully and imaginatively designed, and produced to resemble popular magazines.

Most OU courses have a *radio* and a *television* component. Foundation courses and associate student programme short courses have a weekly radio and television programme. Second, third and fourth level undergraduate courses generally have fewer broadcasts; the University's Broadcast Sub-Committee discriminates between different courses' needs.

The progressive reduction in the amount of available transmission time (pro-rata to the number of courses presented) and the results of evaluation of students' use of broadcasting, together with the development of new technology since the establishment of the OU, have necessitated continuous monitoring of broadcasting and of other media.

Kits are supplied to students to enable them to undertake scientific experiments at home, to carry out field work and to understand the practical application of theoretical principles. In 1981 a total 31,500 kits of 43 different types were despatched. The majority of kits are employed for home experimental work by science and technology students.

Attendance at *residential school* is compulsory for OU students on foundation courses and some higher-level courses. The schools are held mainly on conventional university campuses during the summer vacation. They provide opportunities for learning such as lectures, seminars, field work, laboratory work and informal discussions.

The Open University, United Kingdom

Course Design

Following approval by the appropriate Faculty Board, an undergraduate programme course proposal must receive academic approval from the Courses Committee 24-36 months before the year of presentation of the course.

Courses are written by *course teams* which, regardless of scale of membership and methods of working, have certain roles in common. The chairman, an experienced OU academic, is reponsible for the academic and educational quality of the course. He is assisted in the routine administration and co-ordination of the work of the team by a course co-ordinator or course manager. Course unit authors are OU academics or outside consultants and have various responsibilities to the course team: (1) writing particular sections of the course; (2) planning and presenting broadcasts in conjunction with BBC Open University Productions producers; (3) deciding on set books and recommended readings; (4) designing tests and exercises; (5) developing home experiments; (6) writing supplementary materials including notes for tutors, and (7) reading and commenting on drafts written by other course team members. Authors may well also be part of 'maintenance' course teams, whose task is to ensure the smooth running of the course when the production process is completed and to produce supplementary materials wherever necessary. A staff tutor represents the interests of the student and may also write part of the course. A member of the University's Institute of Educational Technology Course Development Division may have a particular concern with teaching methods and may make arrangements for any developmental testing which is required. It is of vital importance that all of the team's task should be completed on schedule: a special office, Project Control, ensures that the most efficient and effective use is made of the University's production facilities, a complex task in view of the large number of course teams which may be creating courses at any one time.

Following early discussions on course content, responsiblity for particular sections of the course is allocated to course authors. Several drafts of each text are usually written, the later ones incorporating suggestions and criticisms made at course team meetings.

Perry (1976:92) has stated his belief that 'the validity of the course team approach has been proven by the quality of the materials' produced by the OU and that 'a course produced by this method will

178

inevitably tend to be superior in quality to any course produced by an individual' (*ibid*.:91). However, he accepts that 'it is a very expensive way of writing courses, that can be justified only if the course materials are used for a very large number of students' (*ibid*.: 91).

The design and production of courses prepared by the Centre for Continuing Education are frequently undertaken in collaboration with another organisation. Course materials may be written by Centre staff, by staff on secondment from one of the OU faculties or by a consultant or an employee of the collaborating or co-operating organisation. The editing and design functions have also been performed outside the University. The Centre also has the services of a senior BBC producer.

Course Production and Distribution

The finally approved draft is passed to the faculty editor, whose role may be much more creative than that of an editor in a conventional publishing house. The editing and subsequent design processes are both carried out in the University by staff with a specific Faculty responsibility. Printing is undertaken by external commercial printers, with the exception of supplementary materials, which are printed in the University's own print workshop.

The printed course materials are stored in the OU Warehouse at Wellingborough and are despatched to students in regular mailings from the Correspondence Services Division in Bletchley. Kits are distributed to students in the same way.

The BBC produces about 250 25-minute television and 300 20-minute sound programmes (some for radio, some as audio-cassettes) per year in partnership with the University. These programmes are transmitted nationally on BBC1, BBC2, and VHF Radio 3 and 4, mostly at weekends. During the 1981 teaching period the BBC transmitted 35 hours and 25 minutes weekly on television and 19 hours 40 minutes on radio. The amount of radio transmission has recently decreased (from 25 hours and 10 minutes in 1980) as a result of the increased use of audio-cassettes.

In 1982, 36 courses will have only one transmission of television programmes; more than half of these courses will, however, be included in an experimental scheme involving provision of a videocassette borrowing service from Walton Hall and the supply of video playback equipment in students' homes or in study centres. A borrowing service for audio cassettes of radio programmes also operates. Only one third of new courses have radio programmes; many have adopted audio-cassettes, which are popular with both students and producers, instead of radio.

Student Support Services

The OU has divided the United Kingdom into thirteen regions to provide a tutorial and counselling service to its students.

Personal contact with students is maintained by more than 5,000 part-time tutor-counsellors, course tutors and associate student counsellors. Over 260 study centres have been established to provide meeting places and facilities of various kinds, including rooms for watching television programmes and listening to radio programmes, computer terminals and access to libraries.

Co-ordination and supervision of tuition is the responsibility of full-time staff tutors, who are members of faculties but also responsible to Regional Directors. Full-time Senior Counsellors supervise counselling. The work of the regions is in turn co-ordinated by the Director of Studies, Regional Tutorial Services, at the OU's headquarters.

In his first year of study with the OU the undergraduate student is allocated a tutor-counsellor who will tutor one foundation course and will act as counsellor not only in the first year but through the student's University career. The student will have a different course tutor for each subsequent course. Tutorials are intended to be remedial and are not compulsory. Fewer tutorials are held on higher level courses and there may be none at all on low population courses or in study centres with low student numbers. Telephone tutorials or audio cassettes may be employed to link a tutor with a scattered group of students. Correspondence tutoring becomes all the more important where there is no face-to-face tutoring. Guidance on tutoring and on marking assignments is issued to part-time staff by course teams. Post-foundation counselling is maintained through individual interviews at the study centre, by post and telephone, and on occasion by home visits. Associate students are allocated to a course tutor for each course taken, and have access to a counsellor.

Regional offices are located in major cities in each of the 13 regions; some of the larger regions also have sub-offices. Regional staff appoint and supervise part-time tutor-counsellors and course tutors, organise the use of study centres, and allocate students to centres and to tutorial and counselling staff.

Each region operates an advisory service to help interested persons decide whether or not they can benefit from enrolling on a University course, to inform them of the implications of embarking on part-time study, and to give further information on local and national alternatives. Applicants can also be provided with advice on preparing for study, although the University does not offer any preparatory courses.

Assessment and Examination

Most courses taken by undergraduate students, and many taken by associate students, have continuous assessment based on written work submitted during the academic year and a final end of course examination. Certain undergraduate courses require students to undertake project work. The weighting given to continuous assessment and examination grades is determined by the Examination and Assessment Board for each course. Two types of assignments are used for continuous assessment: tutor-marked (TMAs) and computer-marked (CMAs).

TMAs may take one of many forms, from a series of questions requiring short answers to a standard essay. A number of higher level courses employ project assignments which require an extended piece of written work. The assignments are marked and commented upon by course tutors, guided by Tutor Notes prepared by the course team. The course team specifies the relative weighting given to different questions in multiple-question TMAs and indicates marking schemes for each assignment.

The number of TMAs required varies from course to course. In 96 of the undergraduate courses offered in 1981, 75 percent of assignments (those in which the highest grades have been awarded) are used for assessment purposes. In the remaining 36 courses in which TMAs are employed, all the assignments in the continuous assessment components (excluding formative assignments) are used for assessment. Formative assignments are employed in some courses; these are included for teaching purposes only, and grades awarded are not included in the calculation of the overall continuous assessment grade. Completed TMAs are posted to course tutors, who mark them and forward them to the Assignments Handling Office, from where they are returned to the student. The process takes about three weeks.

CMAs do not simply test recall of facts but involve analysis, evaluation and comprehension, and can be time-consuming and difficult to prepare. They are employed most frequently in science and mathematics courses. They are posted by students direct to Walton Hall, processed by computer, and within a week of their receipt the student is notified of his grade.

The three-hour final examinations are held in examination centres throughout the country in October and November. Script markers, drawn from course tutors and course teams, are appointed by individual course Examination and Assessment Boards. Between 15 and 20 percent of all scripts are checked (usually by staff tutors and course team members).

The process of combining examination grades with continuous assessment grades in the OU is known as conflation. The student's position on a computer-produced matrix determines the award of a certificate of credit or a certificate of credit with distinction.

Student Administration: Undergraduate programme

The application period for admission as an undergraduate is from January to mid-June during the year preceding the first course. Applicants are offered places between March and September. Places are in general offered on a first-come, first-served basis so that early applicants stand the best chance of acceptance.

The DES states how many new students may be admitted each year. Quotas are set for each foundation course and to maintain a reasonable balance between applications received and places offered for each region and each sex. Precedence is given to those who applied in previous years.

Advanced standing may be awarded, in the form of credit exemptions or of directly transferred credits, towards part of the credit requirements of the degree on the basis of courses of study successfully undertaken with other institutions.

Students complete Initial Registration within two to three weeks of being offered a place. The initial fee payable in 1981 by students in their first year was £32 per foundation course. Final Registration takes place in March/April when students have already spent 2 to 3 months studying with the OU. The final tuition fee in 1981 was £66 per full credit course. Facilities exist to enable students to pay their fees by instalments, and the University is able to assist a few students who are suffering financial hardship. By returning a completed Conditional Registration form by the end of September the student can guarantee an offer of registration on his chosen courses for the following year, conditional upon results obtained in the current year, and subject to any course quotas which may be applied.

Student Administration: Postgraduate programme

Applicants for part-time external postgraduate study must normally have an upper second class honours degree, although in exceptional cases alternative qualifications may be considered. They are asked to submit an outline of their intended research for assessment by members of academic staff.

If the applicant is accepted, internal and external supervisors are appointed, who meet the student as required and report annually on his work. To be eligible to submit a thesis, students must have completed satisfactorily a required minimum period of study, (normally 18 months for a BPhil., 3 years for an MPhil., and 5 years for a PhD.), and satisfy their supervisors that the thesis is of an adequate standard for submission to the examiners. In 1981, part-time external students were required to pay an initial registration fee of £45 followed by a similar payment at six-monthly intervals, and an examination fee at the end of their studies.

Student Administration: Associate students

Applicants for degree level courses in the associate student programme must be aged 21 or over. They apply between May and October of the year preceding their year of study (which runs from February to October). They are offered a place on a 'first-come, first-served' basis, subject to any quotas which may be in operation. At this stage they are required to confirm their initial registration by paying a £20 fee. Registration is course-based rather than programme-based, in the sense that the students are not (with the exception of the Diploma in Reading Development) expected to study more than the course(s) for which they have registered. Students are required to pay the balance of their fees on demand, although facilities for payment by instalments exist.

Students taking short community courses must be aged 16 or over.

They submit an application form together with their course fee (£16 in 1981) and, subject to any quotas, are offered a place. The courses, which last from 8 to 10 weeks, are usually offered twice in each year (in January and October). The materials are sent to the student about two weeks before the course is due to begin. Students who decide that the course does not meet their needs are able to return the materials in good condition within 14 days, and their fee is then refunded. No tutorial arrangements are made for community education courses, but students may do the optional computer-marked assignments, and if successful in these obtain a Letter of Course Completion.

Organisational Structure and Decision-making

The executive head of the University is the Vice-Chancellor, who is assisted by the four Pro-Vice-Chancellors each with responsibility for a specific policy area,

Organisationally the University is divided into five major areas:

1. The six faculties, responsible for the design of undergraduate and postgraduate courses, research and the teaching of postgraduate students.

2. The Centre for Continuing Education, responsible for the design of courses and teaching packages in the continuing education programme.

3. The Institute of Educational Technology, responsible for educational technology in support of course development and for much of the professionally organised institutional research undertaken within the University.

4. Regional Tutorial Services, responsible for co-ordinating and developing regional activities within the 13 regions.

5. Operations, responsible for course production and distribution (except in so far as this is done by the BBC on behalf of the University in respect of broadcasts).

6. The Administration.

The OU's government structure resembles the bi-cameral model of the conventional British university. Power is shared between two bodies,

Council and Senate. Council, whose members are drawn principally from outside the University, is the executive governing body and is chaired by the Pro-Chancellor. Senate, which determines academic policy, comprises all members of academic staff together with elected representatives of various categories of non-academic staff and of part-time tutorial staff and students and is chaired by the Vice-Chancellor. Senate membership is currently around 800; several reviews recommending restricting the size of this body have been resisted.

Two major boards formulate academic policy: these are the Academic Board and the Student Affairs and Awards Board, which report to Senate. Their areas of responsibility are degree structures and the academic and tutorial aspects of courses, and issues relating to student registration respectively. Planning Board, whose planning activities are undertaken at strategic and at resource allocation level, reports both to Senate and to Council.

Costs

In common with other universities in the United Kingdom, the OU is financed principally from public funds. The University receives approximately 82 percent of its funding from the Department of Education and Science, 16 percent from student fees, and 2 percent from sales of course materials and other sources. The current Government has adopted a policy of increasing the proportion to be contributed by student fees. The Centre for Continuing Education occupies a unique position within the University in that its programme is required to be self financing. 60 to 70 percent of its costs are covered by income from student fees, and the balance by special grants from various agencies. The OU's operating budget in 1981 was £60 millions. The capital cost of the OU to the end of 1981 was of the order of £26 millions.

The economics of the OU have been extensively studied, the literature being reviewed by Rumble (1981: 228-32). A study undertaken by Wagner in 1976 showed that the average cost per student per year was about one third that of the cost in conventional British universities, while the cost per graduate was about one half that of the conventional universities (Wagner, 1977: 374, 377-8).

Conclusion

The University has established itself as a major provider of higher and continuing education during the last ten years. Demand for its undergraduate courses remains high, although there is concern that the increased fee levels which the Government is requiring the University to impose on its students (involving a 22 percent increase in 1982 over 1981 levels) is having an effect on demand, on drop-out, on the rate of throughput of students, and on the ability of certain sectors of society (particularly the lower paid, the unemployed, and women) to enrol. It is now the case that an Open University degree costs considerably more to the student than a part-time degree at a conventional university or polytechnic.

The University has always closely monitored the effectiveness of its production and delivery systems and has introduced many improvements. The development of new technology and the squeeze on broadcasting transmission time may promote the evolution of a very different integrated multi-media system from the one which operates in 1981. It is certainly to be hoped that the OU will maintain its position in the vanguard of distance learning institutions and will continue to work effectively towards meeting the educational needs of those people who can best profit from education at a distance.

References

1. Keegan, D.J. (1980) 'Drop-outs at the Open University'. Australian Journal of Education, 24, 1, 44-55.
2. McIntosh, N.E., Woodley, A. and Morrison, V. (1980) 'Student demand and progress at the Open University - the first eight years'. Distance Education, 1, 1, 37-60.
3. Perry, W. (1976) 'Open University: a personal account by the first Vice-Chancellor'. Milton Keynes: Open University Press.
4. Rumble, G. (1981) 'Economics and cost structures'. In Kaye, A. and Rumble, G. (eds.) 'Distance teaching for higher and adult education'. London: Croom Helm.
5. Sewart, D. (1981) 'Distance teaching: a contradiction in terms?' Teaching at a Distance, 19, 8 - 18.
6. Wagner, L. (1977) 'The Economics of the Open University Revisited'. Higher Education, 6, 359-81.
7. Woodley, A. (1979) 'How open is open?' A paper prepared ... for the Annual Conference of the Society for Research into Higher Education ... Brighton Polytechnic, 19-20 December 1979.
8. Woodley, A. and McIntosh, N.E. (1980) 'The Door stood Open: an evaluation of the Open University younger students pilot scheme'. Brighton: Falmer Press.

Chapter 10

THE UNIVERSIDAD NACIONAL ABIERTA, VENEZUELA

Greville Rumble

COUNTRY PROFILE

Geography

912,417 square kilometres divided into four geographical regions:

A narrow *coastal zone* broadening into the Maracaibo basin in the west and the Orinoco delta in the east contains 18 percent of the population. Main product, oil, based on the Maracaibo basin. Maracaibo is the second largest city in Venezuela (0.8 million).

The *Andean highlands* contain the major centres of population: Caracas the capital, with 2.8 million inhabitants, Valencia 0.4 millions, Barquisimeto and Maracay.

The sparsely populated *Llanos plains*, stretching from the Andean foothills eastwards to the Guyana highlands.

The *Guyana highlands*, occupying 45 percent of the national territory and containing 2 percent of the population. Rich deposits of minerals and iron ore are now being exploited.

Population

13.5 millions (1980 estimate). A young population - 43.2 percent are under 15 years of age and 56 percent under 20. 75 percent of the population lives in urban areas. 4.1 millions are classified as economically active, of which 0.66 million are engaged in agricultural activity. Official figures put the level of unemployment at 5 percent. More than 30 percent of the labour force has no more than third-grade education.

Economy

The economy is overwhelmingly based on the oil industry which provides over 90 percent of exports and 66 percent of fiscal revenue. Government policy is to broaden the industrial base of the economy, and there are some major projects, particularly in Guyana (steel and aluminium plants). Industrial productivity is held back by, amongst other things, a lack of trained human resources. Concentration on huge industrial projects has led to neglect of basic public services, with a marked deterioration of the quality of life in the cities, particularly for the urban poor. Foreign capital and know-how is welcomed. Although Venezuela is primarily an agricultural country as far as the internal economy is concerned, only 3 percent of the national territory is used for cropping agriculture and 20 percent for cattle farming.

Communications

Roads	59,000 km, 20,000 km paved.
Air	There are good domestic air services.
Telephones	969,000 lines (1978).
Television	3 State networks and about 1.4 million receivers (1976).
Radio	State owned Radio Nacional; one cultural station; 143 commercial stations; over 5 million receivers (1976).
Newspapers	Four daily newspapers have a circulation of over 100,000 copies each. There are 56 daily newspapers. (1978).

EDUCATIONAL PROFILE

Structure

Precompulsory schooling exists from ages 3 to 6. Compulsory primary level education covers ages 7 to 13 inclusive. This is followed by secondary education comprising a three year basic common cycle (students aged 14 to 16) followed by a diversified cycle of two years (students aged 17 and 18). Satisfactory conclusion of secondary schooling culminates in the title of *Bachillerato*, which is a pre-requisite for university entry.

Statistics (1975)

School Age population		3,985,000
Enrolments	Primary	2,108,413
	Secondary	669,138
	Tertiary	213,542
	Total	2,991,093

Standards

Wastage rates are high. Only half the students at primary level complete all 6 years. State schools are characterised by large classes, a chronic shortage of teachers, space, furnishings and equipment, an overdependence on rote learning and a rigidly controlled curriculum. The proportion of literates in the population was estimated at 82 percent in 1977.

Higher Education

The development of higher education in Venezuela in the last 20 years has been characterised by the rising cost of higher education, a steady increase in social demand for entry to the universities and the foundation of new institutions to meet this demand. The number of students enrolled in higher education has risen from 95,294 in 1971/2 (88,505 in the universities) to 282,074 in 1978/9 (230,719 in the universities): the participation rate (percentage of the relevant age-group enrolled) has risen from 6.5 percent (1971/2) to 15.0 percent (1978/9). The number of private and state higher education institutions has risen from 13 (1969) to 67 (1979) (Consejo Nacional de Universidades, 1979).

The universities are autonomous. Their overall development is co-ordinated by the National University Council, which is an advisory body. They are, with a few exceptions, highly politicised and characterised by frequent strikes and shutdowns.

In a society in which university education is perceived to be, and to a large extent is, a means towards furthering or maintaining the individual's socio-economic status, the inability of the university sector to meet demands could, it is feared, exacerbate social tensions and unrest.

If frustrated demand is one problem, another facing higher education in Venezuela in the early 1970s was the degree to which traditional university curricula were meeting the needs of the country for educated manpower. The Fifth National Plan (for the period 1976 to 1980) called for increased output of trained scientists and technologists. Universities have in the past needed to concentrate on traditional and socially prestigious degree courses such as law, medicine and engineering.

To meet these needs, the higher education sector not only expanded rapidly (see above) but sought new and innovative approaches towards the solution of the problems facing it. New technological institutes were founded to offer short degree courses of three rather than the traditional five years duration. Some universities instituted Supervised University Studies programmes in which the students study off-campus using written materials such as programmed instructional units, study guides, facsimiles and audio-visual materials, yet have an opportunity through tutorials and counselling sessions to work under the guidance of university staff (Díaz, 1976: 19-30). In addition, the Government decided to establish a distance teaching university.

THE UNIVERSIDAD NACIONAL ABIERTA (UNA)

Origins

The origins of the Universidad Nacional Abierta (UNA) thus lie in the acknowledged need to expand and democratise educational opportunities in Venezuela, while at the same time making the country's educational provision more relevant to the needs of society. The Government viewed its response to these needs as an educational revolution. The then Minister of Education, Luis Manuel Peñalver, argued that "the main purposes and objectives justifying and orientating the educational revolution can be synthesized, in their essential aspects, in three broad principles: (1) Education for Democratization. (2) Education for Innovation. (3) Education for Autonomous Development." (Peñalver, 1976, cited in the Organising Committee Report, 1976: 15). Fulfilment of these principles required that individuals should have real opportunities to continue their education at post-compulsory levels in accordance with their abilities, knowledge and interests. The educational system itself should be transformed from "an elite-orientated system of education into another, able to meet the new demands of massified education. This change will refer to: educational methods, structures, curriculum, attitudes and patterns of prestige" (*ibid*: 15-16).

As part of this process, the Government established in 1975 a Planning Committee for the proposed Universidad Nacional Abierta (Comisión Organizadora de la Universidad Nacional Abierta). The University itself was established in 1977. The Planning Committee hoped that the use of distance teaching methods would enable UNA to achieve the following aims (Comisión Organizadora, 1977: 31-2):

1. To offer real educational opportunities at the higher education level to students from different socio-economic classes in the society

and especially to adults and those members of the working population who have not previously had the opportunity to attend a
traditional institution.

2. To meet in part the social demand for higher education at a standard
   not inferior to those of the best higher educational institutions in
   the country.

3. To contribute to the autonomous development of the country by
   meeting its needs for trained human resources, particularly in
   scientific and technological fields.

4. To establish institutional structures and processes capable of continuous development and of incorporating innovations that will
   optimise the teaching-learning process.

5. To develop a teaching-learning system relevant to the conditions,
   needs and aspirations of its students, and conducive to the stimu-
   lation of the students' capacity for creativity and critical thinking.

6. To support the development needs of the nation in collaboration
   with other relevant agencies and institutions.

7. To contribute to a significant diminution of unit costs in higher
   education.

8. To provide its educational programmes throughout Venezuela.

9. To optimise the productive use of free time by persons following
   its programmes.

UNA's Planning Committee placed great emphasis on the preparation
of a carefully thought out project plan which specified in considerable
detail the objectives, methods and structures of the planned University, and related these to the educational system as a whole (Comisión
Organizadora, 1977). Villarroel (1980: 5-6) has pointed out that the
level of detail attained in the project plan was both advantageous and
disadvantageous. While it provided a point of reference for the detailed
planning of the University, it also tended to act as a straight-jacket that
inhibited creativity when it was taken dogmatically at face value.
However, it is worth noting that a number of the technical staff who

supported the work of the Planning Committee in 1976 and 1977 went on to become members of the University's academic and administrative staff. This continuity between the work of the Planning Committee and the early days of the University proved to be very useful to the new institution.

The Students

Very little demographic data has been published on UNA's students. In common with other distance teaching universities, UNA's students tend to be employed, to have family responsibilities, and to be older than is the case with conventional university students. In 1979, 90.1 percent of them were employed, 56.9 percent were married and their average age was 29. A very high proportion had followed a university level course in the past (92.8 percent) although only 27.8 percent had a university level qualification.

Academic Programmes

Like other distance teaching universities, UNA placed initial emphasis on the development of formal academic programmes at degree level. However, before students can embark on a degree course, they must pass the University's Introductory Course which aims to orientate them to the practice of learning at a distance. They then begin their degree programme, which is divided into General Studies (two semesters) and Professional Studies (six to ten semesters). Students must take a defined number of courses at General Studies level before taking any courses at Professional Studies level. General Studies courses are intended to provide an interdisciplinary foundation that will facilitate their subsequent studies at the higher level.

UNA's Professional Studies programmes are intended to provide students with a professional qualification at one of two levels: full length *carreras* which a student could in theory complete in five and a half years (eleven semesters) and which lead to the award of a licentiate degree; and technical level short *carreras* which can in theory be completed in three years (six semesters).

Seventeen degree lines (*carreras*) were originally envisaged in five subject areas (basic sciences, engineering, agricultural and marine sciences, education, and the social sciences). Subsequently the economic and operational implications of the programme together with a realisation that student numbers on some of the *carreras,* particularly on higher-level courses, would be very low, led to a downward revision of the planned number of degree lines to nine. Two of these *carreras* will initially be developed as short degree programmes, with the possibility that they will be developed into full length programmes at a later date. Table 10.1 gives details.

Table 10.1 : Degree programmes at the Universidad Nacional Abierta

Area	Carrera	Number of credits required		
		at general studies	at professional studies	in total
Administration	Accounting	40	120	160
	Business Administration	40	121	161
	Public Administration	40	120	160
Education	Learning Difficulties (1)			
	i. Short	28	55	83
	ii. Normal	38	116	154
	Maths Teaching	40	125	165
	Pre-School Education (1)			
	i. Short	28	62	90
	ii. Normal	38	106	144
Engineering	Industrial Engineering	40	125	165
	Systems Engineering (2)	40	118	·158
Mathematics	Mathematics	40	124	164

NOTES: 1. initially developed as short carreras with the possibility of subsequent further development.

2. there are 4 options planned for this carrera, in Operations Research, Process Control, Information, and a General Option. Students can also opt to obtain a Certificate of General Competency after six rather than ten semesters work.

193

The basic 'unit of study' is the course. Each course is assigned a credit value which varies within the range 2 to 8 credits - although the majority of courses are of 4 credits. Courses may be offered in more than one *carrera* and a few have different credit ratings depending on the *carrera* in which they are offered. Overall, planning is based on the assumption that students will work one and a half hours per week per credit over an 18 week semester term and will devote an average of 24 hours per week to their studies. This implies an average loading of 16 credits per semester. The average course loading is assumed to be 4 courses per semester in all *carreras* except Mathematics, where it will be three given the higher average credit rating of the course. It is, however, possible for students to register for a smaller number of courses per semester.

UNA's academic year is based on two 18 week semesters. Current assumptions are that each course will be presented every semester over a planned five year course life (that is, ten presentations) and will then be either replaced or remade. Since the complete General and Professional Studies cycle is of ten semesters and since UNA plans to complete its total course offering for the nine planned *carreras* by the end of the tenth semester, this has the advantage that UNA should have completed its current planned course profile before it needs to consider remaking any of its courses.

To date UNA has concentrated its efforts on the development of the Introductory Course and the various *carreras*. The University hopes to offer postgraduate courses and a programme of extension studies courses in the future.

Curriculum, instructional and content design

UNA's planners regarded the University as a vehicle for the professional training of students to meet the manpower needs of the State and so great emphasis is placed on market research as a means of identifying manpower requirements. The process continues with occupational analysis - that is, 'a systematic study of the tasks that typify an occupation, of the conditions in which (the occupation) is carried out, and of the prerequisites necessary for its execution' (Cuadra, 1980: 3). Once this has been done, work starts on designing the curriculum. This process ends with the production of a document specifying the aims and objectives of the programme and its courses, the contents of each course and the instruments of evaluation.

Once the curriculum plan has been produced, instructional designers (whose job is to select the most appropriate teaching strategies given the range of media available at UNA) come together with specialists in the subject area, evaluation and the various media to design the course and brief the academic content specialists who will write the materials. These last may be drawn from the University's full-time academic staff, or may be external academic consultants and writers appointed to prepare the course materials on the basis of the brief that has been given them. At a subsequent stage, the team of institutional, media and content area specialists take the author's draft and transform it into distance-learning modules. Early experience (Villarroel, 1980: 14-15) showed that the separation of instructional design from the job of writing the materials did not work well. Rumble (1981a: 188) reports that course writers tended to respond in two distinct ways to the instructions they received: either they ignored them, wrote what they felt were better texts, and handed these over to production at a stage at which nothing short of cancelling the whole course would allow time for the work to be revised; or they accepted the instructions and wrote texts which they personally felt to be inappropriate, and to which they had lost any sense of commitment.

The response to this situation was 'to simplify the design process by discouraging the overspecialization of each member of the working pair. It encouraged the content specialist to acquire basic knowledge of the instructional design used and the designer to learn about the subject matter of the course he was helping to write' (Villarroel, 1980: 14). In essence, the two specialists were brought together within a project team, the Integrated Design Unit (IUD), which became the basis for the creation of the course. Each IUD is composed of content specialists, instructional designers, evaluators and media specialists, including both full-time employees and contracted staff from outside the University, and is responsible for the development of more than one course in the same area of knowledge.

Villarroel (1980: 15) reports that while it is too early to evaluate the work of the IUDs, they do seem to have fostered integration amongst their members. However, it has been argued that it is 'difficult to co-ordinate the efforts of so many people' and that the functions of some members of the IUDs continue to be unclear. Where external authors are used they seem to be supervised by the internal IUD members rather than integrated as full members of the team in their own right.

Media use, production and distribution

Courses are multi-media. The most important medium is print which may consist of specially designed texts for self-instructional learning, reprints of books and articles, together with commercially published books. The long-term expectation is that highly structured texts will be the exception rather than the rule, being used predominately in lower level courses. The texts are themselves broken down into modules, each of which has specific objectives which the student is expected to master. All courses have associated study guides which contain self-assessment questions and other material. The quality of the printed materials in the Introductory Course and at General Students level has been very high. However, existing design standards will not be maintained in higher level courses where student numbers will be smaller. It is also envisaged that there will in the future be much greater standardisation in the layout and format of the texts. In general, texts will be printed initially for two semesters and then reprinted as a second edition incorporating modifications made as a result of evaluation and feedback obtained during the teaching of the course in its first semester. The texts are printed by commercial publishers on behalf of UNA.

Television programmes, various supplementary printed and audio-visual materials and tutorial assistance support the main texts. Planning is based on the assumption that no course will have more than four television programmes, each lasting 25 minutes. Radio is used for making public announcements to students about, for example, examination timetables. It is not used for teaching purposes.

The television programmes may be bought 'ready-made' or be produced by external production units on behalf of UNA. However, UNA does have its own internal studies and production staff and most of the University's 1980 requirements were met internally. Each course has a budgeted limit of 93,000 US dollars. The television and radio programmes are broadcast free of charge on national channels. Video-cassettes of all programmes are provided for student use in each of the University's local centres.

Printed and other course materials are despatched from the Centre to the local centres, from which the students collect it. At some time in the future it is expected that equipment for experiments will be made available in local centres for students on higher level courses, particularly on engineering courses.

Student Administration and Support Services

UNA has 21 Local or Regional Centres, about half of which are rented. The remainder are either owned by the University or provided free of charge by Municipalities. Students must have a secondary leaving certificate (*Bachillerato*) before they can register on the Introductory Course, and they must have passed the latter before they can embark on a degree programme. Students may apply direct to UNA or be allocated to the University through a clearing operation run by the National Council of Universities. They attend the local centres for registration. In 1980 they paid a matriculation fee of Bolivares 100 per semester (23 US dollars) and a course-based fee of Bolivares 150 (35 US dollars) which covers the direct cost of materials and tuition. In the 1979/80 semester students on average registered on 3.4 courses each. Once registered, they are assigned to a tutor and a counsellor. Great emphasis is placed on providing a counselling service which will help students solve their study problems, and each Centre has a number of full-time counsellors to one of whom the student is assigned throughout his university career. Tutors are also available for consultation at set hours. The tutor's job is to guide and support the student and to contribute towards the solution of their academic problems. Study groups are organised which are voluntary so far as the student is concerned, but at which both counsellor and tutor play a part. Students may also have some individual contact with tutors and counsellors. However, UNA stresses the self-learning nature of its courses, and the role of the tutors, who are contracted on the basis of so many hours work per week, is supportive of the other teaching media. This is underlined by the fact that at General Studies level the overall tutor:student ratio is 1:450. Moreover, while tuition is provided at all 21 centres at General Studies level, at Professional Studies level the numbers per course is not felt to be sufficient to justify its provision in more than six centres (designated Regional Centres for this reason). Also, while at General Studies level the majority of tutors cover only one course, at Professional Studies level the tutors (all of whom are supervised by full-time Subject-area Tutors in the fields of Administration,

197

Engineering, Education and Mathematics) may cover a number of related courses.

As well as having a full-time counselling staff (the number of counsellors being related to the number of students), each Local and Regional Centre has a full-time administrative staff and provides student support services in the form of a small library and video playback machines together with copies of each of the University's television programmes.

Each *carrera* has associated with it one or two periods during which the students are expected to work in an organisation and practice their newly acquired professional skills. These periods of work-study may have associated with them the completion of a project by the students. Given the high proportion of UNA's students who are employed, a particular problem is likely to be faced in trying to arrange work study periods for students who are registered on a *carrera* that has no direct bearing with their current occupation.

Assessment and examinations

With more and more specialised courses on offer, it became impossible to provide specialised tutors in all subjects at all local centres. To make up for this, Villarroel (1980: 16) reports that UNA had by 1980 put into operation a mode of computer assisted instruction known as GLS (Guided Learning System), originally developed at Pennsylvania State University to provide students with individualised instant feedback. The students have access via computer to a centrally located bank of questions which enable them to evaluate their own progress in mastering the objectives of the various course modules.

Students also have to take formal examinations at the local centres. These examinations are the only ones which count for certification purposes. The examination system is very largely based on the use of multiple choice objective tests.

Instructional design and cognitive styles

Escotet (1978), in an article on the problems of transferring distance and open learning systems from one culture to another, has argued that instructional design must take account of the learning styles of the target population. While more research needs to be done, the evidence available tends to support Escotet's assertion that while 'An open learning system requires an independent student with self-discipline and a great capacity for analysis and synthesis, . . . our (Latin American) education has reinforced styles of dependency in learning, of enforced discipline, not self-discipline; and has emphasised amongst other characteristics, memorisation' (Escotet, 1978: 78). Moreover, it seems likely that this divergence in learning styles is likely to inhibit the successful use of distance learning systems which emphasise independent learning. If so, these factors suggest that great thought needs to be given to the tutorial and counselling needs of students learning at a distance - particularly in the Latin American context.

Student progress and drop-out

UNA has not published any information on student drop-out, but there are indications that the level of drop-out is very high. In 1978, for example, 17,160 students registered on the Introductory Course of whom only 3,639 went on to take General Studies in the next semester. Table 10.2 gives details. Escotet (1978:79) has suggested that drop-out is one of the most serious problems facing distance education in Latin America.

Table 10.2 : Student numbers at the Universidad Nacional Abierta

| | Cohort | | |
Semester	1	2	3
1978	17,160		
1979/1	3,639	12,566	
1979/2	2,711	2,315	
1979/80	–	–	11,526

Source: UNA (1980) Compendio de Planteamientos, Appendix I

Organisational Structure and Governance

UNA's organisational structure is based on the *President*, who is directly dependent on the University's supreme governing body, the *Superior Council*. Reporting to the President in a staff capacity are the office of Strategic Planning and Evaluation, and the Audit Department. Dependent on the President in a line capacity is the *Rector* who is the chief administrative and executive officer of the University. Reporting directly to him are three staff officers, the Director of the Budgets and Scheduling Office; the Director of Public Relations; and the University's legal adviser. Six major operating units report to the Rector: The *Institute of Educational Research*, which encompasses both academic and institutional research (including market research); the *Academic Vicerectorate*, responsible for instructional design and the academic development of the University's educational programmes and teaching systems (including those activities undertaken in the local centres); the *Operations Directorate*, responsible for course materials production and distribution, the management of the local centres, and the organisation of tuition, counselling and examinations; the *Administrative Vice-rectorate*, responsible for financial accounting, personnel and general services; the *Secretariat*, responsible for student administration, secretariat services to decision-making bodies, and the management of university archives and records; and the *Information Unit*, which includes data processing, the telephone system and the Library.

Initially, great emphasis was placed on a systems approach to the management of the University. 'UNA was conceived as a system composed of a rationally and functionally defined sub-system network. The authorities were supposed to be managers responsible for the proper functioning and flow within the system, with the concept of private enterprise efficiency being of utmost importance' (Villarroel, 1980: 6-7). In fact, as Villarroel points out, this approach could not be sustained (*ibid:* 10). The governmental and decision-making structures which emerged have their origins in the traditional Venezuelan universities. While power is formally vested in the Superior Council, which has a majority of lay members and is chaired by the President, decision-making effectively takes place in the Directive Council which is chaired by the Rector (Francés, 1980: 100). Apart from the Rector, the Directive Council has three other members: the Academic Vicerector, the Administrative Vicerector, and the Secretary. A high proportion of decisions taken by the Directive Council have been of an administrative nature or related to the allocation of particular resources. Those policy matters considered have tended to be short term. Overall decision-making has been highly centralised, reactive, not proactive; and short-term and localised rather than long-term and global. When important matters have come up, the ensuing debate has tended to be prolonged and decisions have not been made readily (Francés, 1980:100-102).

The managerial structure itself has not always aided decision-making.

For example, conflict has arisen because the local centres are administratively dependent on the Operations area, and not on the Academic area which is formally responsible for formulating policy for the tuition and counselling areas. This has created friction between those who develop the courses and those who are in contact with students at the local centres (Villarroel, 1980: 10-11). A further problem is created by the fact that the Directors of Operations, the Information Unit, the Planning Office, the Budgeting and Scheduling Office, and the Educational Research Division are not members of the Directive Council. While there are committees charged with co-ordinating activities across departmental boundaries, Francés (1980: 53) argues that the managerial and decision-making system would be improved if there was greater lateral co-ordination linked with better defined procedures, delegated powers, planning, scheduling and control.

Costs

UNA's 1980 budget anticipated expenditure of 89.6 million bolívares (20.8 million US dollars). Rumble (1981b) developed a cost model for UNA and projected expenditure against current plans for expansion. This exercise suggested that UNA's total 'steady state' budgetary requirements would rise to about 22.8 million US dollars at 1980 price levels (a 9.6 percent increase) with the number of course presentations rising from 71 in the two semesters of 1980 to 344 in the two semesters of a 'steady state' year. Significantly, student number projections, while fraught with difficulty, suggest that the number of full-year equivalent students registered with the University is likely to fall from about 13,350 in 1980 to 11,650 in the 'steady state'. As a result, the average cost per full-year equivalent student is likely to rise from 1,560 US dollars in 1980 to 1,955 US dollars in the 'steady state'. Significant economies of scale could be achieved if student numbers can be increased. The real question is whether or not UNA can increase the number of students in its system, given the nature of its academic programmes which are designed to appeal to persons seeking specialised professional qualifications, rather than to a wider public. Overall, the current situation, if it continues, will inevitably result in a proliferation of higher level courses with very low student numbers.

Conclusions

UNA is still a very young institution. Villarroel (1980: 18-20) has suggested that the most significant problems faced by the University are the following:

1. The need to find a balance between having a structure, organisation and procedures that allow it to properly fulfil its unique functions and to still be a "university" sufficiently similar to others bearing the name.

2. The need to maintain academic standards and, directly related to this, 'the dilemma of how to keep reasonable standards of scholarship while maintaining an enrolment that economically justifies the university'.

3. The need to solve some problems inherent in distance education - particularly the extent to which students can successfully direct their own learning.

4. The extent to which UNA can prove itself to be cost efficient, while recognising that cost-efficiency is not the sole criteria for judging the success or failure of the institution.

It is not possible at this stage in UNA's development, to reach any conclusions about the success or failure of the institution. While there are a number of critical areas, it is clear that the University's staff have the will to face and solve the problems now facing the institution. If they can succeed in this, then the institution is likely to be assured of success in the future.

Note

1. All prices have been converted to US dollars using a rate of exchange of 4.3 Venezuelan bolivares to the dollar. Prices are at 1980 levels.

References

1. Comisión Organizadora de la Universidad Nacional Abierta (1977) 'Universidad Nacional Abierta: Proyecto'. Second edition, Caracas: UNA.
2. Consejo Nacional de Universidades (1979) 'Boletín Estadístico No. 6, Noviembre 1979'. Caracas: CNU, Oficina de Planificación del Sector Universitario.

3. Cuadra, S. (1980) 'Basamento Teórico - Metodológico Necesita la Educacion Superior'. UNA Opinion 2,2, 3-7.
4. Díaz, L.E. (1976) 'Las innovaciones en educación post-secundaria en Venezuela' Paper presented to the Latin American and Caribbean Meeting on New Forms of Post-Secondary Education, Caracas, September 1976.
5. Escotet, M.A. (1978) 'Factores adversos para el desarrollo de una universidad abierta en América Latina'. Revista de Tecnología Educativa, 4,1,66-83.
6. Francés, A. (1980) 'Diagnóstico de la organización UNA'. Caracas: UNA, Dirección de Planificación Estratégica y Evaluación Institucional.
7. Organizing Committee of the National Open University (1976) 'Venezuela: Preliminary Considerations for the creation of the National Open University of Venezuela (UNA)'. Caracas: UNA.
8. Peñalver, L.M. (1976) 'La Revolución Educativa'. Caracas: Ministerio de Educación.
9. Rumble, G. (1981a) 'Organisation and decision-making'. In Kaye, A. and Rumble, G. (1981) 'Distance teaching for Higher and Adult Education'. London: Croom Helm, 179-199.
10. Rumble, G. (1981b) 'The Cost Analysis of Learning at a Distance: Venezuela's Universidad Nacional Abierta'. Distance Education, 3. In press.
11. Villarroel, R. (1980) 'The Venezuelan National Open University: An Overview'. Paper presented to the Thirtieth International Conference of the International Communication Association, Acapulco, Mexico 18-23 May 1980.

Chapter 11

GENERAL CHARACTERISTICS
OF THE DISTANCE TEACHING UNIVERSITIES

Greville Rumble and Desmond Keegan

INTRODUCTION

The nine DTUs examined in this book operate in very different environments. Of the nine countries, three are characterised by the World Bank (1980) as industrialised, four are middle-income countries, one is a low-income country and one belongs to that group of countries which has a centrally planned economy. The countries range in size from Israel (20,700 square km) to China (9,597,000 square km), and in population from Costa Rica (2.3 millions) to China (1,000 millions). World Bank figures show that the percentage of total population living in urban areas varies from 13 percent (China) and 28 percent (Pakistan) to 85 percent or over in the Federal Republic of Germany, Israel and the United Kingdom (see Table 11.1).

While most of the countries (with the exception of Pakistan) approach universal primary education, the proportion of children of secondary school age attending school ranges from 17 percent (Pakistan) to those countries with over 80 percent participation (United Kingdom, Federal Republic of Germany). At tertiary level, the proportion of the age group participating ranges from 1 percent (People's Republic of China) to 38 percent (Canada) (see Table 11.1).

Clearly the very wide variations in social, economic, cultural and educational conditions in these countries makes it difficult to determine or evaluate the factors which contribute to the success or failure of the nine DTUs studied in this book, and we have not attempted to tackle these wider issues.

GENERAL CHARACTERISTICS OF DTUs

We have selected five general areas for analysis because they seem to us to be particularly important:

1. What have the DTUs been established to do? What are their objectives?

204

Table 11.1 : Selected Development Indicators

Country	Pakistan	Costa Rica	Venezuela	Spain	Israel	United Kingdom	Canada (Alberta)	Federal Republic of Germany	People's Republic of China
Country group	Low-income	Middle-income	Middle-income	Middle-income	Middle-income	Industrialised	Industrialised	Industrialised	Centrally-planned economy
Population (1980/81) (millions)	80.2	2.3	14.5	37.4	3.8	55.9	23.7 (2.1)	61.3	1000.0
Area (thousand sq. km)	804	51	912	505	21	244	9,976 (661)	249	9,597
LABOUR FORCE % of population of working age (15-64) (1979)	51	57	55	63	59	64	67 (67)	66	64
% labour force in agriculture	57	30	19	15	7	2	5 (1)	4	71
industry	20	23	27	40	36	42	29 }(99)	47	17
services (1979)	23	47	54	45	57	56	66 }	49	12
URBANISATION Urban population as a % of total (1980)	28	43	83	74	89	91	80 (80)	85	13
EDUCATION % adult literates (1975/76)	24	90	82	90	88	99	99	99	66
Participation as a % of age group primary (1978)	51	107	106	110	97	106	101 (102)	90	93
secondary (1978)	17	46	38	76	68	83	89 (91)	94	51
tertiary (1977)	2	19	21	22	25	19	38 (28)	25	1

Note: For countries with universal primary education, the gross enrolment ratios may exceed 100 percent because some pupils may be below or above the official primary-school age. The relevant age groups are broadly 6-11 (primary) 12-17 (secondary) and 18-23 (tertiary) but reflect country practices.

Sources: International Bank for Reconstruction and Development (The World Bank) 'World Development Report 1980' and 'World Development Report, 1981'. Washington: IBRD 1980 and 1981 respectively. UNESCO (1980) 'Statistical Yearbook 1980'. Paris: Unesco. Alberta Bureau of Statistics. Case Studies in 'The Distance Teaching Universities' edited by G. Rumble and K. Harry. London: Croom Helm, 1982.

2.   What kinds of students are attracted to the DTUs?

3.   What media do the DTUs use, and to what extent are they actually making use of the 'new educational media', and particularly broadcasting?

4.   How good are their academic standards?

5.   How cost-effective are they?

Objectives

The end of the Second World War was followed by the rapid expansion of access to educational services at all levels in the western industrialised countries, the Central European socialist states and the developing nations of the Third World.

The expansion of the university sector in developed countries and more recently in developing countries was in part motivated by the increasing demand for educated manpower and in part a response to demands for educational equality. At the same time, parents, schools and students increasingly came to recognise the extent to which university education was becoming a pre-condition for upward social mobility and for entry to certain professions and occupations.

The high cost of conventional university education and the reputed potential of distance teaching systems to expand the number of places available at a lower average cost per student has led some countries to regard a DTU as a means of *providing additional university places for school leavers* more rapidly and more cheaply than could be done by other means.. Four of the DTUs studied in this book, the CCTU in China, UNED in Costa Rica, and the FeU in Germany and UNA in Venezuela were established with this as one of their objectives. In contrast the UKOU excludes applications from students under 21 and in this respect is not in competition with the conventional universities.

Far more important has been the recognition that distance teaching enables *new target groups* to be given an opportunity of studying at university. The objectives of the DTUs mention:

1.   *Adults* (AU, UNED Costa Rica, UNA, UKOU).

2.   *Those who for a variety of reasons have been unable to study at a conventional university* (UNED Costa Rica, EU, UNED Spain,

206

UKOU). In the case of UNED Costa Rica specific mention is made of those who for social, economic or geographical reasons cannot enter a conventional university, while UNED Spain set out to meet the needs of those living in remote areas and UNA in Venezuela aims to reach students in different socio-economic classes.

A particularly important group includes those *people who are tied to the home or live in institutions* and for this reason cannot attend conventional universities. The objectives of EU and the AIOU specifically mention such people.

Another important group are *those who want to study at the same time as they continue in full-time employment*. Specific mention of this group occurs in the objectives of UNED Costa Rica, the FeU, EU, the AIOU and UNA. Generally speaking, the flexibility of their teaching systems enables working adults to study more easily than is the case in institutions requiring attendance in classes, although as McCormick makes clear the particular system adopted by the CCTU, involving attendance in class for televised lectures coupled with transmission restrictions, means that only full-time (or nearly full-time students) can do the courses, and makes the CCTU an exception in this respect. Where working adults are enabled to study, the contribution which they make to their country's Gross National Product throughout the length of their university studies is a striking feature of the DTUs.

3.   Some of the DTUs set out *to make up for the past lack of higher educational opportunities in their countries*. As "universities of the second chance" they provide places for adults who were born too soon to reap the benefits of conventional university expansion in the 1960s and 1970s, or whose earlier chances were impaired for other reasons.

In the United Kingdom, the UKOU's planners had in mind not only those qualified school leavers who had not gone on to a university but also *those who had left school without the normal minimal qualification for entry* and who might now wish to enter a university, so the UKOU requires no formal educational qualifications of applicants. The majority of DTUs require applicants to have the normal minimal university entrance requirements of their country (e.g. UNED Costa Rica, UNA), although UNED Spain has special requirements for older students, and AU and EU have open admissions policies in common with the UKOU.

4.   Finally, DTUs have on occasion been seen as a means of keeping students out of the campuses where it is likely that they will be politicised (e.g. the Free University of Iran).

The academic programmes offered by the DTUs reflect both the underlying philosophies that brought them into being and determine in part the kinds of students which they attract. Four considerations seem to have been particularly important in the academic planning of the DTUs, though some of the DTUs have, of course, been influenced by more than one of them.

1.   *The demand for trained personnel.* Some of the DTUs have set out to meet the increasing demand for certain types of personnel. In Venezuela it was hoped that the products of UNA would help to meet some of the shortages of skilled manpower identified in the fifth national development plan (1976-1980). In other countries demand tended to reflect the growing need for credentials and the increasing qualifications sought for entry to certain professions. Frequently demand also reflected the move of a profession (like teaching) from non-graduate to graduate status. Thus UKOU and AIOU planners specifically identified non-graduate teachers as a target group. In Spain, UNED was established to meet the needs of those ambitious for more qualifications. In China the aim was even broader - to promote the modernisation of the country by providing trained graduates.

2.   *Human capital theory.* Human capital theory has greatly influenced educational planning since the 1960s. Its proponents argue that expenditure on education is an investment in human capital which will yield benefits to the individual and to society in the form of increased earning power and productivity. It assumes that one can quantify skilled manpower shortages and then develop educational systems to overcome them. Those DTUs which concentrate on professional and vocational training reflect the dominance of human capital thinking in the formulation of educational aims. Such ideas have strongly influenced academic planning in DTUs like UNED Costa Rica, UNED Spain and UNA.

The theory has recently attracted considerable criticism on the grounds that it is extremely difficult to forecast manpower needs and that it has never been proved that investment in education is a sufficient condition for economic growth. Underdevelopment theorists have also questioned the connection between vocationally orientated higher education and the development of Third World countries.

3. *The liberal arts tradition.* Some academic programmes at DTUs have little or no overt vocational or professional purpose and place emphasis on providing adults with the opportunity to participate in higher education only in the liberal arts. Their objectives may refer to a general mission to raise the educational level of the people (e.g. EU), to provide study programmes in the arts and sciences leading to an undergraduate degree (e.g. AU), or to provide adults who were unable to enter a university when they left school with a 'second chance'.

4. *The concern with lifelong learning.* By the early 1970s another trend was discernible. Increased awareness of the rate of technological and social change was coupled with a recognition of the need for individuals to update their knowledge, not only for the purpose of changing from one stage of employment to another but even for maintenance in present employment. One aspect of this concern is the need to give working adults access to courses. The UKOU has developed some specific courses to retrain and update adults, while a number of the DTUs, (AU, UNED Costa Rica, FeU, UKOU) allow individuals to enrol in degree courses on a "one-off" basis, either for personal training purposes or out of general interest.

One factor affecting demand for educational courses is the relative importance of work and non-work periods in peoples' lives, where work is defined as the proportion of hours per week, weeks per year, and years in a person's life spent in active employment on a job. In many societies the proportion of time spent in work is declining. Factors already contributing to this decline are shorter working weeks, longer holidays, early and enforced retirement, periods of unemployment, late entry into the workforce, and paid study leave. All these factors may have an affect on levels of demand for full or part-time recurrent educational opportunities both on campus and especially at a distance.

The students

Information on the characteristics of students studying at all the DTUs considered in this book is not available, nor is the information that we have necessarily comparable. In assessing data available, one has to bear in mind the extent to which:

1. The regulations of the individual DTUs affect the characteristics of those who apply for entry. For example, the UKOU does not generally accept applications from students aged under 21, whereas UNED Costa Rica has no age bar on entry.

2. The academic programmes offered by the university attract students from particular groups. Table 6.1 (in chapter 6) shows marked variations in the characteristics of students on EU's pre-academic, academic (degree level), adult education and vocational programmes. For example, while the majority of students on the first three of these programmes are female, the vast majority of students (96.7 percent) on the vocational programme are male.

On the whole DTU students are older than conventional university students and a much higher proportion are in employment, married and homemakers than is the case with conventional university students. Again, the situation varies from country to country. Higher education in the United Kingdom is predominantly full-time so the fact that 80 percent of UKOU students are working clearly marks them out from their conventional counterparts. In a country like Costa Rica, however, it is much more common for a student to work his or her way through university and it is not uncommon for students to take up to eight years to gain their degrees. Where evidence is available, the features of distance study that have attracted students have been the flexibility of independent study at a distance, the fact that students can study at home, and the fact that they can study and work.

Table 11.2 provides basic data on students at six DTUs, while further information is given in the case studies. Overall the single most important conclusion to emerge is the degree of heterogeneity of the student body with their wide range of ages and marked differences in life experience, which distinguishes them from the traditional 18-22 age group enrolment of conventional universities.

The Use of New Educational Media

The DTUs have been variously heralded as *open universities* or *universities of the air* and, by their emphasis on the use of new

Table 11.2 : Basic data on students in 6 DTUs

Data Category of Students	AU	UNED COSTA RICA	FeU	EU	UNED SPAIN	UKOU
	All students	New students	All students	All degree students	All matriculated students	All registered undergraduates
Date	1980/81	1979/2	1981	8th semester	1979/80	1980
100% =	3,269 %	2,061 %	36,569 %	7,185 %	45,146 %	61,446 %
Sex						
Male	39	53.6	74.9	44.9	70	57.5
Female	61	46.4	25.1	55.1	30	42.5
Age						
Under age	(24) 19	(22) 25.6	(25) 26.2	(21) 14.4	(21) 4	(21) 4.8
In range (a)	(24-44) 69	(22-26) 32.5	(26-31) 42.3	(21-26) 27.8	(21-25) 20	(26-30) 20.4
In range (b)		(27-31) 20.5	(32-38) 18.5	(27-35) 27.8	(26-30) 28	(31-35) 25.5
In range (c)		(32-36) 11.5			(31-40) 32	(36-40) 16.6
Over age	(44) 12	(37) 8.9	(38) 13.0	(35) 30.0	(40) 16	(40) 32.3
Work status						
In employment	66	75.4	67.2*	74.2	88	80.6
Not working	6	11.5	8.5*	1.2	} 11	} 3.5
Students	-	-	21.5*	12.9		
Housewives/homemakers	8	11.5	2.3*	5.0		15.8
No information /not categorised	20	1.6	- *	6.7	1	0.2

Sources   * On 1980 data (100% = 29,604)
AU: 'Athabasca University Fact Book 1980-81'; UNED Costa Rica: 'Características de los estudiantes admitidos en II semestre de 1979' (Pub. 1980); FeU: published statistics; EU: 'President's Report, 1979/80'; UNED Spain: 'La UNED y sus Alumnos-Curso 1979/80' (pub. 1981); UKOU: 'Statistical Digest 1971-80' and other official sources.

communications technology, have largely thrown off the correspondence image which has characterised many of the mixed institutions
providing university level education at a distance. Indeed, the objectives of a number of the DTUs have specifically required them to use
the new communications technology. AU was established as a pilot
project 'for the application of technology and new procedures to
improve educational opportunities for adults generally'. The UKOU's
Charter specifically enjoins it to advance and disseminate learning
and knowledge "by teaching and research by a diversity of means
such as broadcasting and technological devices appropriate to higher
education, by correspondence tuition, residential courses and seminars
and in other relevant ways". However, while given particular emphasis
in the title of the British Government's 1966 White Paper *A University
of the Air*, broadcasting was never regarded by the UKOU's planners as
being more than one of the elements in a multi-media approach. The
Report of its Planning Committee (1969:6) made this clear:

> It is, however, neither practically possible nor pedagogically
> sound to rely on broadcasting as the principal or exclusive
> means of instruction in an operation designed to provide
> disciplined courses at university level . . . The only method
> of individual instruction capable of being made available
> everywhere, and capable of indefinite expansion as new
> needs arise, is correspondence tuition, which can readily
> incorporate these newer techniques (i.e. broadcasting).

Elsewhere the Report proposed that each course should "make substantial use of correspondence course techniques" which would "form
the nucleus around which an integrated sequence of radio and television
programmes" could be built (1969:18).

In retrospect the distance teaching universities, taken as a whole,
have been marked by a curious mixture of public identification with
and stress on the use of educational broadcasting and the playing down
of their actual basis in correspondence teaching and the use of print.

Part of the enthusiasm for educational broadcasting stemmed from
the general interest that surrounded a number of educational television
and radio projects in the 1960s and which was reflected in books like
The New Media: Memo to Educational Planners by Wilbur Schramm
and his colleagues (1967) and *Open Learning, Systems and Problems in*

Post-Secondary Education by Norman Mackenzie, Richmond Postgate and John Scupham (1975).

Bates (1982) has recently reappraised the role of educational media in twelve distance learning systems (including seven operating at university level) and concluded that:

1. There is a clear movement *away* from using broadcasting by distance learning systems.

2. The range of audio-visual media suitable for distance education is rapidly increasing.

3. The educational potential of audio-visual media still tends to be under-exploited by distance learning systems.

The variety and range of different media or learning methods within each DTU is shown in Table 11.3. However, there is enormous variety in the relative *weight* attached to each medium or learning method. Print is the key medium except in the CCTU. Each of the universities provides local study centres which offer a range of facilities to students. Face-to-face tuition is provided by all the DTUs but the extent of provision in some of them (UNA, FeU) is curtailed with emphasis being placed on the texts. Only the UKOU provides week-long residential schools. Most of the DTUs use television but only the UKOU and the CCTU transmit for a substantial number of hours each week, while the FeU and UNED Spain do not use it at all.

It is clear that television, and radio in particular, are proving to be of less significance in teaching systems or more difficult to use successfully than was originally expected. One of the reasons is the relatively high cost of broadcasting which clearly influences the extent to which it is used in some systems (e.g. AU, UNED Costa Rica, UNED Spain). Another problem is the shortage of skilled broadcasting staff (e.g. at UNA). A third factor is the attitude of the institution towards broadcasting (e.g. the FeU which has adopted the attitude that print is inherently superior).

One of the reasons why broadcasting has not played a greater role in the development of distance learning systems is that education at a distance has been characterised by three major problems: (1) excessive student drop-out; (2) doubts about the quality of learning achieved by distance students; and (3) external acceptance of the quality of the learning and awards by both academics and employers. K.C. Smith has

213

Table 11.3 : Use of Media in the DTUs

	AU	CCTU	UNED CR	FeU	EU	AIOU	UNED S	OU	UNA
Print	+	+	+	+	+	+	+	+	+
Study Centres	+	+	+	+	+	+	+	+	+
Face-to-face tuition	+	+	+	+	+	+	+	+	+
Telephone tuition	+		+	+	+		+	+	
Computer Assisted Instruction (CAI)									+
Access to computer terminals	+		+				+		
Access to laboratories at centres	+	+		+	+		+	+	
Home experiment kits					+			+	
Residential schools								+	
Television	+	+	+		+	+		+	+
Video-tapes	+			+			+	+	+
Radio	+	+	+		+	+	+		
Audio-cassette tapes	+		+	+	+		+	+	

Source: Chapters 2 to 10 of The Distance Teaching Universities, edited Greville Rumble and Keith Harry, London: Croom Helm, 1982.

argued convincingly that to attempt "to devise *learning packages* which will allow students to become completely independent of teachers and other students" at university level "is probably not only futile but mis-directed because it must lead to dehumanising the learning process which for most of us needs to be a social experience as well". For him the essence of success in university distance teaching "is mainly a matter of getting the right balance between elements of independent study and opportunities for direct personal interaction between staff and students" (Smith, 1979: 49).

Another factor is that, as Schwittmann (1982) shows, success in a distance study programme is quite simply a function of the time a student has available to study. When study time is restricted, the components of the course that are viewed as most peripheral are those that are abandoned first. At the university level, where print is the primary medium, this often applies to the audio-visual elements.

Bates (1982) has suggested that in the immediate future the factors which will influence choice of media are:

1. *Accessibility.* The main factor here is the extent to which the medium is likely to be available - or can be provided economically - in most students' homes (although DTUs with an extensive network of local centres may be able to provide more expensive equipment there).

2. *Convenience and ease of use for students.* Those media which students can use when and where it suits them and without extra training arc likely to be the most acceptable.

3. *Academic control over the material.* The easier it is for the academic to design and prepare the material, without training, the more acceptable it is likely to be.

4. *The 'human' touch.* The better the medium is at facilitating the learners' relationship with the teacher, the more acceptable it is likely to be.

5. *What is available.*

On these criteria Bates suggests that print, audio-cassettes and possibly telephone teaching are the 'best immediate bets' although choice is clearly increasing. Nevertheless, the DTUs have on the whole, as Table 11.3 shows, adopted a multi-media approach within a general framework in which the use of print and tuition by correspondence and by personal contact in local centres predominates. However, their use of the 'new' educational media has been a major contribution to their success because broadcasting and particularly television (1) has been politically attractive, (2) has helped gain the DTUs support from planners and policy makers at the national level, and (3) has contributed to their success by throwing off the "correspondence image".

Parity of Academic Standards

The earliest of the autonomous DTUs with which this book deals - the UKOU - set out from its inception to achieve parity of standards with conventional universities in Britain. Jennie Lee, the Minister assigned responsibility for the UKOU project, was adamant that it should have the highest academic status. She scrapped the proposals that had been worked out within the British Department of Education and Science for an experimental College of the Air and pushed forward her own ideas: "The 'University of the Air' was to be an independent university, offering its own degrees, making no compromise whatever on standards and offering an opportunity to all, without entrance qualification" (Perry, 1976.13). The University, once established, accepted the challenge. "Our task was to provide courses that would lead to first degrees equivalent in standard to those of any other British first degree" (Perry, 1981:7).

Perry (1981:7) describes the foundation of the British OU as:

> an act of faith that was remarkable and almost miraculous. This decision was received with scepticism, indeed with scorn and ridicule, by virtually the whole of the academic establishment, by almost the whole of the national press and by at least half the political world. And the biggest cause of that scepticism was the belief in academic circles that higher education was critically dependent on face-to-face tuition.

In Germany the FeU undertook the even more daunting task of achieving degrees that would be interchangeable, both during the study programmes and when awarded, with the degrees of the conventional German universities, themselves heirs of a demanding tradition of academic standards.

All the DTUs have had to establish a reputation for reliability, validity and credibility. Neil (1981: 41) suggests that to succeed they had to: (1) Create and produce learning materials of exceptional quality; (2) Use well-conceived teaching styles, teaching methods and student-support services clearly designed to promote effective independent learning; (3) Design curricula manifestly relevant to specified and real needs for education; (4) Avoid excessive unorthodoxy or adventurousness while maintaining a prudently innovative approach to curriculum design, and (5) Carefully evaluate student performance and consistently analyse and use feedback information to improve their systems.

In the process the leaders of these new institutions initiated periods of intense comparative research, frequently accompanied by inter-institutional visits, to help them with their own decision making.

In fact, comparative research shows that parity of standards between conventional and distance learning systems is achievable in certain carefully structured systems. The evidence from the University of New England at Armidale, Australia, a university with both conventional and external students, shows that distance students can achieve similar results to conventional students on the same university study programmes. The assessment model at the University of New England is so structured that both internal and external students sit the same examinations, are assessed by the same examiners and qualify for the same awards. It is therefore easy to compare the results of the two groups and the evidence shows over the period 1960-1980 that little difference can be discerned between them.

It therefore seems possible that in certain universities teaching by both traditional and distance means, parity of standards between the two groups of students is achievable, though Smith (1979: 33) lays down stringent conditions for the successful functioning of the distance unit:

> Compared with most distance education systems overseas, the New England model has certain cohesiveness and underlying strength that appears to be lacking elsewhere These qualities are derived mainly from the fact that academic staff are responsible for the total teaching/learning process of writing courses, teaching them through a combination of independent study materials and face-to-face tuition and assessing the students by way of assignments and formal examinations. In almost all other contexts, in Britain, North America and Europe, 'teaching at a distance' is a shared responsibility. Courses are generally written by authors on a contractual basis, teaching in tutorial sessions and grading of assignments is delegated to part-time or adjunct staff recruited for the purpose, and assessment often falls between these part-time recruits and the full-time staff of the institution concerned.

Further evidence comes from the performance of students over a similar period at the Centre National d'Enseignement par Correspondance, formerly the Centre National de Télé-enseignement in France, an autonomous distance teaching institution. The CNEC prepares students for the national French competitive examinations, many of which would be at undergraduate or postgraduate university level in other systems. In these examinations not only is the syllabus common to all students but the number of candidates for each award is known and the percentage of students who will be successful is also known before the examinations take place. It is possible, then, when the results are published, to identify the CNEC candidates who studied by correspondence and assess them as a proportion of total candidates. CNEC students have consistently done better than average.

The DTUs, however, had an additional problem. In controlling their own academic standards, setting their own assessment procedures and awarding their own degrees, they have had to achieve parity of standards and convince others that they have done so. The use of a system of external examiners (e.g. at EU and the UKOU) both to assess the examination papers and the marking is one means by which DTUs in common with many conventional universities safeguard standards. In the end, however, what matters most is the institutions' record in enabling students to succeed in their examinations. Tables 11.4 and 11.5 show how the UKOU has met this challenge.

Table 11.4 : The number and proportion of UKOU students continuing from one year to the next

Year	Finally Enrolled Students	Students Enrolling for Next Year	%
1971	19,581	16,186	82.7
1972	31,902	25,744	80.7
1973	38,424	31,300	81.5
1974	42,636	34,528	81.0
1975	49,358	38,763	78.5
1976	50,994	40,251	78.9
1977	55,397	43,156	77.9
1978	58,778	45,725	77.8
1979	60,579	46,985	77.6
1980	61,007	45,558	74.7
1981	59,968	45,347	75.6

Source: UKOU Digest of Statistics/Statistical Bulletins

Table 11.5 : Graduation rates at the UKOU, 1971-81.

Cohort by year of entry	Number of finally registered under-graduate students in cohort	% in cohort graduating with BA (Open) as at 31.12.80	% in cohort still studying in 1981
1971	19,581	56.0	5.9
1972	15,719	50.0	8.2
1973	12,680	49.4	11.3
1974	11,336	46.0	15.5
1975	14,830	37.7	21.3
1976	12,231	29.9	32.3
1977	15,146	20.9	37.9
1978	15,662	11.1	45.1
1979	14,854	1.3	62.8
1980	14,022	–	76.2
1981	14,410	–	100.0

Note: While some of the students studying are working to obtain their BA degree, others have already graduated with a BA and are studying for a BA (Honours) degree.

Source: Academic Planning Office, UK Open University.

Cost-effectiveness

Distance teaching universities require quite complex organisational arrangements before a single student can be admitted. Apart from adminstrative functions, very considerable sums of money have to be invested in materials design, production and distribution, and in student and local support services. The precise level of cost incurred depends on choice of media, the level of local support services provided, and the sophistication of the administrative services (for example, data processing systems) underpinning the university.

These costs are incurred irrespective of student numbers and as such can be regarded as fixed or at least semi-variable in relation to the output of students. However, in general terms, once the structure is in existence, it can meet the needs of very large numbers of students.

While the 'fixed' or 'semi-variable' costs of the system tend to be higher than is the case in conventional universities, the variable or direct cost per student is usually much lower. This difference in the cost structure of distance and conventional educational institutions is well understood (Laidlaw and Layard, 1974). It means that in general conventional teaching systems are cheaper for low numbers of students, while distance teaching systems are cheaper for high numbers of students. The threshold at which the DTUs become economically more efficient (as measured by average student costs) than conventional systems depends both on the extent to which, firstly, the institution's fixed costs are higher than those of conventional institutions and, secondly, the variable costs per student are lower than those of conventional institutions using face-to-face teaching.

Specific comparisons between distance teaching and conventional universities in the same country have been made by Laidlaw and Layard (1974) and Wagner (1972, 1977) in respect of the UKOU and Rumble (1981a) in respect of UNED Costa Rica. An initial study by Collister et al. (1980) on the relative cost effectiveness of the AIOU showed that its average student costs were broadly on a par with those of conventional Pakistani universities. Laidlaw and Layard (1974: 455) showed that the threshold at which the UKOU became more efficient than the average campus-based British university, given 1972 levels of activity, was 21,691 students. Wagner (1977: 364) showed that the unit cost per student at the UKOU was about one third of that at the conventional universities and that the unit cost per graduate was about one half that of the campus based universities. Rumble (1981a) shows that the unit cost per student at UNED Costa Rica is lower than those of the three state-funded conventional universities, but that one of these conventional universities has a cost per credit enrolment which is on a par with that at UNED.

The studies indicate that distance teaching universities can be cost effective in comparison with conventional universities, but that this may not necessarily be the case. Their cost advantage can be undermined if:

1. The investment in media and materials is excessive, relative to the number of students in the system. Rumble (1981b) shows how the average costs at UNA are likely to rise as the number of courses expands without a corresponding increase in its student numbers.

2.   The direct student costs (or variable cost per student) is above or on a par with those at conventional universities - in which case the DTU will *never* achieve economies of scale relative to the conventional universities.

3.   The variable cost per student in a DTU is only marginally lower than that in a conventional university, since in this case the DTU will need proportionately more students if its average costs are to drop significantly below that of the conventional universities.

4.   The DTU can not attract sufficient students to warrant the investment in the development of its materials and systems.

These factors have important implications for the provision of face-to-face tuition. The more face-to-face tuition built into a distance teaching system, the nearer variable student costs will be to those found in conventional universities. Yet, if one considers that the quality of academic provision makes an extensive face-to-face element essential in a distance teaching university, then DTUs with relatively low student numbers (such as, for example, UNED Costa Rica and AU) may not be able both to improve the quality of their provision and retain their present level of cost-efficiency relative to conventional universities in their country or province.

Finally it should be said that, with the exception of the UKOU, none of the DTUs covered in this book have as yet proven their ability to produce graduates at an average unit cost significantly below that of conventional universities in their country. Whether they will be able to do so depends as much on drop-out and repetition rates as on the intrinsic costs of each system.

SYSTEMATIC SIMILARITIES BETWEEN THE DTUs

Superficially the systemic similarities of the DTUs are striking. A systems-based analysis of distance teaching systems has been provided by Rumble (1979: 60-62) and Kaye (1981: 19-22) following the application of ideas originally developed by Miller and Rice (1967).

Miller and Rice use the term *operating activities* to describe activities that directly contribute to the import, conversion and export processes

221

which are characteristic of open systems, and which define the nature of the enterprise and differentiate it from other enterprises. Two major *operating sub-systems* can be distinguished in DTUs:

1. The *courses sub system* is concerned with the design, production and distribution of teaching materials. The course design process converts academic ideas and teaching strategies into a prototype course using appropriate media for achieving defined curriculum objectives. It also defines the instruments of assessment which will be used to measure the students' learning. The course production process turns the prototype course into a finished product, either in the form of a single copy (e.g. a master tape) or in the form of multiple copies (e.g. books or cassettes). Distribution is the process which takes the product from its point of production to the point at which it is available for student use.

2. The *student sub system* is concerned with advertising academic programmes; admitting students and allocating them to courses, tutors, local centres and counsellors; collecting their fees; providing tutorial services (by correspondence or telephone or in face-to-face sessions); counselling; and assessing, examining and certificating students; and maintaining their records.

A third operating sub system, that of *research* may also be found in DTUs. It is not in itself integral to distance education. In addition, *logistical activities* procure and replenish the resources required in the institution (staff, equipment, consumables) and *regulatory activities* relate the various sub systems to each other, and the organisation to its environment through the activities of planning, control and evaluation; and determine policy.

All distance teaching universities can be analysed within this framework. They also tend to share certain characteristics, as follows:

*   A conscious and systematic approach to the design of learning materials for independent study.

*   The use of a wide range of media and other resources to teach, necessitating a variety of production and distribution systems appropriate to the media in use.

* Associated with the use of the various media, a marked role differentiation of staff (Rumble, 1981c: 189-90).

* The centralised design and production of materials, combined with localised learning.

* In a number of systems marked division of labour between those responsible for materials design and production on the one hand, and those responsible for tuition and assessment on the other.

* The provision of two-way communication between students and tutors who generally operate at a distance from the student (correspondence tuition, telephone tuition) but with the possibility of occasional meetings between students and tutors (face-to-face tuition) - thus imposing on the institutions a need to organise and control these channels to ensure both their effective and their efficient operation.

* The introduction into an academic community of a number of quasi-industrial processes which require appropriate management techniques and a hierarchical government structure of management and control which does not always relate easily to traditional foms of university governance (Rumble, 1981c: 179).

* Extensive and well defined administrative areas.

These similarities should not, however, hide the many differences, not only in objectives, but in choice and use of media, teaching strategies, rules regulating student progress and so on which are to be found in the DTUs and which arise in part from the aims of the institutions, but also from the very different settings and cultures within which they operate and from the different levels of human and financial resources which the institutions are able to call upon.

References

1. Bates, A.W. (1982) 'Trends in the use of A/V Media in Distance Education Systems around the World'. In 'Learning at a Distance. A World perspective', edited Daniel, J.S., Stroud, M.A. and Thompson, J. Edmonton: Athabasca University and International Council for Correspondence Education.

2. Collister, P. et al (1980) 'Mid-term Review of ODA's aid to Allama Iqbal Open University, Pakistan'. London: Overseas Development Administration.
3. Laidlaw, B. and Layard, R. (1974) 'Traditional versus Open University Teaching Methods: a cost comparison'. Higher Education, 3, 439-68
4. Kaye, A. (1981) 'Origins and structures'. In Kaye, A. and Rumble, G. (1981) 'Distance teaching for Higher and Adult Education'. London: Croom Helm.
5. Mackenzie, N., Postgate, R. and Scupham, J. (1975) 'Open Learning: Systems and Problems in Post-Secondary Education'. Paris: Unesco.
6. Miller, E.J., and Rice, A.K. (1967) 'Systems of organisation: The Control of Task and Sentient Boundaries'. London: Tavistock Publications.
7. Neil, M. (1981) 'Education of Adults at a Distance'. London: Kogan Page.
8. Open University Planning Committee (1969) 'The Open University'. London: HMSO.
9. Perry, W. (1976) 'Open University. A personal account by the first Vice-Chancellor'. Milton Keynes: Open University Press.
10. Perry, W. (1981) 'The growth of distance learning'. In Neil, M. (ed.) 'Education of Adults at a Distance'. London: Kogan Page.
11. Rumble, G. (1979) 'Planning for distance education'. In Hakemulder, J. (1980) 'Distance Education for Development'. Bonn: German Foundation for International Development.
12. Rumble, G. (1981a) 'The cost analysis of distance teaching. Costa Rica's Universidad Estatal a Distancia'. Higher Education, 10, 375-401.
13. Rumble, G. (1981b) 'The cost analysis of learning at a distance. Venezuela's Universidad Nacional Abierta', Distance Education, 3. In press.
14. Rumble, G. (1981c) 'Organisation and Decision-making'. In Kaye, A. and Rumble, G. (1981) 'Distance teaching for higher and adult education'. London: Croom Helm.
15. Schramm, W., Coombs, P., Kahnert, F., and Lyle, J. (1967) 'The New Media: Memo to Educational Planners'. Paris: Unesco.
16. Schwittmann, D. (1982) 'Time and learning in distance education'. Distance Education, 3,1. In press.
17. Smith, K.C. (1979) 'External Studies at New England - a Silver Jubilee Review 1955-1978'. Armidale: The University of New England.
18. University of the Air Advisory Committee (1966) 'A University of the Air'. London: HMSO, Cmnd. 2922.
19. Wagner, L. (1972) 'The economics of the Open University'. Higher Education, 2, 159-83.
20. Wagner, L. (1977) 'The economics of the Open University revisited'. Higher Education, 6, 359-81.
21. World Bank (International Bank for Reconstruction and Development) (1980) 'World Development Report, 1980'. Washington: IBRD.

Chapter 12

THE Dtus: AN APPRAISAL

Desmond Keegan and Greville Rumble

A FRAMEWORK FOR EVALUATION AND APPRAISAL

Effective contributions to a theory of evaluation for distance education systems have been provided by McIntosh (1975, 1977, 1978), Gooler (1979), Kemmis (1980), and Rumble (1981a).

For our purpose - the macro-evaluation of distance education systems - the approaches taken by Gooler and Rumble provide the most appropriate framework.

Gooler (1979: 46-50) has proposed the following criteria for the evaluation of distance education programmes:

* Access - particularly related to the extension of educational opportunities to new groups of people.
* Relevancy to national, local and individual needs.
* The quality of the programmes offered.
* The extent to which learners achieve (1) the goals set by the institution; (2) their own personal goals; and (3) unanticipated outcomes.
* Cost-effectiveness.
* The impact of the programmes on society, or on other programmes, institutions and individuals in respect of their goals, policies, strategies and behaviour.
* Generation of knowledge of, for example, the nature of adult learners and the use of new educational technologies.

Rumble (1981a: 71-79) advanced a model based on four 'tests':

* The response-time test (or the time taken to produce a graduate)
* The output:input ratio test (or the number of graduates as a proportion of the number of students admitted).
* The correctness of output test (relating the number and quality of graduates to the goals of the institution, the needs of society for educated manpower, the social demand for education, and the needs of disadvantaged sections of society).
* Cost-efficiency and cost-effectiveness measures.

Evaluation may be criterion-based or norm-based. Criterion-based evaluation requires that the qualitative and quantitative judgments derived from the act of evaluation be made in the context of an 'ideal' which has been defined and which can be used as a 'benchmark' against which actual performance can be compared. The standards used to define the 'ideal' and compare performance can be qualitative or quantitative. In both cases the standards should be derived from the purpose and objectives of the institution being evaluated, and hence as evaluation criteria ought not to have universal value.

Norm-based evaluation offers an alternative approach. The norms adopted to evaluate DTUs could relate to standards of performance found in (1) universities in general; (2) traditional universities; and (3) non-traditional universities. The very different cultural, social, political and economic environments in which DTUs operate makes it difficult to draw direct comparisons between them. Usually the comparison made is between the performance of traditional and non-traditional (distance teaching) universities operating in the same country. However, such an approach may overlook differences in the purpose, objectives, and operating conditions of traditional and non-traditional systems.

It is inherently difficult to specify ideal standards of performance, and we have not attempted to do so. In general, we have adopted a norm-based approach in which we compare the performance of the DTUs with that of conventional universities, taking into account the very different social, cultural, and economic environments operating in the countries concerned.

We have not been able to apply the evaluation strategies proposed by Gooler and Rumble rigorously, although they have influenced our approach. This is because the DTUs are relatively recent foundations, and in many cases published data on their performance is scarce or not available. We have been unable to avoid a bias towards the UKOU, for the simple reason that it is the DTU about which most is known, but it can not be assumed that what is true of the UKOU is also likely to be the case for the other DTUs.

Overall, the best we can offer is an initial *appraisal* of the performance of the DTUs since their establishment in the 1970s.

To satisfy those anxious to determine the relative success of the DTUs and the extent to which the investment of public funds has been justified, such an appraisal must attempt to establish

* The 'quantity' of the learning achieved.
* The 'quality' of the learning achieved.

226

* The 'status' of the learning achieved.
* The relative cost of the learning achieved.

THE QUANTITY OF THE LEARNING ACHIEVED

Under this heading we are concerned with:
* The success of the DTUs in widening access, not just in terms of absolute numbers, but in attracting specific target groups.
* Drop-outs
* The quantity of the output relative to the input (the output: input ratio).
* The time it takes to produce the output.
* The DTUs' success in satisfying national, local and individual needs.

The success of the DTUs in widening access

To evaluate the extent to which the DTUs are widening access to higher education, one needs to consider both whether they are meeting social demand, and the extent to which they are equalising educational opportunities for previously deprived groups.

At the simplest level, it is clear that they are meeting a need in so far as students freely enrol on their courses. Thus in 1981 the CCTU had 417,000 students, the UKOU had nearly 86,000, and the FeU over 36,000, although not all the DTUs have so many students: UNED Costa Rica is quite small. It is also clear that many of their students could not study by any other means, so one can conclude that the DTUs are in general widening access to educational opportunities, and meeting *individual* needs. There are also indications that at least one of them (the UKOU) appears to be "providing a second chance to people who are already socially mobile and have already aspired to non-manual jobs mainly through the acquisition of educational qualifications", and is enabling the 'middle class' descendants of 'working class' parents "to secure and legitimate this mobility" (Woolfe, 1977: 80). To this extent the DTUs are clearly increasing and to some extent equalising opportunities for access to higher education. However, this is of limited benefit if the 'open' door is also a 'revolving' door through which ill prepared students pass only to re-emerge as drop-outs.

227

Drop-outs

Distance education systems have frequently been criticised on the grounds that their drop-out rates are unacceptably high.

Comparisons with drop-out at conventional universities are usually made on the basis of the performance of full-time students, many of whom may be in residence at the university. Little data is available on part-time university students attending face-to-face lectures and tutorials, many of whom maintain a position in the nation's workforce. It is with the latter group that more fruitful comparisons with students at the DTUs might be made.

It is also clear that any comparisons must take into account the norms applying in a particular country. Although drop-out is an acknowledged problem for DTUs, the fact remains that it can also be very serious in conventional universities. In his study of UNED Spain James points out that from 50 to 70 percent of conventional Spanish university students desert in the first one or two years of their course.

In Costa Rica a study of student progress at the conventional universities (CONARE, 1980) showed that, out of 316 students who entered the University of Costa Rica in 1971, 82 (25.9 percent) had graduated by the first semester of 1978; 77 (24.4 percent) were still studying; and 182 (57.6 percent) had dropped out. At the National University, the situation was even worse. Of 257 students who entered in 1975, 176 (68.5 percent) had dropped out by the first semester of 1978; 52 (20.2 percent) were still studying; and 29 (11.3 percent) had graduated.

Direct comparison of drop-out between conventional and distance teaching universities may be misleading. The fact that only about 6 in 10 of each UKOU cohort are likely to get a degree, and that this is a lower success rate than that found in conventional British universities, needs to be balanced against (1) the differences between UKOU and conventional British university students, and (2) the effect of the UKOU's open admissions policy compared with those of highly selective conventional British universities. By the end of 1978, over 60 percent of the *qualified* students (that is, students with at least the normal minimum university entry qualification) in the UKOU's first cohort had obtained a degree, but 40 percent of the *unqualified* students had also done so (McIntosh, Woodley and Morrison, 1980: 51-55). The success of the unqualified students represents a real achievement in equalising educational opportunities.

That concern about drop-out is real is shown in the evidence pre-sented in a number of the case studies (e.g. UNED Costa Rica, the AIOU, and UNA), and Bååth (1982: 2) has recently provided an extensive listing of research projects which deal with drop-out in distance education. However, drop-out has not always been as severe a problem as anticipated.

The proposal for a 'University of the Air' led the British *Times Educational Supplement* to comment in its leader of the 4 March 1966: "What would happen in a university of the air? The numbers attracted to it would certainly be out of all proportion to the numbers that stayed in the course. Can we really afford the fantastic cost that this would entail?" But, after ten years experience, drop-out has not been anything like as high as suggested by early critics of the UKOU. Sewart (1981: 12) has claimed that success in reducing avoidable drop-out to an acceptable minimum has been one of the achievements of the first decade of the UKOU. He attributes the success to a cohesive balance between distance teaching (development of high quality learning materials) and distance learning (comprehensive support for student learning from the materials provided). On the other hand, the UKOU is by no means complacent about the number of students who do drop-out, and it, in common with DTUs like the AIOU and UNED Costa Rica (which have more severe problems), is seeking to find ways of reducing the loss of students.

It appears that DTUs can reduce the problem of drop-out to accept-able levels, provided they establish a cohesive system. The characteristics of this cohesiveness are the correct pedagogical structuring of learning materials combined with extensive provision of student support services. There may also be a correlation between rather rigidly paced systems and unusually low drop-out rates (Daniel and Stroud, 1981: 157).

The output:input ratio

With the notable exception of the UKOU, which by the end of 1981 had produced over 50,000 graduates, none of the DTUs had large numbers of graduates. The FeU had produced 66, AU only 29, though UNED Spain had 982 graduates by the end of 1979. In view of this it is not possible to draw any conclusions about the success of the DTUs as a whole in this area.

At the UKOU no fewer than 56 percent of the first (1971) cohort have graduated (1982) with their BA (Open) degree, and a number are still studying. Table 11.5 provides further data on graduation rates at the UKOU.

However, the success of the DTUs can not be measured only in terms of their output of graduates. Not all their programmes lead to a degree level qualification, nor do all their students want to take a degree or even sit an end of course examination. Their success also needs to be judged in the light of an assessment of students' aims and achievements. Success for the individual student may involve 'intangible' and unmeasurable qualities such as increased knowledge, greater fulfilment, improved powers of reasoning and expression, and greater self-confidence. Such benefits are not to be dismissed. On the other hand, it is also the case that taxpayers' funds are not to be allocated lightly to such benefits in preference to conventional education.

The time it takes to produce a graduate

Another indicator of relative effectiveness is the time it takes to produce a graduate at a DTU, compared with the time it takes at a conventional university. Because the UKOU is the only DTU to have produced substantial numbers of graduates, it is the only one which can be evaluated on these grounds.

Over one in three of the present graduates of the UKOU's first cohort of students graduated after three years of study, and over 6 in 10 of them graduated after four years of study. These figures can be compared with the three or four years which are required to graduate as a result of a full-time course at a conventional British university. These figures are somewhat misleading because no distinction is made between UKOU students with advanced standing or credit exemptions, and those without; and only UKOU BA degree graduates, and not those graduating with Honours (which would require a minimum additional year of study) are considered. Nearly 4 in 10 of the students in the first cohort took longer than 3 or 4 years to graduate. While this reflects the part-time nature of their study, it also suggests that at least in Britain, producing graduates by means of a DTU is less efficient *in time* than is the case if students studied full-time at a conventional university.

However, similar findings may not apply in other countries. In conventional Latin American universities the actual time taken by a student to complete his course is invariably longer than the time scheduled - in some faculties more than double. This is because conventional university students frequently only attend part-time (Hennessy, 1979: 152), so that the difference between distance and conventional study found in Britain is unlikely to apply.

The DTUs' success in satisfying national, local and individual needs

Some of the DTUs reflect, in their academic programmes, perceptions about the manpower needs of their countries (e.g. UNA, UNED Costa Rica, AIOU). The extent to which these *national needs* are being met is difficult to judge. If success is measured by the number of professionally-trained graduates emerging from the DTUs who find employment in a job appropriate to their qualifications, then the DTUs have yet to prove themselves.

The DTU with the most graduates (the UKOU) does not set out to produce professionally-trained graduates (although some of them do gain professional recognition of their studies). Escotet (1978: 76-77) believes that the failure of the UKOU to produce professional graduates is its greatest weakness. In this respect there is a distinct difference in approach between those DTUs which aim to produce professionals to meet the manpower needs of a country and those adopting a more liberal-arts tradition.

Even if one could show that the DTUs were turning out graduates with professional qualifications, one would still need to show that these were in fact meeting the needs of employers and the nation. This would depend in part on the extent to which the graduates began to work in areas appropriate to their training; in part on the extent to which the DTUs were providing graduates in sufficient numbers to meet demand (without over-producing them); and in part on the quality of the graduates. We examine some of the evidence on quality below, but it is too early to judge the success of the DTUs in meeting national needs in quantitative terms.

The extent to which the DTUs are satisfying *individual needs* is also difficult to evaluate in specific terms, although it is clear from research at the UKOU, UNED Spain, and AU, that students find the flexibility of studying independently and at a distance an attraction. The fact that students do enrol and complete their programmes (whether it be a single course or a whole degree programme) must be taken as an indication that the DTUs are satisfying individual needs.

THE QUALITY OF THE LEARNING ACHIEVED

We are concerned here with:
* The quality of the learning materials provided by the DTUs.
* The extent to which distance teaching is a suitable vehicle for educating students in certain subjects.
* The extent to which the DTUs provide education as opposed to instruction.
* The effectiveness of learning at a distance.
* The 'intersubjectivity' of learning at a distance.

The quality of the learning materials provided by the DTUs

The quality of the instructional material provided by many of the DTUs (FeU, UKOU, UNED Spain) is generally recognised to be high. Paradoxically, this has led some critics to argue that distance teaching is over-structured and that the student runs the risk of being turned into a passive consumer of "educational commodities - such as packets of knowledge and educational certificates" (Harris, 1976: 44). One can accept that the high cost of designing quality, standardised, mass-produced learning materials makes it difficult to meet the diversity of interests of large groups of adult students. However, there is evidence that some of the DTUs (e.g. the UKOU) are becoming more interested in personalised 'contract-learning' approaches which enable students to choose a project, either from a list provided or of their own devising, and work alone, with a tutor acting as the student's mentor.

One indication of the quality of the learning materials provided by the DTUs is the extent to which they are used by conventional educational institutions and their students.

In the United Kingdom, Moss and Brew (1981) sent a questionnaire to staff in three British institutions of higher education (University College Cardiff, Bristol Polytechnic, and the University of Essex) to determine the degree of familiarity of those staff with UKOU materials, the extent of use of such materials, and the influence of the Open University on teaching ideas and strategies. They showed about eighty percent of conventional higher education staff in those three institutions have had some contact with Open University texts and television programmes, while about 60 percent had listened to some of the radio programmes. Less than half the staff recommended Open University course texts, and ten percent or less of conventional lecturers made direct use of its texts.

Although direct use of materials is not that extensive, there are signs that the DTUs are becoming major educational publishers in their own countries (e.g. UNED in Costa Rica), and there is some evidence that their texts are being bought on the open market by students studying at conventional universities (e.g. in Pakistan).

The extent to which distance teaching is a suitable vehicle for educating students in certain subjects

Those who regard face-to-face teaching as an integral part of higher education often find it difficult to accept distance education at university level.

There are, of course, problems. Holmberg (1981:14) discusses, in relation to an analysis of Bloom's taxonomy, which subjects in the affective, cognitive and psycho-motor domain can and which can not be readily taught at a distance. Some psycho-motor objectives such as surgery or the capacity to handle dangerous chemicals and machinery do not lend themselves to distance study. This appears to be a particular limitation in certain subject areas, but on the whole most subjects can be taught by distance means. Indeed, the effectiveness of distance study as a means of acquiring intellectual knowledge is generally accepted.

Most criticism of distance education focuses on its effectiveness in the affective domain, which is concerned with values, attitudes and beliefs that are 'caught' rather than 'taught'. Many people argue that they can only be 'caught' in a social context, and that this element is not provided in distance teaching systems. Sparkes (1979: 9), however, believes that "teaching in the affective domain requires a form of communication with a strong appeal to the emotions". He cites television, radio, novels and drama as particularly sucessful in this respect. If so, then it follows that distance teaching materials which teach in the affective domain can be created.

Indeed, it is the potential to make use of a variety of complementary communication channels which distinguish distance teaching systems and enable students to obtain a full understanding of a subject and the vocabulary it uses. Sparkes (1979:11) holds that the "key to any academic subject . . . is the vocabulary it uses". In order to achieve a full academic understanding of the subject jargon, one needs to (1) analyse each concept into its *content* (i.e. its component parts); (2) explore its *properties* and *implications*; and (3) establish its setting in the *context* of other concepts and experiences. To do this one requires a rich and varied form of teaching. Sparkes lists, as examples, "print and audiovision for analysis of content, television for context, home kits for synthesis, teleconferencing for tutorials" (Sparkes, 1979: 12).

However, even granted that one can teach at a distance in the affective domain, this still does not fully answer those critics who argue the necessity of having face-to-face contact and a socialising environment.

The extent to which the DTUs provide education as opposed to instruction

Escotet (1980: 11-12, 15-17) examines the DTUs and finds them deficient in the provision of social and cultural learning. He claims that in general these systems have failed to establish a real and permanent contact between the student and the lecturer or professor. He characterises the DTUs as providers of *distance instruction* (the transfer of information) but distinguishes this from *distance education* (which implies a social and cultural contact), and goes as far as querying the possibility of distance education at university level.

Carnoy and Levin (1975: 396) argue that much of the value of a university education is captured in its 'socialization content' and not by the examination per se and that "the average university student receives not only instruction and instructional materials" but "substantially more tutorial services, contact with fellow students, access to libraries, computers and campus lectures than does his (UK) Open University counterpart". They suggest that as a result the quality of the education of institutions like the UKOU may be substantially less.

The effectiveness of learning at a distance

Birkbeck College, London, is one of the constituent colleges of the University of London but differs from others in that it caters exclusively for mature evening class students taking a wide range of subjects in the arts and sciences. Bernard Crick, Professor of Politics at the College, believes that "the (UK) OU system . . . for all the great demand and its skilled response, is not as effective or as rewarding as face-to-face teaching" (Crick, 1982). He would like to see conventional British universities being more responsive to the needs of mature part-time students through, for example, an expansion of evening class provision.

The 'intersubjectivity' of learning at a distance

Educationalists like R.S. Peters, who see learning in terms of "intersubjectivity" of teacher and learner, would seem to have difficulty in admitting the quality of education at a distance:

> At the culminating stages of education there is little distinction
> between teacher and taught: they are both participating in the
> shared experience of exploring a common world. The teacher
> is simply more familiar with its contours and more skilled in
> handling the tools for laying bare its mysteries and appraising
> its nuances. Occasionally in a tutorial this exploration takes
> the form of a dialogue. But more usually it is a group
> experience (Peters, 1973: 100).

The arguments put forward by Escotet, Carnoy and Levin, and Crick, and implied by Peters, are fundamental to any appreciation of the quality of distance education. Yet a major factor in the success of the DTUs has been the extent to which they have achieved a balance between the learning activities the student carries out independently and those which involve contact with other students and tutors. Most of the DTUs place considerable emphasis on the need to provide students with a chance to interact with tutors and other students. For this reason all of them provide local study centres and most of them actively encourage the students to attend these. At the UKOU, students on certain courses are required to attend residential schools. A number of DTUs help to arrange student self-help groups (e.g. UKOU, UNA). Some of them make arrangements for students to contact tutors by telephone (e.g. UNED Spain, UNED Costa Rica, UKOU), while AU goes as far as having a toll free telephone service for students. The UKOU helps to fund the Open University Students' Association. In the process, the DTUs provide an environment for socialization without debarring the independent learner. However, there is a limit to what can be done without undermining the cost advantage of the DTUs and reducing students' freedom and flexibility.

THE STATUS OF THE LEARNING ACHIEVED

Clearly arguments about the quality of the learning achieved have a bearing on its status. If one believes that the quality of distance education is not as good as that of conventional education, then one will not accord it as much status.

Indications of the status accorded the learning achieved by distance students come from:

*   The extent to which other educational institutions recognise the studies for credit transfer purposes.
*   The acceptance of the degrees and diplomas awarded as qualifying students to go on to higher level studies.
*   The recognition of the awards by employers.
*   The esteem in which the distance teaching institutions and their awards are held in the community at large.

The extent to which other educational institutions recognise the studies for credit transfer purposes

A number of DTUs (e.g. AU, FeU, UKOU) have credit transfer agreements with other universities in their countries. This is a sign of their acceptance by the educational community.

The acceptance of the degrees and diplomas awarded as qualifying students to go on to higher level studies

In some countries, first degrees awarded by a DTU are recognised as suitable qualifications for progress to a postgraduate course - a sure indication that their quality is accepted. Swift (1980) reported that a large number of UKOU students have gone on to do research degrees (1,723), taught masters degrees (2,781), professional diplomas and certificates (1,722) and academic diplomas and certificates (492), thus indicating the general acceptability of the UKOU's degree as a passport to professional training and postgraduate work. However, although the BA (Open) has won acceptance as a qualification for postgraduate study in a suitable discipline in conventional British universities, the same is not necessarily true elsewhere.

The recognition of the awards by employers

The UKOU has done some research on the status of its degree in the eyes of employers. McIntosh and Rigg (1979: 1) show that about half of a sample group of employers regarded the UKOU degree as equivalent to one from other universities. While very few felt it was better, a sizeable minority, around 20 percent, said it was not as good. A matter of more concern is the fact that as many as one-third of employers supporting UKOU students by paying some of their fees and nearly one-quarter of those not doing this stated that they did not know.

Those employers who thought the degree was not as good based their view "primarily on the grounds that (1) the degree is not obtained in an intellectual or academic environment" (35 percent); (2) the "older universities are better because they are older and have longer traditions of excellence etc." (31 percent); and (3) the degree is modular and "not the outcome of a period of concentrated study" (25 percent). Those who thought the UKOU degree is comparable in standards to other degrees cited similarity of academic standards (more than half the respondents), comparability of exam standards (23 percent) and syllabi (18 percent), and the better personal attributes and motivation of UKOU students (10 percent) (McIntosh and Rigg, 1979: 2-4).

Another indication of the acceptability of awards made by the DTUs is the extent to which graduates of the DTUs succeed in obtaining well-paid jobs. This is clearly related to general economic conditions and the demand for graduates with particular qualifications, factors which also affect demand for graduates from conventional universities. Another factor is that many distance students already have jobs, so their motivations are likely to be somewhat different to those of students at conventional universities.

At the UKOU, Swift (1980) found that the majority of graduates (83 percent) were in full-time employment on entry. Less than half of them (45 percent) were specifically interested in one or more of the following 'job-related' benefits when they first entered the University: promotion, better pay, or a new occupation. However, the experience of studying encouraged almost two in three of them to try for better pay, promotion or a change of job. Overall Swift found that 38 percent of graduates benefitted solely because of their UKOU qualification,

16 percent indicated that the degree had helped their progress, 15 percent said that they had made progress independently of their qualification, and 31 percent reported no change in their circumstances. Apart from any effects on their career, 71 percent reported that their studies had helped them improve their job skills and their ability to perform their work.

The esteem in which the DTUs and their awards are held in the community at large

There are signs that the DTUs are being accepted by the wider community within which they subsist. In Britain, the presence of UKOU academic staff on government consultancy and advisory bodies; the use of its texts by the general public and on the reading lists of conventional universities; and the attraction of substantial research grants, shows a remarkable integration of this university into the political and educational life of the country.

It is clear that attitudes towards institutions such as the UKOU are less sceptical now than they were when these institutions were being planned.

In general, however, degrees gained at a distance share the fragility of all non-traditional educational programmes - a fact which can be attributed in large part to the innate conservatism of the academic community in general and of educational administrators in particular. While the degree of acceptance varies from country to country, much remains to be done to change the image of non-traditional university degrees both with the community at large and employers in particular. As the graduates of the universities studied in this book come on the marketplace in increasing numbers in the 1980s, their success in 'selling' their qualifications will be keenly observed.

THE RELATIVE COST OF THE LEARNING ACHIEVED

We are concerned here with:
* The cost-efficiency of DTUs relative to conventional universities or to other modes of internal operation which the DTUs could adopt. The more cost-efficient system is the one that is the cheapest means of accomplishing a defined objective, or

which provides maximum value for a given level of expenditure. The assumption here is that the quality of the output is
the same.

* The cost-effectiveness of DTUs relative to conventional
universities. The concept of cost-effectiveness tries to weigh
the relative value of the outputs in qualitative terms.

* The cost benefits of distance and traditional university edu-
cations, in which the costs of the education provided and the
benefits (direct and indirect, financial and social) to the
individual and society are taken into account.

* The opportunity cost of education at a distance.

The cost-efficiency of DTUs relative to conventional universities

Most of the economic studies of DTUs have in fact been studies in
cost-efficiency. They have assumed that the quality of the output
(graduates) from conventional and distance teaching universities is the
same, and have argued that on these grounds distance teaching universities, if they are not already more cost-efficient than conventional
universities operating in the same country (e.g. UKOU), at least have
the potential to be so (e.g. AU, UNED Costa Rica, AIOU) because the
cost structure of distance teaching favours the achievement of economies of scale. The fact that some DTUs would appear to have rising
average student costs (e.g. UNA) does not invalidate the general propo-
sition that DTUs can be more cost-efficient.

The evidence for these statements is summarised in chapter 11 and
does not need to be repeated here. However, critics have argued that
economic studies of the DTUs have very often failed to identify the
true costs of a system because cost-calculations are based on the university's budget and ignore the value of contributed inputs, thus hiding
the true cost of the system. This point is forcibly made by Carnoy and
Levin (1975: 388-9, 395) in respect of a cost study of the UKOU by
Lumsden and Ritchie (1975).

Another point is made by Mace (1978: 305) who asks whether the
UKOU could be more cost-efficient if it changed its internal practices.
"It is a singularly pointless exercise to compare the relative efficiencies
of two systems for producing graduates (external efficiency) and not
consider the internal economies or diseconomies operating within the
system (internal efficiency)". Mace points out that studies of the

internal efficiency of the UKOU have never been published so one is not in a position to judge whether or not the cost-efficiency of the UKOU could be raised, although he believes there is evidence to suggest that it could be (ibid., 308).

The cost-effectiveness of DTUs relative to conventional universities

Economic studies of DTUs have tended to assume that the quality of a distance-taught graduate is the same as one from a conventional university. Although there are indications that the graduates of some DTUs (e.g. FeU, UKOU) are accepted as such, Carnoy and Levin (1975:390) argue that "to assume that the value of an Open University degree will be similar to one from Oxbridge or the 'Red Bricks' . . . simply ignores the credentialing effect of higher education institutions".

We have discussed above some of the factors bearing on judgements about the quality of distance education. The real problem in *cost-effectiveness* calculations is to measure quality and then place a value on it. Moreover, when one is measuring quality, one needs to consider not only the quality of the output (graduate), but also the value-added to the student as a result of his studies. While the problem of measuring the 'quality added' to a student is simplified if all the universities being compared have similar entry requirements for students, there is an added complication in the case of DTUs which have open entry systems (AU, EU, UKOU) in comparing the standard of their entrants with conventional university entrants, while the quality of mature entrants will reflect 'life-experience' as well as academic qualifications.

The cost benefits of distance and traditional university educations

If it were true that the quality of the degree gained at a DTU is not as high as that gained at a conventional university, then it could follow that the benefits to the student of having the degree, or to society of educating him, are likely to be less.

Cost-benefit analyses of education usually concentrate on the 'age-earnings profiles' of workers with different levels of education, and try to assess the financial benefits of the education against which is offset (1) the private costs of studying (e.g. expenditure on fees, books, travel, etc.) and the opportunity cost of students' time as measured by earnings foregone, and (2) the social costs of education (including expenditure on educational institutions and the opportunity cost of students' time, once again measured by income foregone, as a proxy measure for the production foregone by society when students continue their education rather than join the labour market). The costs and benefits are expressed in terms of their present value by using discounted cash flow techniques (Woodhall, 1972: 35-8).

The cost benefit approach to education has its advocates and critics, the real difference between them being over whether or not it is possible to separate out the effects of education and other factors (e.g. ability, social class) on earnings.

Mace (1978: 300) has pointed out that the average age of UKOU graduates (37 years) is much higher than those from conventional British universities (22 years). He notes that "labour market studies suggest that by age 37 most people are established in their jobs" and that this inhibits their mobility. In addition, UKOU graduates will have a shorter earning period in which to reap the benefit of their degree, and hence "the economic benefits of an OU degree will be below those of a (conventional university) degree". He therefore challenges the assumption by Wagner (1977. 379-80) that one of the principal resource costs of conventional university undergraduates is foregone earnings, while the foregone earnings of UKOU students are virtually zero, and that as a result the resource cost per UKOU student is significantly less than that of conventional university students.

The opportunity cost of education at a distance

Strictly speaking, the cost of education is not the money that is spent on it each year but the real resources that are devoted to it and are therefore not available for allocation to any other economic activity (Woodhall, 1972: 23). The *opportunity cost* of education for the individual needs to take into account the cost of earnings foregone (in the case of students who cannot work full-time because of their studies) or of leisure foregone (particularly in the case of part-time students who also have a full-time job).

However, there is the additional point of the opportunity cost to society. One of the most important practical questions here is whether or not the resources spent on DTUs could be better spent on conventional universities. If the conventional universities cannot do the job of the DTUs (for example, educating dispersed student populations who cannot attend a campus), and if this is judged to be a worthwhile use of the resources, then the question does not arise. Such judgements, however, reflect values which are affected not least by the prevailing economic and political climate and the ready availability of resources. If it is thought that the money could be better spent on other activities, then the whole project will be brought into question.

OVERALL ASSESSMENT

We cannot pretend that all the questions raised in the preceding sections have been answered satisfactorily. However, we believe that in general the DTUs have shown that:

* They enable new target groups who cannot attend a conventional university to enter the higher education sector.
* They can solve the problem of drop-out and produce graduates in significant numbers.
* They can help meet national, local and individual needs.
* The quality of their learning materials can be very high.
* They are potentially more cost-efficient and cost-effective than conventional universities.
* Cost-benefit analysis will tend to favour the DTUs because students are able to study at the same time as they are earning and contributing to GNP.
* Their degrees are gaining acceptance from conventional universities, employers, and the community at large.

There seems to be growing evidence that in an educational system, if the learner is separated quasi-permanently from the learning group and from the teacher throughout the length of the learning process, then:

* The quality of the learning is affected.
* The quantity of the learning is affected (because of increased drop-out) and usually harmed, unless one takes careful precautions (as, for example, in the 'consultation model' found in the German Democratic Republic; the 'integrated system' found at the University of New England; and the student support services provided by the UKOU).
* The status of the learning is affected.
* The cost of the learning is changed, and usually made cheaper and hence more cost-efficient (though not necessarily more

cost-effective if the quality is debased as a result).

It is, we suspect, precisely for these reasons that so many distance teaching systems (including those operating at university level) place considerable emphasis on face-to-face tuition and learning groups.

CONCLUSION

This book has chronicled the emergence of new university structures in the decade 1971-1981, and has offered an interim appraisal of their performance in their early years.

As the DTUs enter their 'second decade' there are three questions of vital importance to any student of the evolution of higher education structures which require consideration. These are:

* Will the DTUs survive?
* Are they really necessary?
* Are they genuinely universities?

Will the DTUs survive?

All non-traditional educational structures are characterised by fragility. They are particularly vulnerable in periods of economic recession. Indeed the harsh economic climate of the late 1970s and early 1980s have already swept away a number of the non-traditional educational structures that emerged in the 1960s and 1970s.

When they were established, many of the DTUs faced "profound scepticism garnished with ridicule and hostility" (Open University, 1972: 117). They have collectively survived changes in government which threatened their early existence (UKOU), an uncertain start as a pilot project (AU), and the threat (FeU) and the firm proposal (AU) to move their headquarters.

Now, in the 1980s, there are signs of resilience, a developing sense of identity, and an air of permanence about them. More DTUs have recently been established (in Holland and Japan), and others (in Portugal, Denmark, and Finland) are under consideration. We are confident that the DTUs have a permanent place as providers of university education in the future.

Are the DTUs really necessary?

Given the widespread and far older tradition of providing university level distance education through the distance teaching wing of a

243

conventional university, one can ask whether or not a system of mixed models would be better.

There are, in fact, arguments of both an administrative and a didactic character that strongly support the establishment of DTUs.

Lord Perry, first Vice-Chancellor of the UKOU, claimed that the UKOU's success could never have been achieved by a distance department based within the administrative structure of a conventional university. He was convinced that the establishment of the UKOU as a new, autonomous, and independent university allowed it to "experiment with new patterns of teaching with a freedom that would be impossible to achieve in established universities" (Perry, 1976: 55), while the idea that the other British universities would in 1969 have acted in concert to extend higher educational opportunities on a part-time basis to adults was wholly unrealistic (Perry, 1976: 5).

Daniel and Smith (1979: 64), writing about the foundation of AU and the Télé-université in Quebec, apply Perry's view to argue the need for institutional autonomy:

> Perry suggests that, in order to flourish, an open university operation requires a high degree of institutional autonomy. This is because an open university, whilst it may share with other universities the fundamental missions of teaching, research and public service, undertakes this mission in an entirely different manner. The new teaching/learning system on which an open university is based has repercussions on every other aspect of the operation, from governance, management and leadership to the work of the faculty and the design of physical plant.

There must always be a fear that a mixed institution teaches on-campus students less well because of the diversion of some of its energies to external students, and teaches the latter less well because of the dominating presence of on-campus students.

Educationalists like Professor Otto Peters (1973: 310), the foundation Vice-Chancellor of the FeU, who stress the fundamental differences in didactic structures between conventional education and education at a distance, are likely to favour an institutional separation of the two forms of instruction. Peters' theoretical analysis of distance education led him to conclude that:

> Anyone professionally involved in education is compelled to presume the existence of *two* forms of instruction which are strictly separable: traditional face-to-face teaching based on interpersonal communication and industrialised teaching at a distance, which is based on an objectivised, rationalised, technologically-produced interaction (Peters, 1973: 310).

If Peters is right, there are powerful reasons for regarding distance systems as specifically distinct from conventional ones.

The long record of success of certain institutions teaching solely at a distance, such as the French Centre National d'Enseignement par Correspondance (formerly the Centre National de Télé-enseignement), shows that - provided certain pre-requisites are met - there is no need to mix the two approaches.

While there are many who believe that the two approaches are so similar that mixed provision is both natural and mutually beneficial, we believe that:

* Autonomous DTUs are generally more advantageous for (1) external students, in that they are wholly dedicated to their needs, and (2) the nation, in they they can more readily respond to national needs which can only be met by distance means.

* Autonomous DTUs more readily cater for the needs of distant students to the extent that there are marked differences between them and students in conventional systems.

* Autonomous DTUs are administratively more efficient given the requisite volume of students.

* There is less likelihood of competition between DTUs because, by their very nature, they are costly to establish and hence there is unlikely to be more than one of them in all but the very largest countries. This conclusion ties in with Otto Peters' forecast in the late 1960s that, if DTUs were founded, they would be industrialised organisations with monopolistic tendencies.

* The costs associated with the establishment of an infrastructure for a DTU and the preparation of sufficient course materials to support a degree programme are high, and require a guaranteed annual volume of student enrolments if the system is to be cost-efficient. If sufficient numbers of students can not be

  guaranteed, a mixed system is preferable.

* The number of students at which an autonomous DTU becomes more efficient than a mixed-mode institution depends
on the choice of media, the extent of the student support
services, and the number of courses on offer, as well as the
costs of conventional university education in the country
concerned. It lies at least in the range of 9,000 to 22,000
enrolments a year. We base this conclusion on evidence that
the UKOU became more cost-efficient than conventional
universities with 21,700 students (Laidlaw and Layard, 1974:
455); that with about 10,000 students, AU is broadly cost-
efficient with conventional universities in Alberta, Canada;
and, (based on Rumble, 1981b), that UNED Costa Rica could
meet its academic plans up to 1985 and have an average
student cost similar to that of the most cost-efficient conventional university in Costa Rica, provided it has about 9,400
student enrolments annually.

Are the DTUs genuinely universities?

We believe that the DTUs are generally recognised to be genuine universities of equal status to conventional ones. This is shown by, for
example, reciprocal arrangements between distance teaching and
conventional universities for credit transfer (e.g. FeU, UKOU); and the
fact that the chief executive officers of many of them are members of
the national committees of heads of universities (as at the FeU, UNED
Costa Rica, UNED Spain, and the UKOU).

There are those who believe that some of the DTUs have failed to
achieve full university status because of their concentration on general
as opposed to specialised degrees, and the diversion of resources into
continuing education.

Many of the DTUs (EU, UKOU, AU, AIOU) offer non-degree level
programmes. This has much in common with the American approach
towards the broadening of the curriculum - a marked feature of universities in the USA. Carried too far, such dilution must bring in question the
extent to which an institution is a *university* as opposed to a multi-
level distance education college (as at the Open Learning Institute in
British Columbia). However, we do not wish to preclude the possibility
of DTUs offering programmes at sub-degree level provided, at the same

time, they can demonstrate that the quality of their degrees are comparable with, if not better than, those of traditional universities offering similar degrees in the same country.

A SIGN OF THINGS TO COME

The success of the UKOU, and not least the discovery that even with an intake of 25,000 it could only accommodate about half the students wanting to enter it in 1971, had an immediate worldwide impact on educationalists and educational policy makers:

> A revolution in education was proclaimed with appropriate hyperbole, buses were rented to cope with the international jetset of academic pilgrims descending on Milton Keynes to watch the OU campus rising from the mud and governments of many political hues, noting an open university to be the educational equivalent to an airline in terms of international status, sponsored similar projects for the people (Daniel and Stroud, 1981: 147).

In the 1980s little of this attitude remains. Educational planners and governments are more realistic and more cost-conscious, and they want to know what they are getting for their money.

As we have indicated, we believe that the DTUs have a permanent place as future providers of university level education. We do not believe that they are universal panaceas for the problems of higher education, although we think that they can be successful. A product of adult demand for access to university-level education, they are well suited to their purpose, providing adults with materials of excellent standard which can be studied flexibly and, if necessary, independently at the higher education level. Most of them have gone even further. Given the potential of their teaching systems, they have embraced the concept of community service to provide materials at various educational levels. In so doing, they are recognising not just the potential of their systems as vehicles for educational provision, but the diverse needs of their adult clienteles.

At the present moment, the DTUs are largely print-based, although they are exploiting other media. As new technologies (satellite broadcasting, cable television, cassettes, and interactive computer terminals) are developed and introduced at reasonable price levels, so the DTUs will, we believe, take advantage of them. They will do so because they are already pre-disposed to do so. In the long run, we see them utilising electronic means of communication to provide individualised educational systems capable of giving rapid feedback to persons who are a part of dispersed, heterogeneous student populations.

To some extent, this is already happening, but we believe the next one or two decades will see technological advances which will enable the DTUs to develop the full potential of their systems. In the forseeable future they may become as responsive to the needs of adults facing the problems of a lifetime of rapid technological and social change in the twentyfirst century as the universities of the nineteenth century and early twentieth century were in educating young adults to meet the challenges of industrial society.

References

1. Bååth, J. (1982) 'Distance students learning - empirical findings and theoretical deliberations'. Distance Education, 3,1. In press.
2. CONARE (1980) 'Evaluación 'ex post facto' Proyecto Educación Superior/ BID (No. 2)'. San Jose: CONARE, OPES 03/80.
3. Carnoy, M. and Levin, H.M. (1975) 'Evaluation of Educational Media: some issues'. Instructional Science, 4, 385-406.
4. Crick, B. (1982) 'The system that learned nothing'. The Guardian, 1 March 1982, 7.
5. Daniel, J.S. and Smith W.A.S. (1979) 'Opening Open Universities: The Canadian Experience'. Canadian Journal of Higher Education, 9, 2, 63-74.
6. Daniel, J.S. and Stroud, M.A. (1981) 'Distance education: a reassessment for the 1980s'. Distance Education, 2, 2, 146-163.
7. Escotet, M.A. (1978) 'Factores Adversos para el desarrollo de una universidad abierta en América Latina'. Revista de Tecnología Educativa, 4, 1, 66-83.
8. Escotet, M.A. (1980) 'Tendencias de la Educación Superior a Distancia'. San Jose. Editorial UNED.
9. Gooler, D.D. (1979) 'Evaluating Distance Education Programs'. Canadian Journal of University Continuing Education, 6, 1, 43-55.
10. Harris, D. (1976) 'Educational Technology at the Open University: a Short History of Achievement and Cancellation'. British Journal of Educational Technology 7, 1, 43-53.
11. Hennessy, A. (1979) 'Students in the Latin American University'. In Maier, J. and Weatherhead, R.W. (1979) 'The Latin American University'. Albuquerque: University of New Mexico Press.
12. Holmberg, B. (1981) 'Trends and Status of Distance Education'. London: Kogan Page.

13. Kemmis, S. (1980) 'Program Evaluation in Distance Education: Against the Technologisation of Reason'. Open Campus, number 2. Occasional Papers published by the Centre for Educational Services, Deakin University.
14. Lumsden, K.G. and Ritchie, C. (1975) 'The Open University: A Survey and Economic Analysis'. Instructional Science, 4, 237-291.
15. Mace, J. (1978) 'Mythology in the Making: is the Open University really cost-effective?' Higher Education, 7, 295-309.
16. McIntosh, N.E. (1975) 'Institutional research: needs and uses'. Teaching at a Distance, 2, 33-48.
17. McIntosh, N.E. (1977) 'Evaluation and research. Aids to decision-making and innovation'. International Journal of Institutional Management in Higher Education, 1, 2, 119-127.
18. McIntosh, N.E. (1978) 'Evaluation and Institutional Research: The Problems involved in evaluating one course or educational program'. International Journal of Institutional Management in Higher Education, 2, 1, 5-19.
19. McIntosh, N. and Rigg, M. (1979) 'Employers and the Open University'. Milton Keynes: Open University Survey Research Department. Internal paper.
20. McIntosh, N., Woodley, A. and Morrison, V. (1980) 'Student demand and progress at the Open University - the first eight years'. Distance Education, 1, 1, 37-60.
21. Moss, G.D. and Brew, A. (1981) 'The contribution of the Open University to innovation in higher education'. Higher Education, 10, 141-151.
22. Open University (1972) 'The Open University. Report of the Vice-Chancellor, January 1969 - December 1970'. Milton Keynes: The Open University.
23. Perry, W. (1976) 'Open University. A personal account by the first Vice-Chancellor'. Milton Keynes: The Open University Press.
24. Peters, O. (1973) 'Die didaktische Struktur des Fernunterrichts. Untersuchungen zu einer industrialisierten Form des Lehrens und Lernens'. Weinheim: Beltz.
25. Peters, R.S. (1973) 'Authority, Responsibility and Education'. Third edition, London: George Allen & Unwin Ltd.
26. Rumble, G. (1981a) 'Evaluating autonomous multi-media distance learning systems; a practical approach'. Distance Education, 2, 1, 64-90.
27. Rumble, G. (1981b) 'The cost analysis of distance teaching. Costa Rica's Universidad Estatal a Distancia'. Higher Education, 10, 375-401.
28. Sewart, D. (1981) 'Distance teaching: a contradiction in terms?' Teaching at a Distance, 19, 8-18.
29. Sparkes, J.J. (1979) 'Educational objectives related to the capabilities of various distance communication techniques'. Paper presented to the Open University Conference on the Education of Adults at a Distance, Birmingham, UK, 18-23 November 1979.
30. Swift, B. (1980) 'Outcome of Open University Studies - some statistics from a 1980 Survey of Graduates'. Milton Keynes: Open University Survey Research Department. Internal paper.
31. Wagner, L. (1977) 'The economics of the Open University Revisited'. Higher Education, 6, 359-381.
32. Woodhall, M. (1972) 'Economic aspects of education. A review of research in Britain'. Slough: National Foundation for Educational Research in England and Wales.
33. Woolfe, R. (1977) 'Education, inequality and the role of the Open University'. Adult Education, 50, 2, 77-83.

INDEX